BONDS OF SALVATION

ANTISLAVERY, ABOLITION, AND THE ATLANTIC WORLD

R. J. M. Blackett and Edward Rugemer, Series Editors
James Brewer Stewart, Editor Emeritus

BEN WRIGHT

BONDS

OF

SALVATION

HOW CHRISTIANITY INSPIRED
AND LIMITED
AMERICAN ABOLITIONISM

Louisiana State University Press
Baton Rouge

Published by Louisiana State University Press
www.lsupress.org

Copyright © 2020 by Louisiana State University Press

DESIGNER: Michelle A. Neustrom
TYPEFACE: Adobe Caslon Pro

Jacket illustration courtesy Library of Congress.

LIBRARY OF CONGRESS CATALOGING-IN-PUBLICATION DATA

Names: Wright, Ben, 1983– author.
Title: Bonds of salvation : how Christianity inspired and limited American abolitionism
/ Ben Wright.
Description: Baton Rouge : Louisiana State University Press, [2020] | Series: Antislavery,
abolition, and the Atlantic world | Includes bibliographical references and index.
Identifiers: LCCN 2020013610 (print) | LCCN 2020013611 (ebook) | ISBN 978-0-8071-
7389-3 (cloth) | ISBN 978-0-8071-7451-7 (pdf) | ISBN 978-0-8071-7452-4 (epub)
Subjects: LCSH: Antislavery movements—United States—History—19th century. |
Slavery and the church—United States—History—19th century. | Slavery—United
States—History—19th century.
Classification: LCC E441 .W926 2020 (print) | LCC E441 (ebook) | DDC 973.7/
114—dc23
LC record available at https://lccn.loc.gov/2020013610
LC ebook record available at https://lccn.loc.gov/2020013611

CONTENTS

◇◇◇◇◇◇◇◇◇◇◇◇◇◇◇◇◇◇◇◇◇

ACKNOWLEDGMENTS

◇◇◇◇◇◇◇◇◇◇◇◇◇◇◇◇◇◇

THIS PROJECT COULD NOT have been completed without considerable help from colleagues, friends, family, and a number of generous institutions. Research for the project relied on grants from the Andrew W. Mellon Foundation, Virginia Historical Society, Historical Society of Pennsylvania, Library Company of Philadelphia, Massachusetts Historical Society, Quaker Collection at Haverford College, Filson Library, William L. Clements Library at the University of Michigan, the American Antiquarian Society, Rice University, and the University of Texas at Dallas. These funds enabled me to connect with a number of exceptional librarians and archivists. Special thanks to the professionals at each of these institutions as well as at the Wilson Library at the University of North Carolina, Friends Library at Swarthmore College, Presbyterian Historical Society, Maryland Historical Society, Library of Congress, the Congregational Library and Archives, Widener Library at Harvard University, Boston Public Library, and Huntington Library.

This book began at Rice University under the supportive advising of John Boles. John's enthusiasm for studying the past and his expectation of rigorous academic excellence set an example I will spend my career struggling to approach. Rebecca Goetz offered me an academic example of how I could explore questions that had long gnawed at my soul, namely how American Christianity reflects, reifies, and not-often-enough redresses racial inequality. Caleb McDaniel's own scholarship on abolitionism continues to humble me, and if not for his singular kindness, would paralyze me with intimidation. Generous input from James Sidbury, Alida Metcalf, and Randall Hall likewise encouraged and improved my work.

While I was just a prospective graduate student, John Boles suggested that I would learn more from my graduate cohort than I would from the faculty.

This proved true, and I am deeply grateful for the generous spirit of those colleagues and friends including Zach Dresser, Joe Locke, Andy Lang, Allison Madar, Sarah Paulus, Carl Paulus, Jim Wainwright, Luke Harlow, Wes Phelps, Sam Abramson, John Marks, Maria Montalvo, and many others. After leaving Rice, I found new cohorts that nurtured my work. Colleagues at the Abraham Baldwin Agricultural College, especially Russel Pryor and Alison Mann, demonstrated how scholarly excellence and deep engagement with students can be mutually enriching endeavors.

My colleagues at the University of Texas at Dallas stimulate me daily to read closer, imagine wider, and write clearer. Through generous offers to read my work, share their own, and keep me accountable through writing groups, this book has been enriched by Dan Wickberg, Natalie Ring, Eric Schlereth, Erin Smith, Kimberly Hill, Annelise Heinz, Ashley Barnes, Rosemary Admiral, Erin Greer, Kate Davies, and Anne Gray Fischer. The wider community of Dallas historians has been similarly invigorating. I've been buoyed by learning from Stephanie Cole, Gregg Cantrell, Alexis McCrossen, Guy Chet, Todd Smith, Chris Morris, Edward Countryman, Blake Earle, Lizzie Ingleson, and many others. I found the energy to push myself across the finish line largely through an informal Skype-facilitated writing group with Emily Conroy-Krutz and Gale Kenny, both of whom shared their incisive expertise with gracious collegiality. Other scholars have aided my work through comments, conversation, encouragement, and friendship. Special thanks go to Nathan Jérémie-Brink, Lindsay Chervinsky, Christopher Jones, Nora Slonimsky, and Andrew Wegmann.

I first really felt a historian in 2013 when working with Richard S. Newman on his NEH abolitionism seminar for teachers held at the Library Company of Philadelphia. Rich and the dedicated educators enrolled in the seminar taught me much about the history of American abolitionism and why it must be studied and taught. In the intervening years, dozens of often long and always lively conversations with Rich helped me navigate the thorniest issues in this study. Rich's friendship and mentorship have shaped my work and life even more than his essential scholarship.

I first committed to pursuing a career as a historian while an undergraduate at Bethel University. Among the many debts I owe Bethel's generous and nurturing faculty is a particular thanks to Diana Magnuson for assigning Jim Stewart's *Holy Warriors: The Abolitionists and American Slavery,* a masterful work that transfixed and haunted me as a young student. It has been one of the privileges of my life to work with Jim on revising this book. Jim's fierce faith in the project gave me much needed confidence. Moreover, Jim's untiring approach to scholarship, activism, and organizing will stay with me for the rest of my career. Working with Historians Against Slavery—the collection of academics committed to contemporary abolitionist activism that Jim founded—introduced me to a host of sharp scholars and dear friends including Stacey Robertson, Randall Miller, Matt Mason, and many others. Feedback from Jim's series co-editors Richard Blackett and Ed Rugemer made this a much better book. The staff at Louisiana State University Press are wonderfully efficient, professional, and kind.

Portions of this work have been presented at a number of conferences, symposia, and seminars. I am grateful for all of these audiences, each of which offered thoughtful comments. Much of the third chapter was published in Beverly Tomek and Matthew J. Hetrick's anthology *New Directions in the Study of African American Recolonization* (Gainesville: University Press of Florida, 2017). I thank the editors and readers of the anthology for their helpful comments.

This is a deeply personal book, fueled by my attempts to reconcile the inspiring piety and moral blind spots of the evangelical Christian community in which I was raised. The compulsion to understand and confront injustice comes from faith instilled in me by my parents, Gil and Kathi Wright. In ways they never expected, my parents' moral integrity and insistence on finding value beyond the material led me to a life of historical inquiry. They have been my salvation in innumerable ways. The antiracist lives lived by my aunt and uncle, Karen Thomas and Tony Gaines, helped me recognize elements of white supremacy that my privilege would have kept invisible. Similarly, experiences with the activist community in Dallas have shown me the challenges and importance of agitating for justice. Reading Richard Allen, Maria Stewart, and William Lloyd Garrison while also organizing alongside Dan Sullivan, Marissa Ocampo, Jodi Voice Yellowfish, Kristian Hernandez, Nan Kirkpatrick, and others remind me that activism owes more to hard work than to ideology.

I share my life with another historian, and Whitney Stewart's example of empathy, creativity, and diligence inspired the best parts of this book. Whitney's irrepressible joy alleviated the lonely frustrations of writing, not to mention the emotional struggle of studying the collision of religion and slavery. Watching and reading her scholarship has reminded me of the power of historical research. Over the eleven years I've lived with this project, the support of my family and friends kept me alive, as I reckoned with a few crises both professional and personal. This book is a product of a support system I do not deserve but could not live without.

Finally, I want to thank my students, who remain my greatest source of hope, as well as anyone who takes the time to read this book and ask the question that lies at the heart of this study: How can we find salvation from the inequalities and injustices that continue to haunt our communities, our nation, and our world?

Introduction

Salvation and Slavery

Never go to the southern states of America! They are polluted with slavery, and slavery is the most demoralizing thing under the sun. It is the parent of oppression, the nurse of sloth and guilty passions. It is the bane of man, the abomination of God. Where slavery reigns the human being is made a beast of burthen, or the slave of lust. The poor half-famished negro, trembles at a tyrant's nod, and loses every good quality in the servility of a drudge, or the wickedness of a prostitute. O that this scandal of humanity were annihilated!

—JOSHUA MARSDEN, 1814

JOSHUA MARSDEN NEVER PENNED a petition against slavery, or wrote to a representative in favor of abolition, or joined an antislavery society. Despite describing slavery as "the bane of man, the abomination of god" and earnestly yearning "that this scandal of humanity were annihilated," this Methodist missionary did nothing more than write these seven sentences, buried in a lengthy autobiography designed to celebrate missionary work. Yet he was not alone in his seeming hypocrisy. As the early abolitionist movement scored victories for freedom, few American Christians took organized action against slavery. Marsden and countless others watched on the sidelines as the evil institution grew. How did American Christianity encourage this inaction, and what changed to inspire the later, larger and more active Christian abolitionist movement?

Visions of salvation dominated the dreams of Americans from the very beginning of the nation. These visions clouded out the reality of slavery and the horrifying suffering it inflicted on millions of men, women, and children. In pursuit of salvation, white Christians formed national religious cultures, built national churches, and mobilized national reform networks. To pursue salvation, white Christians built a nation rooted in white supremacy, incapable of recognizing and responding to Black suffering.

Black Christians and their small number of white allies refused to separate visions of national salvation from national emancipation. These Christians railed against the injustice of slavery and the hypocrisy of white American Christianity. Eventually, their tireless activism spawned an abolitionist movement that broke the national consensus that the expansion of salvation must be prioritized over the purity of American churches. The result tore apart the nation's largest churches and set Americans down a road that led to secession, war, and the destruction of chattel slavery. The bonds of salvation both created and destroyed the American nation.

Marsden penned his sole antislavery statement while reflecting on his 1808 experience watching enslaved men, women, and children rake salt on the beaches of Bermuda from sunup till sundown, backs bent under the brutal sun. But despite the dreadful scene, Marsden's attention turned heavenward, and he anguished over the failure of missionaries, bemoaning that the residents of Bermuda "have no meetings of any kind; no professors of religion . . . alas, pleasure seemed their pursuit; money their god, and blindness to futurity their only refuge."[1] Slavery, that bane of man and abomination of God, not only oppressed the enslaved, but it also slowed the spread of salvation on the island. Instead of embracing Marsden's ministry and growing in Christian piety, the white men and women of Bermuda bowed before a false idol of slave-made wealth.

Marsden hated slavery for fostering both brutal oppression and luxurious vanity, but his hatred for slavery paled before his desperate panic that his own church was failing to spread the gospel to those otherwise destined for an eternity of torment. Marsden saw slavery as the barbaric atrocity it was. But he could devote only so much attention to the plight of the enslaved. He had a mission to save the world. Nothing could get in his way, not even the agents of torture empowering an increasingly powerful Atlantic slave system or the impassioned abolitionists agitating for emancipation.

The vast majority of Americans who opposed slavery never took action by participating in the abolitionist movement. White Christians struggled to imagine a biracial kingdom of God, and racism deeply poisoned American Christianity in both overt and subtle ways. But racism was not the only challenge to abolitionism. Marsden saw African-descended peoples as spiritual kin, yet he still refused to participate in the movement aimed at ending their oppression. And he was not alone. Antiracism was and remains much more than the absence of racism. And the very core of American Christianity both inspired and limited the abolitionist movement.

The bonds of salvation kept white Christians from listening to Black Christians and embracing the confrontational political and legal action required to emancipate the enslaved. White Christians saw their work as more urgent and its result as more radically transformative. The spiritual visions of most white American Christians devalued the work of abolitionists and their pragmatic, legalistic, and political agendas. Men and women like Marsden imagined themselves in an international, millennial battle for the spiritual salvation of everyone, enslaved and free. The activism of Black Christians appeared to them a distraction from the more holy work of expanding salvation for all. Marsden and those like him understood themselves as part of a process that would liberate souls both in this world and in the next. For these Christians, it was only worth changing laws if doing so directly enabled the spread of the gospel.[2] Salvation could not wait. The millennium was nigh. Marsden was bringing it. And the world would soon be made anew.

Not even the righteous appeals of the oppressed could compete with these romantic religious dreams. In the minds of Christians like Marsden, tedious lawsuits aimed at liberating the enslaved or divisive politicking designed to undercut the evil institution distracted or even stymied the international salvation that would extend to everyone. And yet a very small minority of white Christians did pursue abolition. For these men and women, their religious visions pursued purification as an essential precursor to the expansion of conversion.

This religious distinction between purification and conversion shaped the ideological possibilities of early American antislavery and of social reform more broadly. Abolitionists worked to purify the nation of slavery, but the majority of white Christians prioritized expanding salvation and accordingly remained outside of the organized antislavery movement. During the 1830s, a new generation of white abolitionists joined their long-active Black coreligionists and shattered the conversionist endorsement of the status quo. By 1845, the collision of abolitionism and salvation destroyed the nation's largest Protestant denominations, and religious leaders encouraged the seething sectionalism that culminated in secession, war, and eventual emancipation.

To understand how Christianity shaped the development of American abolitionism, we must uncover intellectual worldviews that looked to heaven to change life on earth. From the American Revolution through the first few decades of the nineteenth century, many Americans optimistically believed that the world was rapidly improving and that these improvements would advance speedily and thoroughly so long as the gospel of salvation continued to spread. A small number sought to purify the nation before converting others, but in the first three decades after the American Revolution, the voices of these activists were drowned out by those of the conversionists.[3]

Conversion, however, necessitated coordination, and independence from Britain required the creation of new methods of coordination. From 1785 through 1814, the nation's largest Protestant traditions formed new national denominations equipped to carry the gospel across the North American continent and eventually all over the globe. Constructing national institutions required avoiding the divisiveness of slavery, and American denominations worked to contain the agitation of Black activists. Instead, leaders of American denominations bound the nation together in pursuit of expanding salvation.

To further facilitate the expansion of salvation, these new denominational institutions established the many reform organizations historians call the benevolent empire, including the American Colonization Society, which was formed in 1815 to address the problem of slavery. But yet again, salvation structured even this movement, as colonizationists maintained their coalition only by promising to extend salvation to the continent of Africa. Nearly all American Christians believed that setter colonialism was conquering pagan idolatry on the American continent, and countless Christians, North and South, shared the dream of doing the same in Africa.

By the early 1830s, a new national abolitionism emerged in opposition to the colonizationist movement. This movement too relied upon the need to convert the world, and increasingly rancorous conflicts over slavery and salvation tore apart the three largest American Protestant denominations by 1845. In each phase of this process, Americans remained deeply concerned about salvation: the salvation of their families, their neighbors, their churches, and their nation. Throughout the early history of the United States, the bonds of salvation tied the nation together and both inspired and limited American abolitionism.

FOLLOWING THIS STORY CHANGES our understanding of the early republic in at least five ways. First, we see the role of Christian convictions in creating the ideological worlds of the early republic. Second, in seeking to understand the ideas underpinning abolitionist action, we move beyond the old paradigm of gradual versus immediate abolitionism. Third, we see how millennial dreams of salvation structured early American religious and political culture. Fourth, we come to recognize and understand antislavery Americans who have thus far remained outside of the focus of antislavery studies. Fifth, we rethink our broad narratives of American religious history, complicating the emphasis on democratization or diffusion with the recognition that this was an era of institution building, catalyzed by the need to expand salvation and maintain spiritual control of the nation's sprawling population. These institutions both inspired and limited American abolitionism. Eventually, the collision of slavery and salvation destroyed America's religious cultures, enabling the dissolution of the nation itself.

In charting the rise of American antislavery, historians have emphasized status anxieties, market changes, biracial cooperation, and political maneuvering, but few recent studies have foregrounded the pivotal role of religion in structuring the ideological possibilities of the movement.[4] Richard Newman's foundational study of early antislavery, *The Transformation of American Abolitionism,* begins with a caveat that he will not "delve deeply into the religious inspirations of abolitionists."[5] A generation of scholarship has emerged since Newman's study, and subsequent historians have followed Newman in carefully charting the political action of the early movement.

Ideological formations, however, remain understudied. Even Manisha Sinha's magisterial synthesis, which offers considerable insight into the role of religion in American abolitionism, looks primarily to political action rather than to ideological origins; and when she unfolds ideology, Sinha understandably does so to explain the political radicals that drove the movement, not the ideological systems that encouraged so many white Christians to remain politically inactive.[6] By privileging political action over ideological context, recent historiography misses how Christianity inspired and limited American abolitionism.

Black Christians took meaningful action against slavery during the late eighteenth and early nineteenth centuries while the vast majority of white Christians looked the other way. Religious visions of salvation enabled white Americans to ignore the actions and entreaties of their Black coreligionists. Heeding Robert Abzug's caution against "the modern trend toward psychological or materialist reduction" allows one to see the centrality of religious conviction in the transformation of antislavery.[7] Americans fretted over the social welfare of the new nation, but rather than purifying particular sins like slavery,

5

they sought to save everyone. For even those Christians who hated slavery, the only sound more harrowing than the moans of a shackled slave were the wails of a damned soul.

David Brion Davis's distinction between gradualist and immediatist antislavery has structured narratives of abolition for a half-century.[8] Recent studies of the political movement have challenged this format, finding continuities where Davis saw ruptures.[9] When we examine the ideology underpinning the antislavery movement, the distinction breaks down even further. If we seek to understand how religious men and women—particularly those who were opposed to slavery but remained outside of abolitionist movements— envisioned the problem of slavery and sought to solve it, the question becomes not whether a reformer was gradualist or immediatist in their political action, but whether or not they ascribed to the widely shared expectations of conversionist causation or adopted an alternative antislavery of religious purification.

In the late eighteenth century, the very ideologies that turned so many early antislavery white Americans against human bondage in the first place also emphasized the power of religious conversion to save everyone rather than revealing that coercive agitation would be required to free the enslaved. American Christians did not expect this process to be gradual. Christ and the social transformations he wrought would not come like an avenging angel after the plagues of Egypt, but rather the millennium would arrive quickly, in the blink of an eye, like a thief in the night, and the world would be remade. Conversions would save the world.

Conversion, of course, meant different things to different people, but the differences carried less weight than the similarities. Religious studies scholar Tracy Fessenden has described the development of the "nonspecific Protestantism" that enabled reform movements to exert so much pressure by 1830. Similarly, John Lardas Modern describes how, "transcending both doctrinal and denominational differences, a somewhat hazy metaphysics assumed hegemonic status both within Protestant practice and across a number of other sites." These "nonspecific" Protestantisms and their "hazy metaphysics" helped form a still-nascent American culture and laid the ideological foundation for conversionism.[10] Nearly all Americans shared an optimistic expectation in the transformative power of conversion. This expectation often fed millennial energies that allowed white Christians to expect the disappearance of entrenched systems of injustice without the exertion of organized, political pressure.

Christians have expected the return of Christ since the earliest days of the faith, but Anglo-Atlantic Christians in the late eighteenth century directed their efforts toward hastening the arrival of this event with an unusual intensity. Americans embraced millennial optimism as a core component of a shared civic faith, particularly in times of war. Violence has catalyzed millennial religion throughout Anglo-Atlantic history dating back at least to the English Civil War.[11] The American Revolution continued this tradition. Nathan Hatch has argued that Americans adopted a millennial set of expectations that the political upheavals of the era portended more thorough social transformations.[12] Robert Abzug describes the same explosion of millennial energies in the aftermath of the era but claims that postrevolutionary partisanship, the horrors of the French Revolution, and the development of so many new religious groups enervated the enthusiasm of the late eighteenth century.[13] Alongside Abzug's select New England religious virtuosos, however, the millennial spirit endured and grew despite the anxieties he rightly recognizes.

Many Americans optimistically believed they were living on the cusp of rapturous social change. Nicholas Guyatt downplays the millennial energies of the early republic by comparing them to the far more explicit millennial preoccupations of seventeenth-century England.[14] His historical narrative is accurate, but the comparison misses how the strength of postrevolutionary American millennialism flowed not from its systematic orthodoxy but rather from its flexibility. Guyatt usefully distinguishes between apocalyptic and historical providentialism. The former he equates with millennialism and the latter with optimistic nationalism, but historical providentialism also fed a sense of millennial destiny in the early republic. American greatness would hasten the return of Christ, and American greatness depended on the advance of religious conversion.

By focusing on Americans who prioritized national salvation in the late eighteenth and early nineteenth centuries, we can better understand why white Christians struggled to organize serious challenges to human bondage. The dormant antislavery of white men and women like Joshua Marsden, Stephen Grellet, Elizabeth Wilkinson, and John Leland was far more common than the active antislavery of white men like Anthony Benezet, Granville Sharp, or Benjamin Rush. This study, then, does not recount the achievements of the early abolitionists, nor does it foreground the unflagging activism of Black Americans. Instead, it explores how both religious ideas and religious institutions inspired and limited the antislavery movement from the Revolution until the dissolution of the major national Protestant denominations in 1837, 1844,

7

and 1845. Tracking the intersections of Christianity and slavery reveal how the bonds of salvation made and unmade the American nation.

We cannot understand early antislavery without considering religion, and we cannot understand early American religion without foregrounding conversionism. Tracking the eighteenth-century emphasis on conversion not only reconfigures categories of antislavery thought; it also challenges the broad narrative of religion in the early republic. Nathan Hatch's *Democratization of American Christianity* remains the most valuable synthesis of religion in the early republic.[15] According to Hatch, religious energy moved westward, away from traditional sources of religious authority. Old denominational power structures tottered. Upstart revivalists spawned dozens of new sects uniquely designed to meet spiritual needs in a time of unprecedented economic and social change. The market revolution and accelerated migration across the Appalachian Mountains challenged time-honored patterns of social organization. This period of flux brought great opportunity for religious innovators crafting spiritually egalitarian messages. However, despite all of the democratic dispersal correctly chronicled by Hatch, in the first two decades of the nineteenth century American religion experienced concurrent consolidation in new, national denominational bodies designed to coordinate missions of salvation.[16]

Itinerant missionaries were not the only ones aware of the great changes of the day. Rather than standing idly behind their pulpits, the settled clergy formed new networks designed to Christianize the growing nation. These new networks eventually created the national religious cultures necessary for antebellum reform movements, including abolitionism. Our historiography has taught us much about how denominations divided over the question of slavery during the 1840s, but we know less about how these national bodies came together in the first place from 1780 to 1814, much less how their formation enabled the benevolent empire and shaped responses to slavery including the 1815 formation of the American Colonization Society.[17]

Teleologies of sectionalism that look ahead to the 1840s schisms obscure the nature of religion in the early republic and fail to demonstrate how denominations spread and tied various churches together. The story of religion in the early republic then is not simply one of democratization, diffusion, or sectionalism but also one of national development, a process essential for the confrontational abolitionism of the later antebellum period. Understanding the central role of salvation in this process also sheds new light on the nature and consequence of the sectional schisms that paved the way for secession.

INTRODUCTION: SALVATION AND SLAVERY

* * *

THE FOLLOWING SIX CHAPTERS stretch from the American Revolution through secession. The first chapter evaluates the ideological distinctions between conversion and purification in the 1780s and 1790s. A small number of white abolitionist Christians in the late eighteenth century prioritized purification over conversion. The majority of Christians eschewed participation in the abolitionist movement and looked confidently toward the time when salvation would wash away all of the sins of the era. But expanding salvation required new networks of coordination. The second chapter describes how Americans created denominations in order to expand salvation and then how, in the aftermath of the War of 1812, these denominations created the benevolent empire. Attacks on slavery threatened to undermine denominational projects and so abolitionists were increasingly excluded from positions of denominational leadership.

The third chapter chronicles the most powerful national institution formed to address the problem of slavery, the American Colonization Society. It is not a coincidence that this movement drew on denominational networks and emphasized a mission of African conversion in order to maintain its diverse coalition. Despite colonization's popular appeal, critics emerged in the late 1820s, motivated by either proslavery opposition to all hints of emancipation or by Black Christians who had no interest in abandoning the land of their birth. How these opponents of colonization manipulated discourses of conversion forms the subject of the fourth chapter. The fifth chapter unfolds how theological changes and new methods of abolitionist activism in the 1830s destroyed the conversionist consensus. The final chapter tracks how the loss of the conversionist consensus tore apart the nation's churches by the 1840s, and the Conclusion explains how these schisms enabled secession.

The story begins with ideologies of conversion and purification. These different understandings of causation fostered contradictory antislavery strategies in the 1780s and 1790s. In the late eighteenth century, conversionist spirituality made it nearly impossible for the majority of white Christians to confront the realities of their slaving nation. Most Americans opposed to slavery failed to embrace the radical visions of a biracial kingdom of God offered by Black activists and a small number of their white allies.

Some Christians, however, believed that the United States would never take its place as God's chosen nation unless it purified itself of slavery. For Christian abolitionists, national salvation would be impossible unless slavery was destroyed, and so they worked in strategic ways to weaken the institution. And they had reasons to hope. State legislators passed gradual abolition laws in the 1780s and 1790s, freedom suits liberated many wrongfully enslaved men and women, and the nation outlawed the transatlantic slave trade in 1808. All of these advances flowed from desires to save the nation by attacking its most evil sin. Yet abolitionist calls remained unheeded by the majority of white Christians. Many Americans prioritized spiritual salvation over earthly liberation but expected that both would flow from the same missionary labors.

In 1810, Marsden wrote back from Bermuda to Thomas Coke, the coordinator of global Methodist missions, and directly linked his conversionist mission to that of abolition by claiming "posterity will record the name of Coke, with those of Wilberforce and Clarkson, as friends and benefactors of the African race."[18] Marsden believed that he and his fellow conversionist ministers were serving the interests of abolition by liberating souls and spirits, rather than by seeking to transform laws. Other Christians believed that sinful laws tainted the community and hampered the cause of conversion. American Christians were divided over whether to prioritize conversion or purification.

Conversionist causation captured the imagination of the majority of Americans who opposed slavery, but purification directed another response, one that encouraged effective coercive confrontation with slavers. Religious bodies in the eighteenth and nineteenth centuries, like all religious bodies, struggled to balance the imperatives of religious conversion with the need to maintain discipline within their communities. This tension between looking without and looking within, growing or purging, evangelism or discipleship, challenged religious leaders. Most religious communities held both ambitions but rarely pursued both in equal measure. Purificationists removed slaveholders from churches, or at least vigorously pressured members of their religious community to adopt antislavery commitments, but more Americans opted for methods that were less confrontational and more ineffectual. Organizing missionary ventures united more than divided, and conversionism imbued these Christians with the confidence that their labors would conquer sin and save the world.

Independence invited Americans to ask, how do we make the world anew? How do we design a nation and a world in God's image? For abolitionists, the answer was simple. Slavery was evil, and it had to be eradicated. The new nation could never fulfill its spiritual destiny with the stain of slavery making a mockery of American claims to moral leadership. A small number of white Christians, inspired by Black activists, recognized that slavery was a political evil that required political solutions, and so they formed political movements to fight slavery in the 1780s. In the first several decades after independence, most American Christians disagreed with these reformers and sought to inaugurate the kingdom of God and annihilate sin not through changing laws but rather by expanding salvation. For white Christians, the "manifest destiny" of settler colonialism would enable God's outpouring of salvation. They felt compelled to act decisively and they coordinated ever-expansive missionary endeavors rather than agitate internally to purify the nation.

Conversionism had its core in evangelicalism, but conversionist expectation spilled out beyond evangelicals and seeped into the wider Protestant world. Early Americans understood religious conversion in a great variety of ways, but in the development of American antislavery, similarities between American understandings of Christian conversion proved far more consequential than differences. Popular religious discourse from the Revolution to the Civil War was ubiquitous but often theologically ambiguous. This ambiguity did not signal a lack of conviction, however. People in every era, including our own, carry deeply rooted convictions that contain contradictions. The early republic was no exception. But these contradictions did not necessarily pose a problem for those who held them. Historians of theology have too long valued ideological consistency as the measure of theological strength.[19] In the early republic, the theological flexibility of popular evangelicalism proved to be its greatest asset. The explosion of theological systems and ecclesiastical structures during the final decades of the eighteenth century and the dawn of the nineteenth enabled the expansion of evangelical religion. An optimistic expectation in the transformative power of conversion united nearly all white Americans prior to 1830.

These expectations allowed Christians to expect the disappearance of injustice without turning to the law or to political organizing. In the final decades of the eighteenth century, intellectual trends stemming from both moral philosophy and religious revivals encouraged an optimistic expectation that an imminent, millennial expansion of salvation and enlightenment would inaugurate the kingdom of God and the age of reason. These imminent changes would eliminate the most offensive, wrath-inducing sins, including the sin of slaving. This expectation encouraged spiritual warfare rather than political confrontation, and the spiritual weapons of settler colonialism and church building promised to allow the unfolding of enlightenment and the expansion of holiness without triggering the controversies generated by debates over abolition.

In the aftermath of the American Revolution, many white Christians were convinced that God was remaking the world and that divisive political agitation would only get in the way of salvation. Given intellectual trends ascendant in the postrevolutionary era, it is logical that many early American Christians, even those who hated slavery, focused on organizing to evangelize rather than looking to the coercive power of the state. And even when Black activists and their white allies successfully wielded the coercive power of the state to erode slavery through northern gradual emancipation laws in the 1780s and 1790s and the abolition of the Atlantic slave trade in 1808, conversionist expectations continued to provide Christians a way to justify their ambivalence or opposition to the abolitionist movement.

Conversionism captured the imagination of most reformers in the late eighteenth century, but a rival understanding of causation—what I call purificationism—provided an alternative antislavery discourse. We can find purificationist antislavery in the three most influential manifestations of eighteenth-century white antislavery: Quakers, the Congregationalist theologian-minister Samuel Hopkins, and southern evangelicals in the 1780s and 1790s.

With the exceptions of free communities of color and enslaved people themselves, the Society of Friends stood as the strongest and most consistent opponent of slavery in the eighteenth-century Atlantic World. By the dawn of the American Revolution, Quakers had experienced shockwaves of their own making for decades. Reformers in the mid to late eighteenth century encouraged Quakers to strengthen their prophetic voice of protest, but others within the Society of Friends contested these reforming impulses. From the 1750s through the 1770s, Quaker communities struggled to maintain unity amidst the ruptures of the Quaker reformation. Antislavery became a means by which the Society of Friends held their church together despite intense friction. But the Quaker reformation left the Society of Friends as an increasingly marginal sect, and the American Revolution further weakened Quaker claims to power. In the 1770s and 1780s, both religious and secular leaders struggled to reconcile the new language of liberty with the institution of slavery. If purificationist antislavery would capture the national consciousness, it would need a more widely accepted mouthpiece than the marginal Quakers.

Quakers recognized this fact and developed alliances with other antislavery supporters throughout North America, none more influential than Congregationalist theologian and minister Samuel Hopkins, the subject of the second purificationist case study.[20] Hopkins pounced on the critical moment of the American Revolution to solidify opposition to the slave trade in the immediate shadow of powerful and profitable local mercantile interests. But Hopkins, despite his considerable influence, represented a religious tradition that declined in the early years of the new nation. Beginning in the 1770s, insurgent evangelicals swept along the frontier and quickly grew into the nation's dominant religious force. These evangelicals represent the third case of purificationist antislavery. In the 1770s and 1780s, antislavery sentiments spread throughout the growing populations of evangelicals, even in the South. In the 1780s, important institutional declarations against slavery came from both Baptists and Methodists, the two most influential southern evangelical denominations. Baptist minister John Leland and Methodist cosuperintendent Francis Asbury stood at the head of the efforts in their respective denominations and both loom large throughout this study. But a close look at these southern evangelicals reveals the fragility of late eighteenth-century purificationist antislavery and the ease with which it was subsumed by conversionism.

Forward-thinking and nimble, new evangelical churches grew exponentially in the late eighteenth and early nineteenth century as American migrants raced westward. Because of this migration, however, the quest for purification was soon eclipsed by the need to tend to these new communities. The 1770s and 1780s anxieties over sin eroded as a more pressing alarm grew. American clergymen feared that large swaths of the new nation's population would find themselves beyond the reach of existing churches. The demographic challenges of the postrevolutionary era diminished the call for purification, and a new national emphasis on missionary outreach reinforced the importance of conversionism. Conversionist causation let Americans who opposed slavery rest assured that the quest to bring the gospel to the West would also lead to the destruction of slavery. But before the gospel could reach the West, new denominational structures had to form in order to coordinate the effort. And these new structures, beginning in the 1780s and culminating in 1814, would plant the seeds for a new era of antislavery reform.

Missions of salvation drew Americans out of their local contexts and structured the ideas and actions of social reformers. The majority of late eighteenth-century abolitionists, however, remained bound by their region or state, agitating on a local basis. But when attempting to foster conversions, Christians imagined a heavenly host filled with every tribe and tongue. These visions fueled cosmopolitan humanitarianism, religious nationalism, and American imperialism, all essential forces for the age of American reform. American Christians believed that God had a special plan for the United States as the vanguard of this international wave of salvation, and so pursuing the expansion of salvation inspired and shaped emergent American nationalisms. To save the world, Americans had to build a godly nation. These national conversion endeavors transformed ideologies and established infrastructures. While building sprawling religious networks in the early nineteenth century, American Christians developed vivid national imaginations. Informed by these new imaginations, and wielding powerful new religious institutions, both abolitionists and their opponents began to organize on levels previously unimaginable.

By connecting thousands of churches, North and South, East and West, the bonds of salvation tied the nation together in denominations. Abolitionism threatened this national union, and denominations took decisive action in ensuring that neither slavery nor abolition would distract from their visions of expanding salvation. In this way, the denominational focus on salvation tightened the bonds of American slavery. As enslavers increasingly accommodated conversionist missions, abolitionists came to be seen as the true enemies of Christianity by many religious leaders, and denominations expelled anyone unwilling to subdue their hatred of slavery beneath their commitment to extending salvation. No one could interfere with these denominational projects to save the world, and these missions of salvation directly led to the creation of myriad reform organizations. Eventually these reform organizations remade the bonds of the nation and launched powerful new movements. The dramatic results began with the tedious process of institution building following the American Revolution. To understand American reform, we must begin with the institutional history of post-independence denominations. Denominations mattered to early Americans, and if we are to understand how Americans understood and sought to combat social injustice, denominational history must matter to us as well.

Ministers knitted denominations together to expand salvation and serve the saved, but in the nationalist explosions surrounding the War of 1812, the formation of these bodies had the unintended side-effect of pushing denominationalists—both in pulpit and pew—toward social reform. After establishing networks through conversionist groups including missionary, tract, and Bible societies, reformers eventually turned to combat specific sins such as Sabbath breaking, intemperance, and slavery. Inattention to the institutional development of national denominational bodies has led historians to miss how nearly all early American voluntary societies sprang out of national denominational bodies or at least denominational networks.

The competing Christian nationalisms of denominational bodies created the desire and the infrastructure essential for the coercive reform of the benevolent empire. After the War of 1812, the politicization of denominational action eventually added organized social reform alongside conversionism and purificationism as the religious solutions to the era's social problems.[21] These new reform organizations, with their origins in denominationalism, sought to remake the world directly. In this context, new networks of Christian abolitionists stretched across the Atlantic to destroy the international system of slavery.

Historians have recognized these transatlantic networks of reform and highlighted the transnational component of American abolitionism.[22] In so doing, however, the focus on commonalities has missed at least one crucial difference between the United States and other nations. While British reformers flooded Parliament with petitions, speeches, and other forms of legislative agitation, American evangelicals rarely turned to the halls of Congress in the first several decades of the nation's history. Contextualizing religion in Great Britain and the United States reveals that ecclesiastical differences, perhaps even more than political, social, or economic differences, explain the divergent developments of antislavery on both sides of the ocean.

Disestablishment in the United States, beginning in 1776 and culminating in 1833, and the strain of migration prevented antislavery ministers from mustering a unified political assault on slavery. The instability of religious authority in this tumultuous time contrasted sharply with the ecclesiastical context in Great Britain. British reformers successfully harnessed a long-standing national religious culture to tie the 1807 abolition of the slave trade to the very core of British religious identity. Even Dissenters, who did not directly command the state church, could appeal to shared national religious cultures and engage the expectations of Britons who anticipated that national religious discourses would guide national policy. Americans in the late eighteenth and early nineteenth centuries struggled to find a similar discourse for the diverse new republic, and even if such a discourse could be found, who could claim the authority to wield it?

Despite attempts by American Presbyterians to stake a claim as the keepers of the national faith, religious life in the United States could not be driven by any one denomination or any single religious discourse, a fact made clear during the 1812 campaign to halt Sunday mail service. American religious life would be shaped through the competition of churches, ideas, and movements. American abolitionists could not follow the same path as British activists.

Dogged commitments to religious liberty and the sovereignty of conscience worked to stymie coercive denominational attempts at social reform, at least while anxieties over religious conversion continued to haunt Americans.

Despite these setbacks and the belief that salvation would soon obliterate all American sins, denominational action pushed religious leaders to take stands on the great issues of the day. As a result of denominational leadership, religious Americans enlarged their understanding of ministerial spaces from congregations or regional associations to the republic in its entirety. When Joshua Marsden thought about the problem of slavery, he did so explicitly through the lens of his denomination. In 1809, he boasted that if the light of Christianity and its liberatory consequences would reach enslaved men and women, it would do so "by the overlooked, reproached and despised Methodists." Fortunately, for Marsden, he believed that Methodists were up to the challenge. He rejoiced, "Well, glory be to God, the religion of the cross will finally prevail, and triumph over all, and many of the sable sons of Ham, in the great day, will make it evident by whose means they were brought into the family of God." However, Methodists had to take seriously their task, lest they lose out to other Christians in the glorious mission of expanding conversion. When reflecting on the prospects of converting the Caribbean, Marsden was frustrated over Methodists dragging their feet, and he even panicked, wondering, "Shall, in this respect, the Moravian brethren take our crowns?"[23] Surely not! Marsden knew that in order to fulfill the goal of converting the world, Methodists would have to organize and expand their denominational institutions.

The spatial expansion of clerical duty enabled leaders of new national religious cultures to take public positions on the issue of slavery by the 1830s. But denominational formation also bound together coreligionists across sectional lines, making it initially difficult for some northerners to demonize their southern brethren and vice versa. Denominationalism opened the door to national reform, while discouraging that reform from taking an aggressive, coercive shape. Millennial dreams that God would solve the difficult problem of slavery enabled white Christians to focus on expanding salvation rather than on transforming laws. Historians have written extensively on the transformations in American life that resulted from advances in transportation and communication.[24] Indeed, technological advances collapsed space, but long before the railroad or telegraph bound together the continent, denominational affiliation created connections across many of the same great distances.

Just like the telegraph, the spatial expansion of clerical duty did not stop at national boundaries. When American reformers finally created the national infrastructure that could deal with the problem of slavery, they again foregrounded the salvation of souls. From the initial inception of the American Colonization Society in 1815, Americans sought to use African colonization as a tool to inaugurate a global expansion of salvation and solve the problem of slavery. In the early nineteenth century, thousands of Black Americans migrated to colonies in West Africa, eventually forming the nation of Liberia. Many Americans looked to this process as the most effective means of solving the problem of slavery, but a closer look at the movement again exposes the bonds of salvation.

Historians tend to frame studies of colonization in relation to slavery, most recently by emphasizing the colonization movement's antislavery functions.[25] Still others stress the ambitions of African American nationalism.[26] Colonization certainly influenced political debates over slavery, and the movement accelerated the development of African American identity, but colonizationists from 1815 through 1830 invoked another motivation—conversion—with far greater frequency and rhetorical intensity than the explanations emphasized in the existing historiography.

White and Black colonizationists drew strength from a millennial faith in the promise of Psalm 68 that "Ethiopia shall soon stretch forth her hands to God." Sending well-trained African American missionaries across the ocean would realize the Psalm's prophetic promise. Colonization promised salvation for Africa and moral redemption for the United States. The impending conversion of Africa would redeem the sins of the slave trade by repaying the wounded continent with the gift of Christianity. In the minds of early nineteenth-century white Christians, colonization would do more than abolition, as the salvation of an entire continent weighed heavier than the emancipation of several million. Tracing the conversionist ideologies of early colonizationists reveals the goals and expectations of the men and women who invested so much capital, human and otherwise, in this deadly imperial venture. Acknowledging the power of conversionism also illustrates how the widely popular colonizationist movement echoed and amplified the strains of racism and imperialism in the early nineteenth century.

Colonization, despite its popular appeal, could not solve the problem of slavery, and opposition grew in the late 1820s and early 1830s, particularly from Black Americans. Opponents of colonization—including Black Americans, proslavery zealots, and an increasingly confrontational generation of white abolitionists—all recognized the popularity of colonization's missionary ambitions. To attack colonization was to attack the providential salvation of Africa. Opponents of colonization then had to undercut the power of this language and they did so primarily by distinguishing between colonial conquest and missionary outreach. The 1830s battle against colonization was in many ways a battle over the process of conversion. This battle was waged against a backdrop of increasing sectionalist rancor. The national faith in imperial settler colonialism began to falter as debates over slavery challenged the conversionist consensus.

Beginning in the 1830s, a small but loud contingent of radical abolitionists began pressing for new national antislavery strategies rooted in a different set of religious convictions. Years spent saving souls while watching slavery grow had convinced some antislavery Christians to pursue new tactics. No longer tied to conversionist causation, these reformers introduced a new discourse that unraveled the bonds of conversionist antislavery. This is not a story of the cosmos crumbling, but rather a story of how Black and white abolitionists tore it down.

By the end of 1831, the work of David Walker, Maria Stewart, William Lloyd Garrison, and Nat Turner epitomized the new antislavery discourse. The possibility of slave rebellion had long threatened the United States, as the specter of Haiti had haunted white Americans since 1791, North and South. But the 1831 uncompromising vitriol of William Lloyd Garrison, the foreboding threats of David Walker two years earlier, and the realized horrors of Nat Turner's 1831 revolt seemingly made real the nightmares that had haunted both enslavers and the wider white American populace. This new level of confrontation shifted perceptions of the problem of slavery from the hands of providence to a practical matter of national survival.

By 1840, denominational outreach had succeeded, and fears of an unChristian frontier receded. Yet the sins of slavery remained and, in fact, only grew despite the spread of the gospel. Meanwhile, in the early 1830s, revivalists like Charles Grandison Finney inaugurated changes in the process of religious conversion. As Calvinism declined, theologies of increased human agency meshed with increased commitments to popular democracy among white men. The reform movements that grew out of earlier denominational conversionist projects had politicized northern Christians. Meanwhile, theological and ecclesiastical changes in the United States allowed white Christians to hear the appeals of Black Christians anew, and during the 1830s a new generation of abolitionists turned against older tactics and instead embraced a national, confrontational abolitionism, emboldened in purifying the nation of slaving.

Conversionist appeals continued, but the antislavery of men and, increasingly, women challenged the causation of conversion. In the 1830s, white Christians began to look anew to political agitation as a means of reform. Moderate antislavery conversionists responded to the new abolitionists with hostility, seeing the new agitation as a distraction of the work of salvation and therefore a distraction from the surest means of achieving emancipation. For these men and women, abolitionists threatened to hinder the work of missions, thereby delaying the expected day of deliverance from sin and slavery. But the new generation of agitators would not be thwarted by these old arguments. This left conversionist discourse in the hands of proslavery apologists who contrasted southerners spreading the gospel with abolitionists spreading the seeds of slave rebellion and disunion. These tensions frayed and then snapped the bonds of denominational unity by 1845. The conversionist consensus no longer held, and the nation tore itself apart, beginning in its churches.

The nation's three largest Protestant denominations splintered over questions of conversion and slavery. The Presbyterians in 1837, Methodists in 1844, and Baptists in 1845 all divided over the question of how to expand salvation in a slaving nation. In the Presbyterian case, theological disagreements regarding revival drove the conflict, but slavery loomed over these debates and contributed to the spirit of distrust that northern and southern divines harbored against one another. In the Methodist and Baptist cases, slavery was more directly tied to their purely sectional schisms. But here too, slavery itself was not enough to destroy the union of national denominations. Denominational fracture for both the Methodists and Baptists occurred when northern Christians came to believe that slaveholders would no longer make effective agents of American salvation. The loss of these denominations destroyed the best hope of avoiding war, and the nation hurled headlong into an increasingly rancorous sectional crisis. This crisis only culminated when the way of death wrought by slavery was replaced with the hellacious body counts of the Civil War and the final arrival of emancipation.

* * *

RELIGIOUS AMERICANS IN THE late eighteenth century expected a new world to appear with the expansion of Christian conversion. A prophetic few adopted an alternative antislavery of purification, but these cries were either muted by the limitations of their source (i.e., the marginal Quakers or declining Calvinists) or else drowned out by the challenges of rapid migration in the aftermath of the American Revolution. The challenges of this migration caused conversionists to focus energies on missionary outreach, resulting in the consolidation of religious authority in new denominational bodies by 1814.

These new religious bodies created an opening for reform but restricted it from taking an aggressive, coercive shape. Colonization appeared to promise a solution to both slavery and abolitionism and the movement built a diverse coalition of supporters by foregrounding the conversion of Africa. By 1830 it became clear that religious conversion would not solve the problem of slavery. Conversionist antislavery turned into a conservative weapon used by proslavery apologists, who wielded the weapon so well that abolitionists eventually broke the bonds of religious unity by denying enslavers positions as sanctioned missionaries. National religious cultures forged by dreams of conversion were undone by the inextricable connection between conversion and slavery. The pursuit of salvation motivated the formation, development, and dissolution of national American religious cultures. Emancipation only arrived via the deadly apocalypse of civil war. Yet, for nearly a century prior, antislavery was inextricably tied to visions of American salvation.

Uncovering the theological worldview of early American social reform explains not only how Christians like Joshua Marsden could hate slavery and yet seemingly do nothing; it also clarifies the ideological underpinnings of American antislavery, recasting the political strategies of gradualism and immediatism as cosmological worldviews privileging purification or conversion. This is a story of how Christianity structured what was ideologically possible as Americans reckoned with the nation's sin of slavery. Understanding the limitations of those possibilities explains how antislavery Christians enabled the expansion and entrenchment of human bondage, necessitating the cataclysm of war to finally secure emancipation.

Joshua Marsden's antislavery was not hypocritical nor was it apathetic. Marsden hated slavery and looked with great anticipation for the day when God would fulfill his promise of deliverance for all creation. Marsden staunchly believed that the hours of study, preparation, and active ministry that occupied his time served to accelerate this glorious day. And he expected that day to come soon, for, as he wrote in 1814, "the Redeemer's kingdom is gloriously near. If the world is to be reformed, God will doubtless employ his Son—his Son

INTRODUCTION: SALVATION AND SLAVERY

will employ the gospel as the brightest transcript of his divine, gracious, and holy nature." Marsden dedicated his life to missions that he believed were "in the hands of a wise providence, capable of doing infinite good."[27]

But these hopes and expectations hinged on a converted populace. Achieving this goal required a responsive, active church that bound together both enslavers and antislavery Christians. Conversionism provided an expectation of emancipation, but also a challenge to meet the needs of the age through institutional development, organization, and ultimately social transformation. Each stage of this progression shaped the worlds of American antislavery. By foregrounding ideas of religious conversion and religious purification, we can begin to understand the problem of slavery and its potential solutions as did the men and women whose lives included both dreams of salvation and the nightmare of American slavery.

◇◇◇◇ 1 ◇◇◇◇

Conversionist and Purificationist Antislavery, 1776–1800

VIRGINIA BAPTISTS SOUGHT TO purify their state of slavery in 1789. John Leland, a locally respected minister who claimed to have baptized seven hundred souls and preached three thousand sermons, took up the charge of his nascent denomination to denounce slaving and call for emancipation.[1] The ministries of Leland and many of his fellow Baptists challenged racial hierarchies in Virginia, by seeking to promote salvation among both white and Black, free and enslaved. Of the seven hundred baptisms Leland performed, many involved enslaved men and women. From his experience spreading the gospel in Virginia, Leland believed that "the whole scene of slavery is pregnant with enormous evils," and he emphatically prayed that "would to heaven" the new government "liberate them at once."[2] Unlike Joshua Marsden, however, he was willing, at least for now, to turn his ideas into actual abolitionist action.

Through Leland's pen, Virginia Baptists lambasted slavery as "a violent deprivation of the rights of nature." For these southern Christians, the spirit of the American Revolution, fought under the authority of the rights of man and the will of God, left slavery "inconsistent with a republican government." God's plan for universal salvation was underway, and the American state was part of that plan. Yet to fulfill its destiny, the nation had to purify itself of the sins of the British. Due in part to Leland's own activism, the United States was already overcoming the sin of established religion. Slavery was the next abomination to conquer. Leland and his Baptist allies called on all Virginians "to make use of every legal measure to extirpate this horrid evil from the land," particularly "our honorable legislature," who "may have it in their power to proclaim the great Jubilee."[3]

Virginia did not proclaim a jubilee, great or otherwise, but partly owing to the success of evangelical revivals and revolutionary rhetoric, manumissions increased in the aftermath of the Revolution. Slavery, however, endured and gained new life when the rise of cotton exploded the demand for enslaved labor. Black Virginians sought their own emancipation, but after a failed attempt at rebellion, Virginia abolished abolition rather than slavery. By 1806, it became impossible for enslavers in Virginia to repent and free their enslaved laborers unless they could send them out of the state. Rather than restoring liberty to its captives, the Old Dominion instead enriched itself, shattering families by selling human chattel into the cotton kingdom's engine of death.

The abolitionist southern evangelical moment soon passed as well. Leland left Virginia two years after penning the Baptist antislavery petition. For the remainder of his life, he reverted to the same conversionism of Joshua Marsden and in fact went even further, devoting more energy and ink combating what he saw as the sin of abolitionism rather than maintaining his witness against the sin of slaving. The purificationist attempt to purge the new nation of slavery had failed, but ideologies of conversionism enabled antislavery Christians like John Leland to remain confident that slavery would eventually dissolve through a divinely ordained expansion of salvation.

Prioritizing salvation meant shunning Black Christians who refused to wait on God. The majority of white antislavery Christians largely ignored the Black activists who consistently campaigned against slavery. Throughout both his purificationist and his conversionist phases, Leland was more concerned with the purity of white Christian souls than with the very real suffering of Black Americans. In fact, when addressing enslaved men and women in 1791, he discouraged them from taking any action to undermine the institution that was destroying their families, telling Black Baptists that there was nothing they could do "to move God to send you deliverance so effectually as to obey those who have the rule over you."[4]

Salvation for Leland, and for the vast majority of late eighteenth-century white Americans, had to begin with the soul and not with the exploited bodies of the enslaved. Bodily liberation would ensue, but damned souls required spiritual salvation first. Anything, especially Black activism, that distracted from the orderly conversion of the nation threatened the safety and salvation of all. By prioritizing the salvation of the soul over the liberation of the body, antislavery evangelicals like John Leland entrenched white supremacy and sowed the seeds for what would later blossom into both the abolitionist and proslavery movements.

To understand Leland and his fellow white Christians, we must begin to uncover an intellectual world very different than our own. In the late eighteenth century, theological understandings of causation redirected early Americans away from the coercive action required to destroy slavery. Yet Americans, including those opposed to slavery, remained optimistic. After the defeat of Great Britain, nothing seemed impossible. Surely God was behind this miraculous event. Through the expansion of salvation in the newly independent United States, God would redeem the world.

Historian David Brion Davis begins his foundational study of Revolutionary-era abolitionism by considering "what the abolitionists were up against."[5] Davis chronicles the centuries of Western thought and legal precedent, as well as the powerful, entrenched economic interests defending slavery in the Atlantic World. But a close look at eighteenth-century ideologies of progress, rooted in both the Enlightenment and nascent evangelicalism, adds another obstacle to abolition.

Abolitionists in the 1780s and 1790s confronted a widely shared cosmology of progress that hindered the recognition of Black suffering and discouraged the actions required to eliminate American slavery. Intellectual currents privileging either head or spirit led to the same optimistic expectation that the world would inevitably improve without resorting to coercive purification. In the minds of most white Christians of all political persuasions, nothing would do more to improve the nation and the world than expanding opportunities for salvation. However, some Americans refused to rest in the confidence of inevitable improvement and instead labored to purify their communities of slavery. Conversionism and purificationism sometimes overlapped, but when it came time for direct action against the problem of slavery, Americans usually selected one or the other, and by 1800, conversionism dominated religious responses to the powerful American system of slavery.

As purificationists and conversionists offered their own spiritual solutions to the problem of slaving, the brutality and suffering of the peculiar institution only grew. Black activists did not sit passively amid this oppression, but white Americans trained their eyes to the heavens, drowning out their Black coreligionists with an imagined angelic chorus of global redemption. Understanding the development, limitations, and consequences of conversionism and purificationism exposes how Christianity inspired and limited American abolitionism.

This chapter begins by unfolding the expectation of progress that suffused the intellectual world of the late eighteenth century. These expectations of progress enabled white Christians to ignore the activism of their Black coreligionists and instead focus their efforts on expanding salvation. The chapter then considers three case studies that merged purificationism with confrontational abolitionist action, offering both an emancipatory moment in the late eighteenth century and presaging the radicalism of later antebellum abolitionists: the Quakers in the 1750s and beyond, Samuel Hopkins in the 1770s, and southern evangelicals in the 1780s. The third case study merges the worldviews of purificationism and conversionism, for in the aborted abolitionism of southern evangelicals like John Leland, we see how by the first decade of the nineteenth century, conversionism conquered purificationism and in turn muted the antislavery witness among these former radicals.

Americans, evangelical and otherwise, venerated the sovereignty of conscience and looked with suspicion on all methods of coercion. This veneration drew on wider intellectual currents to create understandings of causation that discouraged the kinds of coercive reform required to root out the institution of slavery. And so, in the early nineteenth century, American Christians busied themselves with launching campaigns of conversion to bring salvation to all corners of the new nation. These endeavors required the construction of new denominational structures, which in turn fostered new understandings of causation and new opportunities for reform that together eventually enabled a new white abolitionist movement to recognize the activism of Black Christians and together confront slavery in more effective ways. But all of this began with a preoccupation with conversions and the anticipated revolutions they were sure to bring.

Inevitable, Imminent Progress

American slavery could only be eradicated through coercion applied by the force of law. Slavery depended on the state, and so too would abolition. Indeed, there was not a single instance of slavery's disappearance in the modern world without the intervention of the state.[6] Moral suasion was only useful in that it generated support for political action. This principle proved true in both the gradual emancipation laws of the 1780s and 1790s and the so-called age of emancipations in the nineteenth century.

This realization was not so obvious, however. Slavery appeared to be in retreat. The chaos of the Revolutionary War brought liberty to tens of thousands of men and women who emancipated themselves.[7] Virginia passed legislation easing manumissions in 1782. For reasons of religious awakening and revolutionary political conviction, the peaceful granting of freedom to formerly enslaved persons began to rise in this largest and most wealthy slave state.[8] Dropping tobacco yields appeared to foretell a decline in demand for enslaved laborers.[9] Gradual abolition laws beginning in 1780 and culminating in 1804 marked the beginning of the end of slavery in the North.[10] More importantly, intellectual trends of the time placed considerable faith in the citizenry to commit itself to the cause of justice without the use of governmental power. God was working in the world, and the church had a role to play in extending the gospel.

Early antislavery existed in a world filled with both anxiety and hope. Many Americans believed that the conversion and enlightenment of hearts and minds would soon reform the world. The overturning of time-honored authorities and the dangers of revolutions alarmed Americans, yet many of these same processes promised a new era of salvation. Disestablishment and the achievement of religious liberty radicalized evangelicals during the Revolution, but the defense of religious liberty also created discourses that discouraged aggressive, political reform. Anxieties only increased with the violent terror of the French Revolution and the radicalism of the Haitian Revolution.

As Americans moved further from their own revolutionary moment, white Christians grew increasingly suspicious of political upheaval. More importantly, in the late eighteenth century, evangelicals, particularly Baptists, believed that simply securing religious liberty would unshackle American souls. Without the corrupting influence of false religion, the inevitable progress of salvation and virtue would transform the world. This confidence in progress undergirded conversionism, and evangelicals were not alone in their confidence. The expectation of inevitable progress formed the seedbed that allowed revivalism to sprout into conversionism. Put another way, evangelical revivals tapped into Enlightenment expectations of progress in order to create confidence that conversions would continue and soon remake the world. In this way, conversionism stemmed both from evangelical assurances and the Enlightenment philosophy echoing throughout the American Revolution and its aftermath.

Moral optimism suffused intellectual currents in the eighteenth-century Anglo-Atlantic World. The decline of Hobbesian pessimism in the first half of the century was followed by increased interest in the work of Scottish moral philosophers such as Henry Homes (Lord Kames), Francis Hutcheson, and Adam Smith. These thinkers fueled confidence in the progressive triumph of virtue. Francis Hutcheson built on Anthony Ashley Cooper's (Lord Shaftesbury) *Inquiry into the Original of Our Ideas of Beauty and Virtue* to argue for an independent, innate "moral sense" in all of humanity.[11]

These assurances provided powerful balms for Christians in colonial North America who anguished over the state of their souls and their safety in an age of revolutions. This anxiety transcended theological boundaries and extended both to Calvinists, convinced of their total depravity and the irresistibility of grace, and to Methodists, who strove for spirit-led sanctification and perfection. Denominational identities created rivalries and anxieties between Christians, but nearly all Americans remained convinced that the spread of their religious tradition would offer the surest and most effective means of social improvement.[12] For white Christians, governmental action could never compete with the redemptive power of the cross.

Conversion was a rigorous process but regardless of the sincerity of one's conversion experience, the true evidence of salvation manifested in righteous living. Moral philosophy, then, became a way of understanding and evaluating the evidence of conversion. Christian piety encouraged a constant, rigorous level of introspection. Diaries from the eighteenth century are riddled with intense, anguished self-evaluation.[13] Moral philosophy sought to externalize this process with rational laws about human behavior. Deference to the authority of tradition declined. The world was being made anew, and American Christians needed evidence of their salvation and assurance that God was advancing his cause in the new nation. The optimism of Scottish common sense moral philosophy offered both.[14]

By reading moral philosophy, accepting academic instruction, or simply attending church services, Americans absorbed ideological expectations of progressive social improvement. Americans celebrated Scottish common sense philosophy mostly because it served their religious purposes. In the dedication to his *Inquiry into the Human Mind on the Principles of Common Sense*, Thomas Reid attacked David Hume's *Treatise of Human Nature* by labeling it "a system of scepticism which leaves no ground to believe any one thing rather than its contrary."[15] American Christians needed to believe things, and they needed to believe that those things were true. Hume's work called everything into question, but Reid's brought clarity and, more importantly, assurance.

Reid's work reached the United States primarily through his student Dugald Stewart's *Elements of the Philosophy of the Human Mind*. This work formed a key component of American education, particularly in the curriculum of influential Presbyterian educator John Witherspoon. Both as an individual teacher and as president of Princeton from 1768 to 1794, Witherspoon did more than anyone else to spread Scottish moral philosophy in the United States. His students then carried the same curriculum to Presbyterian schools across the nation, both North and South. From Reid through Stewart and Witherspoon, Americans gained intellectual confidence in the reasonableness of their faith and the expected progress of virtue.[16]

Few Americans had heard of, much less read, these thinkers. However, historian Sarah Knott has convincingly argued that the development of sensibility was an active process of identity creation, particularly for middling Americans, and through this process Enlightenment ideals suffused several strata of society. Knott also demonstrates how women likewise consumed and perpetuated expectations of progress, particularly through accessible works designed for both sexes.[17]

Whether through an expansion of the Enlightenment or through the fires of revival, Americans remained optimistic that the world was on the cusp of rapturous change. The kinds of coercive agitation required to destroy slavery threatened to divide white Christians and interrupt these inevitable, liberatory processes with distracting division. The fear of these divisions led many white Christians to willfully ignore the Black activists that constructed abolitionist movements. Other white Christians sympathetic to the Black freedom struggle simply could not risk sidetracking their missions of salvation.

The very same intellectual currents that challenged the morality of slavery also contained optimistic expectations of progress that discouraged the kind of agitation required to end the institution in the United States. Confidence in progress coexisted with pessimism about the dangers and challenges of the human condition. Scottish moral philosophy maintained its grip on Americans for a century after its apex in the mid-eighteenth century.[18] This body of thought merged head and heart, reason and piety, and it did so by reinforcing confidence in the progressive triumph of virtue, enlightenment, and salvation. Faith in the future coexisted with beliefs in human depravity. Enlightenment notions of progress meshed well with evangelical confidence in the spread of salvation. God was at work in America, and his work would save souls and remake the world in his image.

Optimism accelerated during the American Revolution in ways that discouraged organized legislative challenges to slavery. Americans saw God's providence in the war and anticipated an outpouring of salvation that would save the world. But salvation would not come from government nor from divisive political agitation. It would come from God. Independence freed God's people from tyranny, and Americans would use that freedom to expand salvation. Timothy Dwight celebrated the miraculous victory at Yorktown in 1781 by claiming that God was bringing "an entire separation between civil and ecclesiastical things" and that the millennium would approach not because of political change but rather by "an extensive diffusion of holiness, the work of his Spirit."[19] Three years later, the same year that the Confederation Congress abolished slavery in the Northwest Territories, the Baptist Warren Association in New England remarked that the real purpose of the Revolution was to "advance the cause of Christ in the world," thereby "bringing the glory of the latter day."[20] Of course, the era was not the bastion of religious liberty implied by this rhetoric, and white Christians used a host of political and cultural pressures to maintain their hegemony.[21] But prior to the War of 1812, these same hegemonic forces discouraged the political organizing that national abolition would require.

In the early republic—an age of intense politicking—powerful countercurrents pulled the faithful away from expecting holiness to flow from legislation or legal rulings. Even as Americans joined political parties, they often did so with a sour taste in their mouth, fearing that divisive factionalism might sunder their revolutionary experiment. Fortunately, in their view, confidence in the rising tide of salvation funneled the humanitarian sensibility away from political coercion and toward religious conversion. Most Americans did not believe that the Revolution itself nor the political changes it unleashed would inaugurate the millennium; rather, these events would enable the expansion of salvation that would bring true, lasting, divinely directed change. Americans had defeated British tyranny, leaving the gospel manifestly destined to spread across the continent and rebound back across the Atlantic.

Confidence in inevitable progress was shared even by men who doubted the divinity of Christ. Thomas Paine promised in 1792, "The present age will hereafter merit to be called the Age of Reason, and the present generation will appear to the future as the Adam of a new world."[22] After the Revolution, the decidedly non-evangelical Richard Price also predicted a steady improvement in the world. When he looked to the past, the Fellow of the Royal Society confidently proclaimed, "The world has hitherto been gradually improving." He found more reason for optimism in the future: "Such are the natures of things that this progress must continue."[23] These values were shared by both Enlightenment deists and pious evangelicals.

The American clergyman and educator Timothy Dwight proclaimed in 1781, "It is the tendency of human affairs, unless interrupted by extraordinary incidents, to be constantly progressive towards what may be termed natural perfection."[24] This confidence, however, did not lead to a political push for new laws. Intellectual currents that emphasized individual religious regeneration inspired many to look to heaven rather than to the legislature or the courthouse for social improvement. In 1788 Salem, South Carolina, Presbyterian minister Thomas Reese concluded that "human laws will be found but a weak fence against the violence and injustice of men."[25] For Reese, and so many others, the expansion of religion provided the only hope for a stable and prosperous nation. And that hope would soon be realized by spreading salvation. Instead of listening to the calls of their Black coreligionists, white Christians remained optimistic that simply expanding salvation would solve all of the problems of the age.

In May 1783, after the surrender at Yorktown but before the Treaty of Paris, Ezra Stiles delivered a sermon before the General Assembly of Connecticut with the title "The United States Elevated to Glory and Honor." Stiles predicted that the end of the war would inaugurate the "accomplishment of the *magnalia dei*—the great events in God's moral government designed from eternal ages to be displayed in these ends of the earth." Stiles saw God's fingerprints in demographics, rejoicing that as the white population was "increasing with great rapidity, and the Indians, as well as a million Africans in America are decreasing as rapidly . . . an unrighteous slavery may at length, in God's good providence, be abolished and cease in the land of liberty."[26]

It is worth noting that Stiles still used the term "abolished" and not a more passive term like "disappeared" or even "eradicated." Still, the agent in his sentence is God's good providence, and men like Stiles rested confident that God would solve the problem of slavery without divisive, human-led political agitation. Even more notably, Stiles's vision of abolition involved the disappearance of African-descended peoples. Stiles, and many others like him, could not imagine a biracial nation. The piece did, however, include a few calls to action. The first was to preserve and extend religious liberty. The second was to continue the work of spreading the gospel. Stiles also included an implicit third call to invade and conquer the West, a process most Americans understood as part of God's divine plan for expanding salvation. Through these actions, and not the work of attacking social sin, the United States would fulfill "the *magnalie-dei,* the great events in God's moral government."

At the end of the eighteenth century, the English Methodist Joseph Benson's millennial musings refused to tie providential deliverance to political upheaval and instead turned to personal piety and expanding salvation as the only true roads to progress. Benson lived in what historians now call the age of revolutions, a transformative moment where ancient systems of oppression were overturned with startling speed and terrifying violence. In editions published on both sides of the Atlantic, Benson dismissed these "revolutions which are continually happening" as "events which short-sighted mortals deem of consequence." What mattered more was "the grand revolution of universal nature; the glorious exaltation of the Prince of the kings of the earth." To truly change the world, Christians should not meddle with policies nor support violent revolution. But Benson was not discouraging all action. Instead, he called on Christians to "delay no longer, but while thy glass of time is not yet run out" all should look to their soul and to the souls of their countrymen.[27] Suspicions of political radicalism only grew when the age of revolutions shifted from what Americans understood as their orderly, pious independence movement to the licentious infidelity of the French Revolution and to the overthrow of slavery and white supremacy in Haiti.

Americans increasingly divorced their visions of social change from political radicalism as the French Revolution devolved in terror and the Haitian Revolution horrified white Americans ever aware of the potential for slave rebellion. Against this backdrop of political anxiety, enthusiastic beliefs in radical personal transformation generated a cheerful expectation that true, lasting, and orderly change would best be wrought through individual conversions and through settler colonialism, a form of violence embraced by white Christians as an agent of salvation.

Under the logic of conversionist causation, what we might identify as conservative strategies were for contemporaries the very embodiment of world-altering radicalism. They believed themselves engaged in a revolutionary project of a different sort that would remake the world while avoiding the blood and death of the French and Haitian Revolutions. Of course, this radicalism yielded little effectual change, and conversionist causation did more to entrench American slavery than to weaken it. On the ground, human bondage deepened its grip on American life, while white Christians of nearly all political persuasions ignored Black activists and instead looked confidently to the heavens.

John Blair Smith addressed the inaugural meeting of the Northern Missionary Society in Albany, New York, on January 11, 1797, a time that was in many ways a world apart from the optimism of the early 1770s. However, we see that despite the terror of the French and Haitian Revolutions, optimism endured when constrained solely to missions of salvation. In this missionary address, Smith proclaimed that the expansion of conversions would ensure that "the order and happiness of the creation be best secured." Smith's ministry moved through Pennsylvania, New Jersey, Virginia, and New York as he pastored numerous churches, fostered revivals, and held the presidency of Hampden-Sydney College in central Virginia and that of Union College in upstate New York. In all of his homes and in all of his vocations, he held a consistent anticipation of a gospel-driven social transformation. He repeated this sentiment throughout his address to the Northern Missionary Society, calling his audience to aid the society in their efforts "to obtain the increase and stability of the Redeemer's kingdom." The end of slavery would be a component of these radical changes, but antislavery and other matters of social reform must begin with conversion not only because eternal salvation took priority over temporal happiness, but also because the expansion of salvation promised the surest route to a godly social order.[28]

These thoughts were not Smith's alone. In fact, Smith considered them so commonplace as to negate the necessity for their publication. When the society pressed Smith to allow his remarks to be published, Smith insisted that a foreword acknowledge its contents as "so familiar and common." Smith wanted to be known for uttering impressive ideas and found it embarrassing to be associated with what he found to be oft-repeated banal truths. The foreword again expressed the wish that readers would nonetheless benefit from these "common topics and arguments."[29] Though this belief of conversion's potential to enact social change was so prevalent in the turn of the century as to make him wary of overburdening his reader with commonplace assumptions, historians have not reckoned with the widespread belief that conversion would solve the problems of the day. The widely held conviction that conversion would bring God's kingdom to earth enabled the men and women who made up an early American antislavery consensus to drift along with the tide of the times without mounting a serious challenge to increasingly entrenched systems of slavery.

Black Americans would not be so patient. Rapidly growing communities of free Black people in northern cities organized against slavery while their white coreligionists turned away.[30] The same month that Smith foretold the transformational power of salvation, Black Christians in Philadelphia sought to advance human liberty in another way. On January 30, Congressman John

Swanwick of Pennsylvania presented a petition signed by Jupiter Nicholson, Jacob Nicholson, Joe Albert, and Thomas Pritchet. These men were formerly enslaved in North Carolina before being freed by their owners, enabling their migration out of the slave society of their birth. Now residents of Philadelphia, the four enlisted the help of Absalom Jones, leader of the African Episcopal Church of St. Thomas. Through Jones's pen, these Black activists petitioned the United States legislature to protect emancipated peoples from capture and resale. After a raucous discussion, the House voted 50 to 33 to ignore the petition.[31] Black Americans continued to appeal to the power of the federal government, and the federal government, like white religious denominations, continued to ignore them. Meanwhile, white Christians remained optimistic that the world would improve not through politicking, but rather though expanding opportunities for conversion.

This same confidence in the liberatory power of salvation directed the responses of religious bodies to the sins of slavery. In May 1787, while the Constitutional Convention was just underway down the road, the Synod of New York and Philadelphia met in Second Church, Philadelphia. These Presbyterians produced a curious antislavery tract proclaiming, "The Synod of New York and Philadelphia do highly approve of the general principles in favor of universal liberty, that prevail in America, and the interest which many of the states have taken in promoting the abolition of slavery." This enthusiastic praise for the progress of abolition was followed not by encouragement for further action, but rather caution. The synod asserted that "men introduced from a servile state, to a participation of all the privileges of civil society, without a proper education, and without previous habits of industry, may be, in many respects dangerous to the community."[32]

While this alarm certainly illustrates how Presbyterians shared the ubiquitous racist anxieties of the era, their concern implies more than a lack of antislavery zeal. It also indicates a deep confidence in the inevitability of mass manumissions. These Presbyterians felt assured that slavery was passing away. In their minds, the tide of freedom had begun to sweep across the continent. The American Revolution marked a shift in the millennial timeline, and an era of holiness was nigh. From their perspective, the Synod did not need to encourage further action except for coordinating campaigns for conversion. Divine agency promised to continue the work of abolition, and from their vantage point, economic trends, religious convictions, and political currents all proved that God was well at work in securing abolition. The question for these Presbyterians was not whether the United States would abandon slavery but rather what a postslavery nation would look like. It was here that the Presbyterians sought to act.[33]

Presbyterians implored the faithful to Christianize and educate their soon-to-be-freed slaves. The members of the Synod "earnestly recommend it to all the members of their communion, to give those persons who are held in servitude such good education as may prepare them for the better enjoyment of freedom." According to the republican ideology common in the late eighteenth century, freedom required the ownership of property, so Presbyterians entreated their members to provide their slaves with "some share of property to begin with, or grant them sufficient time, and sufficient means, of procuring by industry, their own liberty, at a moderate rate; that they may thereby be brought into society and those habits of industry that may render them useful citizens." Only after these directives did the authors conclude with a call for churchmen "to use the most prudent measures, consistent with the interest and the state of civil society, in the parts where they live, to procure, eventually, *the final abolition of slavery in America*."[34]

These antislavery sentiments came from the Synod of New York and Philadelphia two years prior to the formation of the General Assembly, the national Presbyterian denominational body. Tying the national church together required compromise, particularly on the question of slavery, and northern clergymen must have worried about how their southern brethren would react to even veiled antislavery language. In 1793, the same year that Congress passed the first Fugitive Slave Act, Presbyterians were at the height of their effort to maintain national unity in order to coordinate missionary efforts. Despite the need for continued unity, the General Assembly unanimously approved the earlier resolution and apportioned money to be spent in reprinting and publicizing the declaration. The statement left enough room for slaveholders to offer their support without offering any foreseeable threat to the institution. Paternalist fantasies enabled pious slaveholders to imagine their mastery as a means of preparing slaves for freedom without actually taking steps toward manumission, much less abolition.

Whether they understood themselves as Adams of a new world or John the Baptists presaging the reign of Christ, many Americans believed that theirs was an auspicious age and they expected an outpouring of salvation. The American nation had much to do with the expected transformations, but primary agency was generally placed in the providence of God and not the energy of the American state. Enlightenment radicals and antislavery evangelicals marched confidently toward an age when evils like slavery would vanish before the impending glory. Yet revolutionary confidence proved a mirage and expectations of progress collided with the realities of a nation rooted in slaving.

Despite the powerful pull of conversionism, the late eighteenth century also included a fledgling movement of purificationist abolitionists who would not passively wait for God to remove the sin of slavery. While conversionists busied themselves with the millennial expansion of salvation outside their congregations, other antislavery Christians looked within, laboring to purify their communities, or even the entire nation, of the sin of slavery. Purificationists mounted serious attacks on slavery for a variety of reasons. Most were more interested in ensuring the holiness of their own souls rather than in alleviating the suffering of Black Americans. But whether from internal piety or outward-facing compassion, purificationists sought to use power to eliminate slavery. Tracking the three most influential cases of purificationist antislavery shows the limitations of this ideology and the process that led most white antislavery Americans to turn instead toward conversionism as the less confrontational solution to the problem of slavery.

The first case analyzes the most-consistent opponents of antislavery in the era, the Quakers. Transatlantic activism motivated by Quakers and secured the largest and most influential early nineteenth-century abolitionist victories in both Britain and the United States. Reformers in the mid to late eighteenth century encouraged Quakers to strengthen their prophetic voice of protest, but others contested these reforming impulses, and the community of Friends struggled to maintain unity. Antislavery became a means by which the Society of Friends held their church together. But the Quaker reformation of the eighteenth century left the Society of Friends as a marginal, often persecuted sect. The American Revolution further weakened Quaker claims to power, and the Quakers began to search for other allies to carry forth their crusade.

One of the most influential partners in this process serves as a second case study: the Congregationalist theologian and minister Samuel Hopkins. In the aftermath of the Revolution, both religious and secular leaders struggled to reconcile the new language of liberty with the institution of slavery. Hopkins utilized the rhetoric of revolution and the emergent Black antislavery movement to mount an assault on the slave trade in 1776, and he did so in the immediate shadow of powerful and profitable local slaving interests in his home of Newport, Rhode Island. Through a series of tracts and treatises published in

the middle of the eighteenth century, Hopkins developed a powerful reputation as a formidable theologian. But his commitment to Calvinism ultimately
muted the effectiveness of his antislavery appeal and prevented him from directing the destiny of the nation in the way he desired. The heirs to the Great
Awakening slowly moved away from the rigors of Calvinism and the activism
of purificationist abolitionism, leaving Hopkins as a lone, marginalized voice
crying in the wilderness.

New, louder voices in the South and West captured the national consciousness in the era. These evangelicals serve as the third case of purificationist antislavery. Southern evangelicals mounted a short-lived challenge to the slave system in the 1780s, as both the Baptists and Methodists issued condemnations of
slaving and excluded slavers from active religious fellowship. In the tumultuous
time of the Revolution, religious leaders North and South, from denominations
expanding and contracting, processed revolutionary hostility to slavery in terms
colored by geographic location and religious values. The revolutionary language
of liberty combined with the values of late eighteenth-century religion to ig-
nite a purificationist purge of slavery in the newly independent United States.
This purge would be short-lived, however, as evangelicals concluded that conversionism provided a more comfortable and less confrontational solution to
American slaving. By the second decade of the nineteenth century, southern
evangelicals devoted far more energy to purifying their communities of abolitionism than to getting rid of slavery.

The Quaker Reformation

It is nearly impossible to exaggerate the influence of Quakers in advancing the
cause of abolitionism.[35] With the sole exception of enslaved people themselves
and free Black communities, no other group in the Atlantic World did more to
embrace abolitionism as a component of their self-identity or did more to turn
that identity into meaningful action. Historian Christopher Leslie Brown has
shown how American Quakers emboldened British abolitionists in abolishing
the transatlantic slave trade in 1807. To understand the abolitionist prowess of
Quakers on both sides of the Atlantic, however, we have to move back at least a
half century to understand how abolitionism came to be an integral component
of membership in the Society of Friends. The American Quakers that Brown
credits for motivating British abolition were themselves motivated by British Quakers several decades earlier. Tracking these ocean-traversing reformers

reveals how and why Quakers sought to purify the Society of Friends of all manner of sins, including the sin of slavery.

Quaker abolitionists grew out of what scholars have called the Quaker reformation, a watershed development that transformed the Society of Friends from a small, scattered community into a globally informed countercultural movement. The Quaker reformation commenced as Friends relinquished their power in the colonial Pennsylvania government in the 1750s and instead tightened Quaker disciplinary policies across the Atlantic World.[36] As they moved further from sources of political power, Quakers called for increased discipline on a host of moral issues ranging from Christian parenthood to material asceticism to abolitionism. This communal cleansing allowed many marginal Quakers to drift away to other sects, while emboldening those who remained by the time of the Revolution. The smaller, more committed group emerged with a zealous belief in their moral purity, and Quaker identity became increasingly connected to adherence to these reforming principles, most notably abolitionism. By the end of the eighteenth century, it became nearly impossible for enslavers to maintain active membership in a Quaker meeting. The purificationist impulse had worked within the Society of Friends, and slavery all but vanished from Quaker communities.[37]

In 1720, British Quaker Thomas Chalkley offered perhaps the most succinct distillation of the doctrine that informed the movement. He wrote, "Christ says, 'be ye perfect as your Father who is in heaven is perfect.'" Chalkley unflinchingly claimed that any who resisted reformation "mock[ed] the Almighty," and "they will be much mistaken in the day of the righteous judgment of God." Chalkley, much like the later Garrisonian abolitionists, was not shy in calling out sins and demanding radical, immediate transformation. He and the reformers who came decades after him would not relent in their quests to purify the Quaker community.[38] They could not imagine mocking the Almighty and they persistently confronted others who did. Chalkley published his call for purification in 1747, and Quakers throughout the Atlantic World reprinted the text and employed his message as a powerful argument for reformation. Other British Quakers would carry this message personally through several important transatlantic missions of reform.

John Storer, a British Quaker, traveled to North America in 1759 with the goal of encouraging American Quakers in their reformation. In early May 1760 Storer began a collaboration with John Woolman, the American Quaker mystic. The two met in Newport, Rhode Island, a principal port for slaving activity in eighteenth-century British North America. The continuation of the slave trade tortured Woolman, and his time spent in Newport only amplified his discomfort. Woolman hoped to present a self-penned essay against the slave trade to the state legislature. Local Quakers dissuaded him from this plan, pressing him to instead purify the local community by encouraging Friends to emancipate their slaves. Woolman complied but soon grew distressed as several respected Newport Quaker elders refused to free their slaves. Woolman turned to Storer for help, and the two quietly and patiently confronted these elders to press for manumissions. Following the meeting, Woolman rejoiced, confident that "a good exercise was spreading among them," and that slavery would soon disappear from the community of Friends in Newport.[39] This pattern repeated itself throughout Quaker communities and informed the lessons that parents taught their children.[40]

Quaker women took on a particularly important role in the Quaker reformation due to the emphasis on raising pure, faithful children. Elizabeth Wilkinson, another British Quaker who traveled across the Atlantic to encourage the Quaker reformation, reached northern Virginia in the early 1760s. As she surveyed this slave society, her primary focus was not on the suffering enslaved people she encountered; instead, she fretted that slave ownership prevented parents from raising their children properly. At a meeting held just outside of Petersburg in 1762, Wilkinson advised Quakers who delayed in freeing their enslaved laborers to at least require "servants and negroes to call their children by the names they had given them and not master and mistress."[41] Wilkinson and many others feared that children raised around enslaved laborers would be filled with pride and other perhaps more dangerous sins. Saving her harshest language for women, she berated the attendees of a women's meeting in Nantucket, blaming them in part for the "many hurtful things [that] had crept into the society." Questioning the women's ability to maintain Quaker identity, she challenged all "to look well to their own families each one, so that a reformation might be begun by the present generation."[42]

Wilkinson continued trumpeting this message at a Philadelphia meeting in 1763, joining fellow British itinerant Quaker Hannah Harris. According to George Churchman, the two women prepared Americans to "repair the wall broken down, through the backsliding of their predecessors and themselves in the day of ease and outward prosperity."[43] This emphasis on the relationship between slavery and raising Christian children endured among Quakers even after the Revolution.

While ministering to Virginia Quakers in 1788, Job Scott wrote to his wife, Eunice, "Negro slavery has almost ruined this country, both as to religion and the outward soil of the earth." The primary problem with slavery, according to Scott's observations of Alexandria, Virginia, was that "Friends' children have been brought up in idleness." Unlike the children of "happy New England" who "have to do for themselves and are not so generally endangered by that idleness," children in the South were "scarcely called on to do an hour's business of any kind. From infancy to settlement in families of their own, they have spent much of their time in riding about for pleasure. The consequence has been almost the extinction of society."[44] It is true that Quaker purificationist antislavery often prioritized the spirituality of white members over the alleviation of Black suffering; nonetheless, the purifying spirit was sufficient to mount a serious challenge to human bondage. The fear of personal corruption was enough for many Quakers to renounce slaving and support meaningful action to secure abolition.

For some Quakers, their identification with abolitionism became even stronger than their identification with Quakerism. During the same trip where he fretted over the corruption of children, Scott found some non-Quakers who had not suffered the scourge of slavery to such an extent. While still ministering in northern Virginia, Scott rejoiced over "a glorious meeting" held with Methodists. His Quaker partisanship kept him suspicious of Methodist enthusiasm, but when he compared his time with antislavery Methodists with his despair at enslaving Quakers, Scott seemed to privilege moral purity over doctrinal orthodoxy. When meeting with Quaker enslavers, Scott seemed to "suffer almost unto death" but among Methodists in 1789, he rejoiced that "this day, in a special manner, the streams of life flowed plentifully and sweetly to my great satisfaction and comfort and to the refreshment of many minds."[45] Slavery threatened true spirituality, and faithful Quakers had to purify themselves and their communities of human bondage. If they failed to do so, they risked surrendering their moral superiority to other antislavery Christians, like these late 1780s Virginia Methodists.

Even Friends who sought converts privileged purity over evangelism. John Fothergill traveled to North America in 1754 to grow the Quaker church. His explanation of why he failed to spread salvation in Virginia reveals how most Quakers understood the close, and perhaps inextricable, relationship between purity and conversion. Fothergill claimed that though the "meeting house in Surry County was pretty large," the impiety of this community prevented their further growth, as the "want of living to the Truth, stood in the way of the Gospel Life and hindered its prevalency among the people."[46] According to Fothergill, unless these Virginia Quakers first purified their congregation, growth would remain impossible. That same year, British Quaker Benjamin Holme framed purification as essential for the Quaker witness, suggesting in his "epistle to Friends in America" that if the weaker members of the community were "drawn away with loose company," then the Quaker witness would suffer, "bringing dishonor to the truth."[47] Holme wanted conversions to grow the community, but he believed purity to be an essential precondition.

For some Quakers, adding members to the society was not a reason for celebration but rather a cause for alarm. When ministering in New York in 1762, Elizabeth Wilkinson chastised Quakers about their recent success in recruiting new members. As she wrote in her journal, "I apprehended it my duty to caution our Society that they were spreading in the Land." For Wilkinson, the desire to see Quakers fully purified led her to warn against attracting novice converts who might become "stumbling blocks to any inquirers."[48] The strength of the Quaker witness would come from the community's unique purity, and nothing, not even generating new converts, should jeopardize that purity.

John Churchman's commitment to purity pressed him to sacrifice even divinely ordained opportunities for evangelization if it meant inconsistency with his moral code. Despite feeling assured that the Inner Light was calling him to minister in Barbados in 1760, Churchman refused to travel when he could find passage only on warships. Churchman was sure that God was moving in the Caribbean and that he could be a part of a great and holy work, but he would not sacrifice his uncompromising commitment to pacifism.[49] For Churchman, conversions might save the world, but salvation could not occur in the first place unless the bearers of the gospel had purified themselves. Conversions mattered for nearly all of this era's religious Americans, but for some, holy living mattered even more.

The purificationist antislavery of some Quakers like John Parrish led to open confrontations with slaving Quakers, an intimidating prospect for those whose piety was in question. In an undated letter, Parrish informed James Thornton that he was traveling to Maryland, "taking some meetings on the Western Shore and spending some time at Annapolis with the assembly on account of the oppressed Africans before the Yearly Meeting comes on."[50] By 1780, Parrish believed that his work had been so successful that he began to turn his antislavery ministry outward, beyond the community of Friends. What began as a series of "Notes on Abolition" eventually was published as *Remarks on the Slavery of the Black People*. Between the first draft and the published piece, Parrish watered down much of his rhetoric, but he nonetheless addressed all of the "inhabitants of the land of my nativity" and described slavery as "a national evil."[51] This focus on slavery in a wider national context, rather than on a local community level marked an important shift in Quaker antislavery. Even as Quaker antislavery grew more national, the purifying spirit remained.

The new American republic made a perfect target as Quakers sought to extend the purification campaign. To do so, however, required new allies. American Friends found a perfect candidate in perhaps the unlikeliest of all places: Newport, Rhode Island, a hub of the Atlantic slave trade. The prevalence of slavery in Newport thoroughly disgusted John Parrish, just as it had distressed John Woolman decades earlier. Parrish called the cosmopolitan port "a dark place and on the decline at present." But he was excited to make the acquaintance of "a veritable aged Presbyterian parson." This famous minister was well known to Parrish and others throughout the Atlantic World for his work as "a warm advocate for the liberation of the Black people as well as for stopping the trade." While their theologies diverged wildly, the two shared a commitment to purge the new republic's sins, and both appealed to the discourse of purification to do so. Parrish rejoiced after the meeting, which he believed "was to our mutual satisfaction."[52] This minister was no Presbyterian, but rather the prominent Congregationalist theologian and antislavery advocate Samuel Hopkins.

Samuel Hopkins and Revolutionary Abolitionism

Samuel Hopkins returned the affection of John Parrish, having glowingly written fifteen years earlier, "The Quakers, who have done more than any others to acquit themselves of the guilt of the slave trade, and have discovered more humanity and regard to the laws of Christ, in [the antislavery struggle], than any other denomination of Christians."[53] Unlike Parrish, Hopkins did not have the support of a deep denominational commitment to antislavery. His conversion to antislavery did not come from a position of denominational unity, but rather from a place of denominational rivalry. However, Hopkins did not seek to save his denomination; he sought to save his nation, and he was prepared to listen to the Black men and women in his church and elsewhere calling for an uncompromising break with slavery.

But first Hopkins had to reckon with the battle waging in his own city.

By 1761, Hopkins's rival Congregationalist minister, Ezra Stiles, calculated that Newport boasted sixty shops on Main Street and one in three buildings in the entire city served as a warehouse or commercial establishment.[54] Nearly all of this economic growth was tied to slavery. Hopkins himself asserted that "the inhabitants of Rhode Island, especially those of Newport, have had by far the greater share in this traffic of all these United States. This trade in the human species has been the first wheel of commerce in Newport."[55] Indeed, Newport was among the most influential slaving cities in the Atlantic World.[56] Abolitionists in Rhode Island, particularly in Newport, battled wealthy, powerful slaving interests, and upon moving to Newport in 1770 to take up the position of pastor at First Congregational Church, Hopkins plunged right into the middle of the fight, eventually pairing with Providence-based Quakers in forming a powerful Rhode Island abolitionist axis.[57]

Before he earned fame as an abolitionist, Hopkins first made a name for himself as a theological troublemaker, defending Calvinism and articulating a radical view of divine sovereignty that credited God for making everything happen, including sin.[58] After his move to Newport, he continued to rankle Congregationalist clergymen with his intellectual prowess and commitment to social justice. From a frontier theologian to the most active antislavery divine in the new nation, Samuel Hopkins developed a new theology of social reform that both reflected and shaped the contested meaning of American freedom.

Throughout this process, Hopkins broadened his sphere of influence from Congregationalist ministers to local leaders in Rhode Island, before ultimately seeking to direct the destiny of the nation as whole. As an heir of the theocratic New England tradition, Hopkins was not shy about wielding Christianity in attempt to graft abolitionism onto the new nation. He was an outlier, however, and nearly all of his colleagues failed to pick up his call for social transformation. Nonetheless, Hopkins demonstrated how dreams of Christian purity could inform radical abolitionism, and his failure shows the challenges faced by those who adopted those purifying principles.

Hopkins's principles were as fiery as any Garrisonian a generation later, as he cursed slavers, claiming that they were "unworthy [of] the privileges of freemen" and ought "to be considered as enemies to mankind, and murderers of their brethren for the sake of gold, and real pests and plagues to society."[59] Opposition to the slave trade caught on much quicker than opposition to the practice of slavery itself, and some Americans argued that while great guilt was incurred by the traders who stole Africans from their homes, present slave owners were merely suffering from an incorrigible arrangement that left them no option but to try to treat their slaves with compassion. Hopkins had no tolerance for those who imparted different levels of guilt upon slave traders and slaveholders, thundering to the latter that their human chattel "have been stolen and sold, and you have bought them, in your own wrong."[60] Hopkins would not tolerate any union with enslavers, even for the purpose of expanding salvation. In his eyes, the nation was stricken with the sin of slaving, and it must purify itself.

Hopkins's commitment to purificationist abolitionism developed from three sources: his rivalry with Ezra Stiles's Second Congregational Church, his theology of disinterested benevolence, and his experiences with Black activists. Through his opposition to "the first wheel of commerce," Hopkins distinguished himself from his cross-town rival, Ezra Stiles. Stiles held the pulpit at the Second Congregationalist Church in Newport, while Hopkins was at the First Congregationalist Church. Despite the two names there was no doubt that Stiles's congregation was first in rank. On any given Sunday, the pews of Second Congregational in Newport would swell with the town's elites, while Hopkins preached to a smaller, less distinguished collection of white and Black congregants. This disparity caused little concern for Hopkins, confirming the purity of his humbler flock. From his early years in the backwoods of Housatonic, Massachusetts, Hopkins developed a deep distrust of those wielding wealth and power. His relocation to Newport accelerated his public criticisms of material comfort. While eventually Hopkins would cooperate with Stiles on a number of conversionist missions, their rivalry endured and guided First Congregationalist's antislavery witness.

Hopkins's theological inclinations toward abolitionism began with his rejection of self-love. In the mid-eighteenth century, liberal Calvinists drew on recent trends in moral philosophy to use the concept of self-love as inspiration for moral living. Instead of berating selfishness, these ministers praised enlightened self-interest that demonstrated how righteousness benefited both earthly and heavenly pursuits. For consistent Calvinists like Samuel Hopkins, these doctrines raised alarm bells; the church must be purified of all forms of selfishness.

Hopkins saw himself as a faithful defender of his mentor Jonathan Edwards's theology, but, in reality, he had moved well beyond his teacher. Edwards granted self-love a role in what he termed "secondary virtue," whereas Hopkins relegated all manifestations of self-love as sinful, instead embracing disinterested benevolence.[61] Best understood as a rejection of self-love and an emphasis on unselfishness, disinterested benevolence was a virtue Hopkins found sorely wanting in the world around him, particularly after his relocation to the slaving city of Newport. This virtue provided an ethic for social reform much as the Quaker reformation provided an ethic that supported Quaker abolitionism. Hopkins put his social ethic to quick use in mounting an attack on slavery. Only three years after advocating the value of disinterested benevolence, Hopkins sought to purify the selfishness of his community by attacking the slave trade.

And yet, if we pay close attention to the discourse of Hopkins's abolitionism, we see that his theological commitment to disinterested benevolence was not sufficient to motivate his antislavery. Instead, Hopkins's abolitionist rhetoric had far more in common with that of Black activists than with his earlier theological writings. Unlike most other white Christians of the era, Hopkins listened to his Black coreligionists, including those in his own congregation, which included many Black Christians, and his activism reflected both his theology and these biracial relationships.[62] Among his many Black correspondents, none were quite as famous as Phillis Wheatley, who sent Hopkins several volumes of her work in 1774 and met with him several times while visiting her good friend Obour Tanner, a parishioner at Hopkins's First Congregational Church.[63] But while Hopkins valued his correspondence with Wheatley, his worldview was shaped more by quotidian interactions with his parishioners and local Black leaders who recognized the hypocrisy of the American Revolution.

The bulk of Hopkins's 1776 abolitionist pamphlet drew heavily on the spirit of the American Revolution and on the prior activism of Black New Englanders. As an heir to the New England theocracy, Hopkins was comfortable in seeking to direct the nation's religious destiny, and he deployed the rhetoric of providential nationalism to purify the republic of its greatest sin. This use of providential nationalism echoed the earlier writings of Caesar Sarter, a formerly enslaved man in Newburyport, Massachusetts, who in 1774, as tensions with Britain accelerated, offered his own purificationist jeremiad. Sarter declared to white New Englanders that he sympathized with their agitation against Britain, but reminded them that "slavery is the greatest, and most consequently most to be dreaded, of all temporal calamities." If Americans were to gain victory over Britain, they first must ensure their own righteousness. Sarter declared. "Would you desire the preservation of your own liberty? As the first step let the oppressed Africans be liberated; then, and not till then, may you with confidence and consistency of conduct, look to Heaven for a blessing on your endeavors."[64]

Hopkins echoed all of these themes, labeling the Revolution as a providential message condemning the sin of slavery: "God has raised up men to attempt to deprive us of liberty, and the evil we are threatened with is slavery."[65] "This whole contest," Hopkins wrote, "was suited to bring and keep in our view, and impress on our minds, a deep and lasting sense of the worth of liberty, and the unrighteousness of taking it from any man, and consequently, of our unrighteousness and cruelty towards the Africans."[66]

Hopkins clung strongly to this providential logic after the Revolution, crediting the 1774 temporary ban on the importation of slaves as the cause of American victory. Hopkins wrote in 1793, "With this resolution we entered the combat, and God appeared to be on our side, and wrought wonders in our favor, disappointed those who rose up against us, and established us a free and independent nation."[67] Yet without further progress in the abolition of slavery, Hopkins warned that divinely ordained penance was inevitable, for slavery was "a national sin, and a sin of the first magnitude—a sin which righteous Heaven has never suffered to pass unpunished in this world." He had carried this even further in 1793, asking "is this not Heaven frowning upon us *now?*" His evidence for God's displeasure at America was plentiful, including the decline in trade, the vast public debt, the depredations of the Barbary Pirates, and "a spirit of discontent and murmuring, and jealousy of our rulers . . . and in some places insurrections, and open, violent opposition to government."[68]

The struggles of the new nation, according to Hopkins, were the direct result of divine punishment for the sins of slavery. These ideas drew directly from protests echoing out of the Black community. Phillis Wheatley, for example, wrote in a published letter to Samson Occom in 1774 that "God grant Deliverance in his own Way and Time, and get him honor upon all those whose avarice impels them to countenance and help forward tile Calamities of their fellow Creatures."[69] Hopkins and Wheatley both anticipated calamities to occur unless the United States purified itself from the sin of slaving.

Hopkins turned to purificationist abolitionism as an extension of his doctrinal commitment to disinterested benevolence, much like generations of later evangelical abolitionists including Charles Grandison Finney, Theodore Dwight Weld, and many others. However, when asking Americans to embrace the emerging abolitionist movement, Hopkins did not ask his readers to abandon their self-interest. Rather, he threatened that refusing to abandon slavery would lead to divine punishment. In this antislavery work, Hopkins chose to appeal more to self-interest than to religious piety. Disinterested benevolence had been replaced with the fear of divine judgment as the motivation for social reform. Gone was his earlier view that even sin was a divinely ordained illustration of God's unlimited sovereignty. Instead of the divine will driving historical events independently of human action, we find a system of causation that hinged on human obedience or disobedience. To purify the nation, Hopkins modified his theological convictions

By 1784 Hopkins had nurtured his congregation in his commitment to disinterested benevolence and the desire to distinguish themselves from the affluent at Second Congregational. In this spirit, the church voted "that the slave trade and the slavery of the Africans, as it has taken place among us, is a gross violation of the righteousness and benevolence which are so much inculcated in the gospel; and therefore we will not tolerate it in this church."[70]

Yet, it was not only the rich and powerful that Hopkins implicated in the sins of slavery. In his close study of scripture, he found and shared three verses that backed up his claim that "a heavy, dreadful woe hangs over the heads of all those whose hands are defiled by the blood of the Africans, especially the inhabitants of that state, and of that town, who have had a distinguished share in this unrighteous, bloody commerce!"[71] Every citizen of Newport, whether the high and haughty of Second Congregational, the pious and penitent of First, slavers or those committed to their liberation—all were exposed to the imminent wrath of God. Purification was inevitable. It would result either from the principled actions of pious Americans or from the wrath of a righteous God. As a cleric in the New England tradition, Hopkins was more comfortable telling politicians what to do than other evangelicals. His impassioned pleas and thunderous warnings were echoed by future generations of Black activists, perhaps none so directly as Lemuel Haynes, a Black Calvinist abolitionist.[72] White Americans, however, largely ignored him.

The frontier theologian had found a place in Newport through an embrace of moral reform. While his motivations were rooted in his distaste for the self-love of rival members at Second Congregational, his commitment to the success of abolition transformed his theology from a consistent Calvinism focused on disinterested benevolence to a contractual providentialism emphasizing human effort and the self-interest of avoiding divine wrath. Samuel Hopkins was one of the most brilliant and prolific participants in the revolutionary antislavery crusade, yet because of his geographical location and theological persuasion, his voice could carry only so far. By the era of the Revolution, the stronghold of American slavery lay southward, beyond the echoes of Hopkins's protestations, where great religious change dethroned the established church of England and replaced it with surging frontier evangelicalism.

Southern Evangelicals and the Triumph of Conversionism

Conversion always held a higher priority than antislavery among southern evangelicals; however, for a short but consequential period, the two ambitions marched hand in hand. Evangelicals cared deeply about the souls of enslaved men and women, and when they saw slavery as an opponent of their conversionist mission, they worked to purify the South from its stain. However, when enslavers accommodated the conversionist mission, evangelical abolitionism declined in the South, and the bonds of salvation tightened the bonds of slavery. This transformation occurred as southern evangelicals morphed from an embattled minority into a hegemonic power at the very center of southern life and culture. By the late antebellum era, Baptists and Methodists made up a core constituency of fire-eating secessionists. But in the late eighteenth century, southern evangelicalism was in a precarious position.

Rhys Isaac first described the arrival of evangelicals in 1750s and 1760s Virginia as a cultural insurgency, and historians like Donald Mathews and Christine Heyrman similarly emphasize the countercultural elements of late eighteenth-century evangelicalism before chronicling a capitulation to southern slavery.[73] As Heyrman puts it, southern evangelicals dropped their prophetic witness as they adapted to the slaveholding South. More recently, historians have downplayed the countercultural tendencies of early southern evangelicalism. Charles Irons illustrates how the antislavery convictions of a few Virginia Baptists easily melded into the proslavery defenses of the antebellum era.[74]

But from the 1760s through the 1780s, antislavery sentiments spread throughout the swelling new southern evangelical sects, as both Baptists and Methodists offered institutional purificationist declarations against slavery in the 1780s. With Baptist minister John Leland and Methodist superintendent Francis Asbury at the head of the charge, the two sects that later grew into the most influential churches in the South both employed the discourse of purification to attack slavery before ultimately capitulating to ineffective conversionism. Certainly, the imperatives of conversion ultimately shaped the social positions of both Baptists and Methodists, but for a brief moment both denominations sought to purify themselves and the new American nation of the sin of slavery. The failure of this moment reveals the frailty of white purificationist abolitionism and the dominance of ineffective conversionist antislavery.

This story begins in Virginia. Anglicanism, the established church of the Old Dominion, permeated the colonial social fabric, maintaining the dominance of the gentry and their place at the apex of the slaving social structure. Two patterns emerged in Virginia's religious establishment: first, public financial support for the Established Church, which remained consistent with practices in Britain; and second, an empowered vestry, a significant innovation that further tied the Church to the slaving gentry. Because a bishop was never sent from London to Virginia, the legislature functioned as a sort of proxy, regulating the actions of both clergy and laity. For future dissenters, these close entanglements made Virginia hostile territory.

Despite the ties binding Anglicanism to the local slaving power structure, evangelical itinerants found Piedmont Virginians receptive to their version of the gospel. The presence of Anglican churches mirrored the presence of wealth clustered around the enslaving tidewater plantations. Virginians further west often had to travel great distances to the nearest parish. As a result, many of the non-elites in the Piedmont found the religious establishment lacking. Into this spiritual vacuum came northern missionaries, including the influential Baptist John Leland.

Leland left his native Massachusetts for Virginia in 1775, successfully itinerating throughout several counties in the central Piedmont and building a strong base in the north-central counties of Orange, Spottsylvania, and Culpepper. After a ministry of fourteen years, Leland had earned admiration or ire throughout the state.[75] In addition to his effective preaching, Leland labored hard to erase any establishment of religion as a perversion of both gospel and government. He led the Baptist charge in the fight for disestablishment beginning in 1776 and culminating with his 1785 collaboration with James Madison in securing Thomas Jefferson's Virginia Statute for Religious Freedom, the policy that set the mold for the First Amendment. In 1788, he likely proved decisive in nominating Madison to the Virginia convention to ratify the Constitution.[76]

Just one year later, he penned the Baptist abolitionist petition. When he arrived in Virginia in 1775, Baptist ministers were regularly jailed for preaching without licenses. By the time he returned to his native Massachusetts in 1791, he had helped redefine the relationship between religion and politics, in the process creating a network of Baptist churches that continued to grow into the nineteenth century.

Leland's lifetime cause was that of religious liberty, but he also fretted over the problem of slavery, and for several years he labored to purify both his church and his state of the sin of slaving. John Leland despised enslavers and believed that exposure to slavery warped the mind, even his own mind. Upon leaving Virginia in 1791, Leland confessed, "I am not as shocked to see [slaves] naked, gaunt and trembling, as I was when I first came into the state."[77] In an era dependent upon the expansion of the moral sense, this desensitization scared Leland. He himself, had to be purified of the corrupting effects of slavery, and he sought to protect others from this dangerous perversion.

Leland did care for the suffering of the enslaved, but he also identified the institution as a danger to all, Black and white, enslaved and free. In addition to desensitization, Leland wrote in 1790 that slavery afflicts masters with "enormous evils" such as "pride, haughtiness, domination, cruelty, deceit and indolence."[78] Throwing in a jab against the effeminacy of southern slaveholders, Leland presaged later arguments made by free labor advocates by claiming that a "hard hand and a meek heart are preferable to a soft hand [and] a turbulent, fretted, disappointed heart." In a Fourth of July oration in 1802, Leland went so far as to label enslavers "despotic masters," a label which, in the context of a celebration of liberty from the British, carried considerable weight.

For Leland, slavery transformed virtuous men into compassionless despots. It was a terrible sin and the body of Christ must be purified of its stain. Many Christians worried about the righteousness of the republic and blamed slavery for inspiring a great many vices. Daniel Chapman Banks, a native of New Hampshire ministering in Louisville, expressed this viewpoint, writing that "the effects of slavery are here very manifest as it is in all parts of the State of Kentucky. Idleness and destitution and want of enterprise and improvement are the consequence."[79]

Upon leaving Virginia in 1791, Leland reproduced and even amplified his earlier attacks on slavery, writing with an intense vitriol that the institution "in its best appearance, is a violent deprivation of the rights of nature, inconsistent with republican government, destructive of every humane and benevolent passion of the soul, and subversive to that liberty absolutely necessary to ennoble the human mind."[80] In 1789, under the authority of the Virginia Baptist General Committee, Leland challenged other religious bodies, referred to as "our brethren," to "make use of every *legal* measure to extirpate this horrid evil from the land." Moreover, the resolution prayed that "our honorable legislature may have it in their power to proclaim the great Jubilee, consistent with the principles of good policy."[81] When the "honorable legislature" of Virginia failed to "proclaim the great Jubilee," Baptists turned to conversionism as the sole solution to the problem of slavery.

Leland spoke about slavery as "a violent deprivation" and as "destructive of every humane and benevolent passion." He likened enslaved Americans to Old Testament Israelites and imagined Moses leading slaves to liberty just as he did for the Israelites. Leland continued to use biblical imagery to imagine a "halcyon day" when slaves will "march out of bondage," asking, "what would be more elating, to see the power of the gospel so effectual" that "the names of master and slave be buried—every yoke broken and the oppressed go free?"[82] But for Leland, in all eras of his life, the agent of emancipation was "the power of the gospel." And so, despite his antislavery sympathies, he never again pressured a legislature for emancipation. In fact, as the nineteenth century progressed, Leland's antipathy to slavery was replaced by an antipathy to New England abolitionists, and this prioritization of conversion enabled the former antislavery activist to seamlessly shift into an aggressive antiabolitionist. In all of his later political work, he held fast to conversionist antislavery and criticized abolitionist tactics, writing in 1836, "the measures of the abolitionists are reprobated by every friend to his country."[83] The confrontational activism of abolitionists was at best a distraction from the holy work of conversionist antislavery and at worst a dangerous encouragement of violence.

Leland's path from moderate antislavery to vigorous anti-abolitionism mirrors wider patterns among southern Baptists. After the overwhelming majority of Baptist associations abandoned opposition to slavery, the purificationist strain endured, but with a new target and a new goal. Instead of rooting out slavery, southern Baptists instead began to root out abolitionists. They were not alone in this process. Another force in southern evangelicalism spread widely and soon offered an additional purificationist assault against slavery before also capitulating and surrendering its antislavery witness. This challenge came from what would become the largest denomination in the South, the Methodists. We see the move from purificationism to conversionism in the career of Francis Asbury.

No one saw more of early America than Francis Asbury. The first bishop of American Methodism left his native England for the colonies in 1771, remaining in the post-Revolution United States even after the majority of British Methodists had left. Asbury tirelessly traveled the new nation, covering an average of 6,000 miles a year as he grew his denomination from a small contingent of Anglican evangelicals to the most popular religious group in antebellum America, a group that would come to exert an almost hegemonic influence on the American South. There were few corners of early America that did not witness the road-weary minister passing through to exhort and organize the growing flock. Asbury's diary demonstrates a keen eye and soft heart as he could not help but notice and frequently agonize over the plight of Black Americans both slave and free. From 1771 until his death in 1816, Asbury led the Methodist charge against slavery, before retreating to an uneasy accommodation in the face of massive resistance.[84]

In 1785 Francis Asbury faced the full passion of the slave debate during the first annual meeting of the North Carolina conference of the Methodist Episcopal Church. Waking early to a spring sunrise, Asbury was in high spirits, but as the events of the day progressed, his heart sank. The harmonious proceedings of the conference stalled as a contingent of angry southerners protested the prohibition of slave owners from Methodist fellowship. As Asbury's colleague Dr. Thomas Coke rose to defend the church's position, a colonel began cursing and issued threats. The crowd dispersed to allow time for tempers to cool, but the next day began with an equal amount of vitriol as the irascible future schismatic James O'Kelly angrily denounced slavery and its supporters. O'Kelly's tirade whipped the crowd into a violent frenzy. Asbury gratefully reported that despite the intensity "we . . . came off with whole bones."[85] But while Asbury's bones remained intact, unity in American Methodism suffered. The divisiveness of antislavery clearly threatened the rapid rise in Methodist conversions.

The conflict between slavery and conversion was similarly fraught for Asbury's co-superintendent, Thomas Coke. One year after the near violence in North Carolina, Coke traveled to the Caribbean to supervise the conversion of the West Indies, both white and Black, slave and free. Coke recognized that the only way to convert the large enslaved population was with the blessing of enslavers. After returning to North America in 1787, Coke wrote in his journal, "however just my sentiments may be concerning slavery, it was ill-judged of me to deliver them from the pulpit."[86] Denouncing slavery may have made Coke feel better, but the fate of all of those souls weighed heavy on his mind, and as a result, he discouraged confrontation with enslavers and instead encouraged Methodist ministers to "have great Compassion on the poor Negroes & do all you can to Convert them." Despite this change in tactics, Coke continued to "long for the time when the Lord will turn their Captivity like the Rivers of the South."[87]

Francis Asbury underwent a similar process, and his commitment to conversionism conquered his stand against slaving. A notable turning point occurred in January 1798 when he lamented, "Oh! To be dependent on slaveholders is in part to be a slave, and I was free born. I am brought to conclude that slavery will exist in Virginia perhaps for ages; there is not a sufficient sense of religion nor liberty to destroy it; Methodists, Baptists, Presbyterians, in the highest flights of rapturous piety still maintain and defend it."[88] Asbury himself had become ensnared by the power of the institution. He could not attack it head-on without losing access to the lost souls he sought to save. Never before did Asbury articulate such despair, and from this point forward he did not relate any serious confrontations with slaveholders. In fact, only two months later, he shifted his focus away from encouraging enslaving among church members and instead simply tried to keep preachers from purchasing enslaved laborers.[89] Asbury backtracked further in 1808, when he appeared resigned to slaving clergymen and championed a regulation that simply ensured "that no member of society, or preacher, should sell or buy a slave unjustly, inhumanly, or covetously."[90] If Methodism was to destroy slavery, it would have to do so solely by expanding salvation.

Methodist growth slowed in the last decade of the eighteenth century, and Asbury pressed both settled ministers and itinerants to continue ministering to slaves. This pursuit was always dependent upon the whims of masters, and Methodists worked hard to maintain access. In 1801 Asbury felt downtrodden at the arrogance of South Carolina planters, writing, "The rich among the people never thought us worthy to preach to them." Methodists had earned a reputation as hostile to slavery, and many South Carolina planters threatened to deny their slaves the opportunity to attend Methodist meetings.[91] This proved to be the ultimate weapon of the planter class in nullifying the southern evangelical antislavery witness. All evangelicals privileged conversion and would do everything in their power to maintain access to enslaved souls, even if that meant abandoning antislavery principles. In 1809, Asbury again appeared frustrated that so many "masters are afraid of the influence of our principles" and wondered "[w]ould not an *amelioration* in the condition and treatment of slaves have produced more practical good to the poor Africans than any attempt at their *emancipation?*"[92]

Asbury witnessed the begrudging discontent that enslavers exhibited when allowing their enslaved laborers to attend Methodist meetings and he anguished over the fact that Methodists offered the only opportunity for some enslaved people to hear the gospel. When faced with the reality that antislavery action would close off Methodist access to enslaved populations, Asbury abandoned the bold stance offered in the Revolution's aftermath and settled into a process of accommodation and, later, assimilation to southern demands for a proslavery Christianity. Asbury was dealt a difficult hand. Methodism could either abandon their purificationist antislavery witness or lose access to both enslavers and the enslaved in the South. The logic of conversionism enabled Asbury and others to reconcile the two. Ministers would drop the purificationist purge of enslavers and instead rely on the transformative power of salvation. The result let to a renewed explosion of Methodist growth in the early nineteenth century.

Francis Asbury displayed tremendous skill in building the national Methodist church. Independence brought a new era of westward migration and Methodists developed an unparalleled ability to coordinate outreach among far-flung frontier settlements. The church grew exponentially but not without cost. Methodists could not afford to both purify existing communities while also aggressively seeking to save souls in the West. What good would it be to create a small, pure, godly community while the new nation was allowed to sink into infidelity and licentiousness? The ancient tension between evangelism and discipleship inherent in all Christian traditions challenged Methodist leaders, and the powerful nationalism of the Revolution led Methodists and others to work earnestly in ensuring the new nation would fulfill its duty as the Lord's republic of righteousness. The logic of conversionism enabled antislavery Christians to bridge the gap and avoid the conflict that came with purificationism. The salvation of the frontier took greater precedence over the purification of the church, and enslavers continued to present critiques of human bondage as dangerous agitation that would only end with rebellion and race war.

The fear of violence was ever present as white Americans considered the problem of slavery. Slavery only survived through the brutal use of force, and the possibility for revolutionary backlash never disappeared. In 1800 this possibility nearly became reality in Virginia when an enslaved blacksmith named Gabriel offered his own vision of how to end slavery. Well-read and steeped in both the political and religious context of the era, Gabriel and his followers sought salvation through violence. Rebels planned to set fire to the city's warehouse district while others kidnapped the governor, James Monroe, and still others would seize the city armory.

Religion offered both an ideological vision and the practical infrastructure for rebels like Gabriel and his associates. The image of Exodus echoed throughout countless expressions of enslaved people's resistance, and Gabriel recruited more to his cause at various religious meetings. Due to the Methodists and Quakers' record of purificationist antislavery, the rebels agreed not to kill white Methodists or Quakers. They added Frenchmen to this list as well, owing to the antislavery spirit ascendant in the French Revolution. The Baptist Hungary Meeting House provided a rallying point for the rebels. At this meeting house and elsewhere, Gabriel's brother Martin arose as an important spiritual leader. According to a white Virginian familiar with the brothers, Martin was respected by his brother and others in the enslaved community because of Martin's extensive knowledge of the Bible. This knowledge proved particularly important when the rebels gathered to debate whether flooding meant they should postpone their plan. Martin wanted to proceed, and in trying to persuade the others, he proclaimed, "I read in my Bible where God says, if we shall worship him, we should have peace in our Lands, five of you shall conquer an hundred and a hundred, a thousand of our enemies."[93] Despite Martin's prophetic appeals, the rebels did delay, and in the delay, their plan was exposed. Twenty-six enslaved men were hanged, including Gabriel and Martin. The rebellion rocked the Old Dominion. Voluntary manumissions came to a crashing halt, and by 1806 any newly freed slaves would be forced to leave the state or face reenslavement.

The violence portended by Gabriel's planned rebellion contributed to a violent repression of southern antislavery agitation. Expanding conversion increasingly became a mechanism to redirect antislavery energy while maintaining national unity. When white Christians confronted the potential of slave rebellion, national salvation became a matter of national survival. Compelled by the imperatives of expanding salvation, an era of denominational formation commenced. New networks stretched across vast spaces, uniting the new republic, North and South, East and West. At the same time, economic trends and Black activism eroded slavery in the North while the rising power of the cotton kingdom entrenched human bondage in the South.

Denominational networks strengthened, but the national context changed. As reformers attempted to bend the new national denominational structures toward the antislavery cause, they faced a new paradigm of sectionalist tension. This tension strained and eventually snapped the conversionist consensus, leading to the renewed purificationist push of the post-1830s era. But from the vantage point of late eighteenth-century white Americans, there was little evidence of this fate: the gospel of Christ would soon stretch deep into the continent. Salvation and enlightenment were manifestly destined to spread according to divine direction.

Conversionist antislavery was a dead end, but if we are to understand the ways that white Christians in the late eighteenth and early nineteenth centuries understood the problem of slavery and its potential solutions, we must account for ideologies of conversionist causation. Despite the inability of conversionism to mount a serious challenge to slavery in the era, it did inaugurate a consolidation of religious authority that ultimately created the infrastructure for the kinds of coercive reform that developed in the 1830s and beyond. The imperatives of conversion in post-Revolutionary America required a new approach to expanding salvation. The millennium still loomed, but to bring the kingdom of God into reality, Americans would have to create new denominational structures to meet the changing realities of the new nation. In so doing, they transformed both the nation and the fight against slavery.

◇◇◇◇ **2** ◇◇◇◇

National Churches and National Reform, 1800–1815

A S THE NINETEENTH CENTURY began, a thickening cloud of white supremacy smothered visions of emancipation. The purificationist abolitionism of Samuel Hopkins died with him, and Black activists met heightened opposition in a nation increasingly defined by whiteness. Gradual abolition stalled, and legislators criminalized manumissions, halting the slow wave of Southern emancipation. Easy credit invigorated the cotton economy and the family-shattering domestic slave trade. Demands to purify the nation from slavery quieted, while calls to convert the continent amplified. Political and religious leaders declared that to be American was to be white, and new national institutions defended white supremacy through slavery, settler colonialism, and the consistent erosion of rights and privileges held by the growing communities of free Black Americans. White supremacy rapidly extinguished the radical expansion of liberty that had enabled purificationist abolitionism during and immediately after the American Revolution.[1]

The nation faced a spiritual crisis. Migration, deism, political conflicts between Federalists and Jeffersonians, British incursions, abolitionism, and the constant threat of slave rebellion made real by Gabriel and his conspirators in Virginia—all of these terrors seemed to imperil the spiritual promise of the United States.[2] To save their nation, Methodists, Presbyterians, and Baptists created national denominations through the Methodist Episcopal Church, Presbyterian General Assembly, and Baptist General Convention.[3] These bodies expanded the national consciousness of countless men and women. For many Americans, denominational relationships formed their first national identities, and membership in a national denomination offered the first opportunity to belong to a national institution.

Following the War of 1812, these denominations created the ideas and infrastructure for the benevolent empire. Missions of conversion in the first decade of the nineteenth century became missions of social redemption in the second. Denominations directed both, but debates over slavery threatened national networks, and denominational leaders purged abolitionists from their ranks. Black agitators and the few white abolitionists would not be silenced. Enduring activism forced newly formed national denominations to reckon with slavery, and by 1815 they had their solution in the trans-sectional conversionist mission of African colonization.

Despite the proliferation of scholarship on religion in the early republic, denominational institutions receive scant attention. Ideas matter, but so too do institutions that nurture ideas and transform them into action. This process was not always smooth. Samuel Haselby has shown how established elites and frontier revivalists warred over control of the West and the soul of the United States.[4] American Christians of nearly all classes and geographies, however, shared commitments to settler colonialism and white supremacy. Christian leaders organized to expand salvation by subduing idolatrous Native Americans and the untamed wilderness.[5] Whether through frontier circuit riders, well-educated missionaries, or conscience-triggering tracts, denominational collaboration bound the nation together in pursuit of salvation.

American nationalisms were not born overnight in 1776; they coalesced over many decades. Political parties aided this process, but considerable opposition arose to these organizations.[6] Voluntary associations formed another method for political organizing, but in the late eighteenth century, the republican tradition discouraged voluntary associations, as they were associated with revolutionary work and therefore seen as dangerous to national unity and stability.[7] Associations designed to expand salvation, however, elicited far less opposition than political associations. By the early nineteenth century, the focus on salvation deflected much of the earlier hostility to voluntary organizations, paving the way for the benevolent empire of the post–War of 1812 era.

This chapter chronicles how the bonds of salvation structured three phases in the development of American denominations, American nationalisms, and American reform. The first phase created American denominational bodies in the 1780s and 1790s. The second spawned denominationally affiliated mission organizations in the first decade of the nineteenth century. Finally, during and immediately after the War of 1812, denominations provided the imagination and authority for the benevolent empire. Dreams of salvation drove every phase of this process, and when abolitionists within their ranks sparked agitation, denominational leaders invoked the exigencies of salvation to purge them from positions of influence within these new Protestant networks. Yet the problems of slavery endured, and so as the spirit of benevolent reform swept across the nation, denominational leaders appealed again to salvation to address slavery without risking internal division. The American Colonization Society, born out of denominational networks, promised to end slavery and secure white supremacy through a millennial, international expansion of salvation. We see all of this in the ministry and activism of Robert Finley.

Robert Finley: Revivalism, Denominationalism, and Reform

In early 1803, the Presbyterian minister Robert Finley bemoaned the stalled spread of salvation in New Jersey, lamenting, "all was still, nor was there a voice heard." The community "was full of dry bones." Finley and countless other ministers understood the United States as God's chosen nation, millennially destined to fill the continent and save the world. Stillness would not do, and so Finley began coordinating with other Presbyterian ministers to foster revival by traveling the region in teams of two. Through a carefully planned process of denominational cooperation involving dozens of ministers stretched across New Jersey and New York, "the day of deliverance was at hand." Denominational coordination had done what Finley could not do alone. Together, these Presbyterians harvested hundreds of souls. Salvation had come.[8]

Ashbel Green, the national coordinator of Presbyterian missions, enthusiastically reprinted Finley's gripping account of this revival in the denomination's newly formed missionary magazine. Through this new national organ, ministers from Massachusetts to Georgia read how denominational cooperation brought salvation to the mid-Atlantic. According to Finley's antebellum biographer, the revival and his new national denominational leadership "seemed to animate, direct, and characterize, all his subsequent life, in public and in private."[9] Finley's name spread throughout the sprawling national network of Presbyterians, and six years later he delivered the General Assembly's national missionary sermon, calling his brethren to work together in bringing salvation to distant lands.

Inspired by this taste of national leadership, Finley began to dream more boldly, envisioning his flock sprawling out from New Jersey and New York to the rest of the nation and even across the ocean. He sought to save the United States and the rest of the world from all that ailed it, including human bondage. After another six years, Finley finally took action against slavery through the logic of conversionism. Again, his denominational connections proved pivotal when a network of Presbyterian Princeton alumni promised to fulfill prophecies of global salvation while simultaneously encouraging emancipation, reducing the threat of slave rebellion, and eliminating free Black communities.

The similarities and differences between Finley's response to slavery and the purificationism of Samuel Hopkins are revealing. Finley's national leadership enabled him to see slavery as a serious national problem much like Hopkins did decades earlier. Unlike Hopkins's situation, however, where he wielded neither an effective national discourse nor a national network, Finley's position as a Presbyterian leader connected him to the people and power necessary to act on a national level. But along with Finley's new power came new responsibility.

For denominationalists like Finley, visions of a unified, converted white Christian nation blotted out the reality of Black suffering. Hopkins had listened to his Black parishioners, whereas Finley looked past contemporary injustices and instead trained his eyes toward a millennial horizon of salvation. Denominational leadership left Finley with both an inability to prioritize Black suffering over salvation and an institutional position that valued national unity over the pursuit of justice. Hopkins eagerly lambasted the sinful slaving of his fellow Newport residents during and immediately following the American Revolution. In the aftermath of the War of 1812, Finley and other denominational leaders knew that doing the same would sacrifice the conversionist potential of their national networks. As a result, Finley and other aspiring white denominational leaders refused to hear the call of Black activists as Hopkins had and instead labored to fulfill the nation's spiritual destiny by expanding American salvation.

Shunning the prophetic abolitionism espoused by Hopkins and countless Black Christians, Finley approached slavery through the unifying promise of salvation. Inspired by his expanded national vision and aided by his denominational connections, Finley became the spiritual father of the American Colonization Society (ACS), the widely influential national attempt to reckon with slavery through a millennial, global expansion of salvation. According to Finley, colonization promised salvation for Africa and redemption for the United States.

The ACS and other reform organizations emerged through denominational networks for the purpose of expanding salvation and eliminating sins. The goal of eliminating sins redefined salvation as more than just conversion. In the second decade of the nineteenth century, salvation for reformers came to mean

59

both conversion and escape from the sins of the era. Christians, acting through their denominational channels, fostered an empire of benevolence. These new reform networks eventually yielded both a new powerful, confrontational abolitionist movement and a religious discourse that opposed these activists. But all of this began with dreams of salvation and the national denominations formed to make those dreams real.

American Denominational Formation

American denominational formation began when American Christians could no longer rely on British religious authorities for the coordination of missionary work. This process began with the disruption of the American Revolution and culminated with the War of 1812. Independence and then the renewal of war less than forty years later severed both political and ecclesiastical bonds.[10] No longer supported by their British brethren, American Methodists, Congregationalists, and Presbyterians built their own national organizations during the 1780s. During the War of 1812, a national Baptist denomination joined them. All of these denominations considered adding abolitionism to their list of goals, with the aforementioned Presbyterian resolution of 1787 and the 1784 Methodist Christmas Conference coming the closest.[11]

But ultimately, all white denominations prioritized national conversion over purifying the nation of slavery. Some religious leaders, however, began to broaden their understandings of salvation. The second war with Britain ignited a new outburst of American nationalism, fueled by denominational identities, that stirred religious leaders to expand missions of salvation to not only convert the world but also purify it from a host of sins, including intemperance, Sabbath-breaking, and eventually enslaving. But before any of this could occur, Americans first created their national religious bodies that would later inspire reform organizations.

The Methodist Episcopal Church formed in the United States only as a result of national independence. English Methodists remained members of the Church of England until the death of John Wesley in 1791; however, Wesley himself arranged for the separation of Americans into the independent Methodist Episcopal Church in 1784. The famed Christmas Conference, held in Baltimore on December 24, 1784, began with a nationalist message of American superiority. Thomas Coke, himself an Englishman, likened the Church of England to "the drunkard, the fornicator, and the extortioner, triumphed over bleeding Zion."[12] Coke's ordination of Francis Asbury, naming both of them as cosuperintendents of American Methodism, concluded by proclaiming that God "will carry his gospel under thy direction from sea to sea, yea, perhaps from one end of the continent to the other."[13] This pairing of nationalism and conversionism informed the origins of all American denominations. Yet, as we've already seen, the antislavery of John Wesley, Francis Asbury, and other Methodists threatened to limit the potential of Methodist growth, particularly in the South. In order to fulfill their mission of carrying the gospel from sea to sea, Methodists abandoned purificationist abolitionism and instead relied on an ineffectual conversionist antislavery.

Congregationalists, by virtue of the ecclesiology that earned them their name, did not believe in any earthly religious authority beyond each congregation. Fiercely independent Congregationalist churches would only surrender even a shred of autonomy for the holy purpose of expanding salvation. And so, for Congregationalists in Massachusetts, missionary societies served as the closest thing possible to a denominational body. By the time war reached New England, the most influential missionary organization in North America was the Scottish Society for the Propagation of Christian Knowledge (SPCK). When the Revolution separated New England Congregationalists from the SPCK, the vacuum threatened to halt the growth of salvation. And so, after independence, Massachusetts Congregationalists formed their own North American missionary society, the Society for Propagating the Gospel among the Indians and Others in North America (SPGNA). The Massachusetts General Court issued a charter in 1787 "that the Gospel should be sent into the dark, benighted parts of the land," and the SPGNA began its work as an extension of and organizing institution for Massachusetts Congregationalists.[14]

Beginning in at least the early 1780s, the General Association of Connecticut Congregationalists collected money for missions, and by 1798, the General Association formalized these activities as the Missionary Society of Connecticut.[15] This society included many of the most distinguished Connecticut clergymen, including Timothy Dwight, Joseph Huntington, Cotton Smith, and Jonathan Edwards Jr. It did not take long for Connecticut Christian leaders to make the move from missions to social reform. By 1791, these same clergymen helped to establish the Connecticut Society for the Promotion of Freedom and for the Relief of Persons Unlawfully Holden in Bondage. For most American Christians, the journey from missions to organized antislavery took far longer. However, like many other American organizations, the Connecticut Society was limited by its reliance on denominational imperatives, and it never took consequential action against slavery or racial persecution.[16]

Presbyterian attempts to form a national denominational body began as early as 1774. These early efforts focused on the coordination of missions work, but considerable opposition mounted among those fearful of how a powerful, centralized church might enforce theological conformity. Presbyterians remained divided over the conversion tactics espoused during the revivals of the Great Awakening that began in the 1730s, even after a previous schism had been resolved in 1758.[17] Anticlerical strains among supporters of the revival worked to minimize ministerial qualification requirements and to reserve ordination powers in presbyteries rather than the General Assembly. Despite these concerns, Presbyterians constructed a national denominational body by 1789 and eagerly anticipated their role in guiding the spiritual destiny of the United States.

John Witherspoon, president of the College of New Jersey, opened the inaugural 1789 meeting with a sermon that set the theme for the assembly and for the new denomination. Witherspoon focused the sermon around 1 Corinthians 3:6, "I have planted, Apollos watered, but God gave the increase." The text of Witherspoon's sermon has never been found, but we can surmise from the scriptural reference that the assembly opened with a reflection on evangelism. Just as the Apostle Paul wrote of his efforts in spreading the fledgling Christian church, so too these American Presbyterians understood themselves as laboring to sow the seeds of a national faith.[18]

To assert their national orientation, the Presbyterian General Assembly drafted a letter to the great symbol of the new nation, George Washington. In an encomium to the new president, Presbyterians sought to claim Washington as a crypto-Presbyterian and stake their claim as keepers of the national faith.[19] To the local presbyteries, the General Assembly encouraged their annual participation in the larger body by warning them that "without a common intelligence, and concert in our measures, our respectability will be diminished and our efforts for the public good, and for the promotion of religion will be weakened by becoming divided."[20] The United States needed Presbyterians, and for the church to best serve the nation, national denominational unity had to become a priority.

Baptists remained fragmented longer than Presbyterians, Methodists, or Congregationalists, but when they finally came together, in 1814, they did so for the purpose of organizing missionary labors. In 1776 the Warren Association, comprising dozens of churches in New England, sought to organize "a general meeting of delegates from our societies in each colony" for the purpose of fighting for religious liberty.[21] In 1799 the Philadelphia Association, the most active Baptist association in commissioning missionaries, resolved to "invite the general Committee of Virginia and different Associations on the continent to unite with us in laying a plan for forming a missionary society."[22] All of these actions came to nothing, however, as friendly correspondence was not enough to convince Baptists to risk establishing a national body, at least not yet.

By 1812, the greatest enthusiasm for unity emanated from the South, long after John Leland had returned to Massachusetts and the brief southern Baptist dalliance with abolitionism had come to end. Richard Furman, influential minister at First Baptist Charleston and future proslavery polemicist, along with his protégé, William Bullein Johnson, then of First Baptist in Savannah, both voiced their support for a new national body. Johnson circulated a letter on behalf of the Savannah Baptist Society for Foreign Missions that wished that "delegates from [all of the Baptist missionary societies in America] convene in some central situation in the United States." This meeting would allow "the energies of the whole Baptist denomination, throughout America," to combine "in one sacred effort for sending the word of life to idolatrous lands."

Johnson thought in huge terms, dreaming of "100,000 to 200,000 souls all rising in obedience to their Lord, and meeting by delegation in one august assembly."[23] There was not really a "Baptist denomination," only Baptist churches, with a few localized ministerial and missionary associations. A convention would have to do more than draw together the denomination; it would have to create one. With that challenge, Baptist ministers from around the nation gathered in Philadelphia's First Baptist Church in 1814 where they achieved more diverse geographic representation than any other denomination in the early republic. Both antislavery and proslavery Baptists united in order to pursue national salvation, and the appeals of Black Baptists were largely ignored.

The experience of denominational leadership eventually politicized many white Christians. Black denominational leaders did not need politicizing. Since at least the mid-seventeenth century, when Black skin became equated with enslavement, the very existence of free people of color challenged the logics of slavery. Similarly, the faith of Black Christians challenged the white supremacist assumptions and structures of American religion. And so while most white Christian reformers first gained experience organizing at the denominational level, the political and religious context for Black Americans reversed the pattern. Throughout the antebellum era, many Black denominational leaders achieved positions of spiritual leadership after first organizing politically to protect their communities from the many threats of American white supremacy. We can see this pattern in the Black communities of Philadelphia, Boston, and New York.

Richard Allen, called by his biographer Richard S. Newman a "Black Founding Father," is most famous for founding the African Methodist Episcopal Church.[24] Allen's denominational leadership is usually dated either to the founding convention of the AME denomination in 1816, when he assumed the position of bishop, or to the formal creation of Mother Bethel AME Church in 1793. However, a close look at the Free African Society (FAS), formed in 1787 Philadelphia, reveals the relationship between Black political activism and Black spiritual leadership.[25]

The common origin story for Allen's ministry centers around his famed walk-out in 1793.[26] At St. George's Methodist Church, white parishioners interrupted the prayers of Absalom Jones and Allen and attempted to remove them to the balcony. In response, Allen and Jones led Black parishioners out of the church. But this event occurred after the FAS began its work in April of 1787. The FAS created a mutual aid society to help widows and other impoverished Black Philadelphians. It also created a burial ground, organized a school, performed marriages and funerals, and much more. All of these functions soon were taken up by the new Black churches led by Jones and Allen. Jones's African Episcopal Church of St. Thomas was formed in 1792. Allen created his own congregation, Bethel African Methodist Episcopal Church, in 1794, and in 1816 he launched what became the largest Black denomination in the nation. The pattern of Black political organizing spawning Black denominations repeated itself elsewhere.

In Boston, Black residents drew strength from the African Masonic Lodge, formed in 1775 by Prince Hall. Masons were sometimes attacked as anti-Christian, but this was surely not the case for Black Bostonians, and eventually Hall's work mirrored that of other denomination builders. The African Masonic Lodge in Boston organized a host of Black civic and religious organizations and, according to historian Christopher Cameron, "this fraternity acted as an antislavery society."[27] Indeed two years after forming the lodge, Hall organized a petition drive to the state legislature.

In this 1777 wave of petitions, Hall and other Black Bostonians decried the hypocrisy of having a "great number of blacks detained in a state of slavery in the bowels of a free and Christian county" and called for "an act of the legislature to be past whereby they may be restored to the enjoyments of that which is the natural right of all men and their children who were born in this land of liberty."[28] Hall continued to organize a series of political petition drives throughout the last decades of the eighteenth century. Eventually, Hall was asked to sponsor additional African Lodges, and a coalition of Black Masons emerged, united by Hall's administrative leadership.

The African Masonic Lodge met several needs of Black Bostonians, including Christian worship, particularly through the ministry of John Marrant, a Black Mason and minister who connected Masonry and Christianity in a series of 1789 sermons.[29] Membership in Masonic Lodges was available only to men, however, and so in 1796 another organization emerged in Boston, modeled off Richard Allen and Absalom Jones's Free African Society. The Boston-based African Society formed that year to support poor Black Bostonians and encourage Christian worship. Prior to this point, Christians in Boston had no choice but to worship under white ministers.

In 1800, the First Baptist Church in Boston began holding separate services with Black leadership. Five years later, First African Baptist Church in Boston was created, with Thomas Paul as its minister. The church quickly also began housing the recently formed African School, an institution providing educational opportunities for Black children. Paul then traveled to New York to help organize the Abyssinian Baptist Church. From there he helped create a denomination of sorts for Black Baptists, mostly directed through the Boston Baptist Association, which coordinated missionary work. He also formed the Baptist Education Society, which supported schools like the African School.

Abyssinian Baptist in New York joined an already vibrant community of Black Christians, which would eventually sprout both the African Methodist Episcopal Zion denomination and the Episcopal Parish, St. Phillip's African Church. Yet again, we see that political organizing predated denominational formation in New York. While still worshiping under the leadership of white Methodist and Episcopal ministers, Black Christian New Yorkers created the New York African Society. This organization in turn spawned independent Black religion in New York. According to historian Craig Steven Wilder, "The NYAS founded the black church."[30] Despite the work of Allen, Jones, Hall, Paul, and numerous other Black denominational leaders, most white denominational leaders ignored Black Christian activism. Rather than joining the work of their Black coreligionists, most white Christian leaders continued to pursue their conversionist missions while slavery only tightened its grip on the nation.

Denominationalism and Conversionist Organizing

In the first decade of the nineteenth century, lofty hopes of a godly republic confronted the reality of a nation racing West ahead of its churches. Independence exploded westward migration and inaugurated a new birth of religiously sanctioned settler colonialism. Numerous Americans, including Thomas Jefferson, believed that the expansion westward would replace slave societies with a nation of virtuous yeoman famers.[31]

Christian leaders looked at western expansion as both fulfillment of God's manifest destiny for the United States and a source of anxiety over declining religious authority. Churches scrambled to fulfill their desired role as the directors of American expansion by converting Native Americans and meeting the spiritual needs of settlers. If the United States would fulfill its destiny as God's agent for international redemption, the nation needed the church, and the church needed greater coordination. The threat of "heathen" Native Americans and uneducated white settlers rushing to the West alarmed the new nation's clergy and pressed them into action, sparking a new era of denominational organization.

In order to convert the nation and then eventually the world, Americans created new ecclesiastical structures, including reform organizations. Reform bodies in the late eighteenth and early nineteenth centuries fell into one of two organizational categories: associations and societies. Both were deeply enmeshed in denominational structures. Associations were almost always direct extensions of denominational bodies, but an overwhelming number of voluntary societies owed their roots to denominational action as well. Missionary work began in associations but shifted primarily to societies by the early nineteenth century; however, American missionary societies differed from English organizations in maintaining greater congregational independence.

Almost all Americans remained suspicious of denominational consolidation, and theological fault lines continued to divide the nation. American Christians could occasionally work across denominational barriers in launching missions to Native Americans but creating churches for white Americans highlighted the differences between denominations. These divisions nearly always proved too powerful to overcome. In aiding the settler-colonial project of dispossessing Indigenous peoples and extracting resources from the environment, denominations could collaborate, but when it came time to direct the destiny of the nation beyond extending white supremacy and American imperialism, theological divisions usually stymied ecumenical action. Internecine theological squabbles both challenged and catalyzed denominational formation.

The first purportedly ecumenical American missionary society was formed as a direct response to actions across the Atlantic. The London Missionary Society (LMS) was formed in 1795 by evangelical Anglicans. Americans looked to the LMS with admiration and envy and attempted to form their own societies in its image. The LMS emphasized ecumenism. The society's bylaws promised "not to send Presbyterianism, Independency, Episcopacy . . . but the glorious gospel of the blessed God."[32] The LMS called on Christians to prioritize salvation over theological division.

When news of the LMS reached New York City, local ministers sought to create their own missionary society.[33] The New York Missionary Society (NYMS) held its first meeting on November 1, 1796, in the Middle Dutch Church. Alexander McWhorter, Presbyterian minister in Newark, gave the opening sermon and characterized the mission of the society as "sending God's salvation to our desolate frontiers, and the gloomy regions of paganism."[34] The NYMS, following in the footsteps of the London Missionary Society, successfully maintained an ecumenical leadership.[35] The society's primary endeavor included the establishment of a missionary settlement in the Chickasaw territory of western Georgia, but that mission struggled and was abandoned after five years.[36] The NYMS had greater success in cosponsoring the missionary outreach of Elkanah Holmes among the Iroquois, but Holmes's primary sponsorship came from the more denominationally partisan New York Baptist Missionary Society.[37]

In Massachusetts, doctrinal divisions between liberals, Calvinists, and Hopkinsians limited the constituencies for various societies, as male members of these factions continually described the others as corrupting the gospel. Men in New England were less successful than women in maintaining ecumenical organizations. The SPGNA continued its work, but Hopkinsians formed a society of their own in 1799, called the Massachusetts Missionary Society (MMS).

The MMS claimed to deemphasize "party objects" and "refuse to suffer any political interest." Nathaniel Emmons ecumenically titled the circular letter announcing the society "To all who are desirous of the spread of the gospel of our Lord Jesus Christ." But the document itself included partisan rhetoric, claiming that the society was composed of "those who cordially subscribe to the divine authority of the Holy Scriptures, and candidly admit the leading doctrines which they contain, as all Christians must be supposed to do." The "leading doctrines" that he chose to emphasize included the claim that "the whole human race is in a state of apostasy from God . . . and exposed to the eternal punishments." The MMS clearly did not welcome liberal Christians.[38]

Emmons ended the tract, however, with a millennial promise invoking the logic of conversionism by claiming the "glory of God which is so largely predicted in the scriptures, that the world shall shortly be filled will essentially consist in the universal and legitimate influence of this Gospel." When the world is under the sway of the true gospel, the great sins of the age will fade away, for "the virtue and happiness of mankind are really always in proportion to the influence which the Gospel has upon them."[39] The MMS successfully partnered with the Northern Missionary Society in reaching Indians and sent its own missionaries to frontier communities throughout New England, New York, and even into Canada. It was easier for societies to partner with one another than it was for denominations to collaborate. However, the legacy of denominational identity continued to shape missionary societies, and collaboration remained limited.

A few Baptists joined the MMS, but in 1802 they formed their own society. The Massachusetts Baptist Missionary Society (MBMS) held no formal affiliation with the association of New England Baptists, called the Warren Association, and the society allowed non-Baptists to advance as far as the level of trusteeship as long as at least eight of the twelve trustees remained Baptists.[40] The MBMS tried to attract non-Baptist members and listed their purpose as "to promote the knowledge of evangelical truth," but the membership rolls included few if any non-Baptists. At its very first meeting on March 26, 1802, the MBMS commissioned missionaries to western New England, New York, and Upper Canada. The society focused its efforts on white Americans, but due to the efforts of missionary Elkanah Holmes, the society partnered with the New York Baptist Missionary Society to support his work among the Iroquois.[41]

Historian Charles Chaney describes the MBMS as "the most extensive and effective missionary society that Baptists formed for churching the wilderness." He finds far greater success in the MBMS than in similar organizations in Philadelphia or Charleston.[42] Baptists in the northeast responded to the problem of migration with societies, while their brethren in the South directed missions from within local or state associations. North and South, missionary efforts channeled the desire to expand salvation into a project to consolidate denominational authority.

The Massachusetts Society for Promoting Christian Knowledge (MSPCK), formed in 1803 to supplement the missionary work of SPGNA. The MSPCK fretted over the plight of the unchurched along the frontier, but back at home they waged partisan wars against liberal Congregationalists and Baptists. The first words of their constitution lamented "not only the increase of irreligion and infidelity among the inhabitants of our native land in general, but also the decay of evangelical piety among professors of Christianity."[43] This last clause revealed their animosity toward liberal Congregationalists and transformed the MSPCK into a surrogate orthodox Congregationalist denominational body. While not all missionary societies evinced this highly partisan character, the overwhelming majority of missionary societies drew on denominational networks or, as in the South, simply were extensions of local denominational authorities.[44]

Philadelphia Baptists experimented briefly with ecumenical missions, trying to form an interdenominational Philadelphia Missionary Society in 1798. Presbyterians failed to join, however, so by 1803 the Philadelphia Baptist Association formed a missions society solely supported by their association.[45] In the United States, conversionist work and effective reform organizing would have to begin with denominational bodies. Conversionism and denominationalism developed together in mutually constitutive relationships.

Women's reform societies as well as Black activist organizations of the early nineteenth century followed a very different pattern than those of their white male counterparts. Women's societies and Black organizations managed to both foster ecumenical action and connect the expansion of salvation with the purification of the nation's sins. While white male organizations frequently depended upon denominational identities and networks, societies of white women or Black Americans maintained a surprising ecumenism and looked to attack sins as an earlier extension of their missionary organizing.

Since the earliest days of the republic, women had played prominent roles in nearly every major reform movement of the era, beginning with missionary societies. The activism of American women, like that of their male counterparts, began with the pursuit of religious conversions before spreading out to other benevolent causes. Nancy Cranch, John Adams's niece, exemplified the desire and limitations of female reform when she described her membership in the Ladies Missionary Society of Washington, DC, by exclaiming, "Tho' I cannot become a preacher of the gospel in public—why may I not at least endeavor to increase the knowledge of God and religion in my little circle?"[46] The "little circles" of American women, however, became increasingly larger, and, unlike their male counterparts, often transcended the boundaries of denominational identity. Denominationalism was a powerful force in the early republic, yet not as powerful as the segregating power of patriarchy.

In the first two decades of the nineteenth century, women's activism fueled missionary expansion, but their efforts often remained submerged under institutions dominated by men. One of the most successful early women's groups spawned from the labor of Mehitable Simpkins, who in 1802 called women to donate a single penny per week for the cause of missions. The tremendous outpouring from women all over New England filled the coffers of the Massachusetts Missionary Society, where Mehitable's husband, John, served as treasurer.

The modest donations enabled women to participate directly, and the single cent harmonized well with the parable of the widow's mite, the Bible story of an impoverished widow who gave two mites to the temple, all she had in the world, earning the praise of Christ. In the parable, the donation of a wealthy man is ignored, while the modest donation of an impoverished woman is lauded, and Simpkins explicitly played on just this theme in her 1802 broadside.[47] Participation in the Cent Society promised a similar spiritual reward for pious women eager to transform the new nation with the message of the gospel. Cent Societies, also called Mite Societies, sprang up throughout the republic as women took an active role in fundraising for the missionary cause.

Just two years prior to Mehitable Simpkins's work, another woman in Boston, Mary Webb, formed the first woman's missionary society. Webb and fourteen other Congregationalist and Baptist women met on October 9, 1800, and formed the Boston Female Society for Missionary Purposes (BFSMP). Webb's group, like Simpkins's organization, donated their proceeds to the Massachusetts Missionary Society.[48] Inspired by women like Webb and Simpkins, dozens of new women's missionary organizations formed, and in 1812 the BFSMP initiated correspondence with other women's organizations. By 1818 ninety-seven other women's missionary organizations coordinated their activities with those of the BFSMP.[49] This success resulted in a small number of women being admitted to the ranks of the Massachusetts Missionary Society.[50]

The ability of female missionary societies to sidestep the divisiveness of denominationalism is most apparent in fractious New England. While many male missionary societies merged with denominational structures, including those in Connecticut, Vermont, and New Hampshire, female societies not only remained independent of denominational control but also avoided the theological schisms that plagued many male organizations. The minutes of male associations in New England are filled with wrangling between orthodox and liberal Congregationalists. These trends are wholly absent in the records of the Massachusetts female societies. In fact, Mary Webb's path-breaking Boston Female Society for Missionary Purposes held together a coalition of Baptist and Congregational women.

Early in its organizational fundraising, the BFSMP donated all proceeds to the Congregationalist-dominated Massachusetts Missionary Society. Even after Baptist men formed the Massachusetts Baptist Missionary Society, the BFSMP held together its collection of Congregationalist and Baptist women. Instead of dividing, the women of the BFSMP agreed to split their funds evenly between Congregationalist and Baptist groups.[51] For women excluded from denominational leadership, the bonds of gender and the commitment to missionary activity proved stronger than the tensions of theological or denominational rivalry.

Black religious activism similarly maintained surprising levels of ecumenism. Richard Allen and Absalom Jones continued to cooperate even after the two created their own rival churches. Allen and Jones held the same kind of theological and ecclesiastical differences that caused white clergymen to condemn one another as infidels, yet these two pillars of the Philadelphia community continued working together. By 1794, Allen led a congregation at Mother Bethel African Methodist Episcopal Church and Absalom Jones presided over St. Thomas African Episcopal Church: this same year the two men nonetheless collaborated in writing an important explanation of how Black Philadelphians helped to serve the city during a deadly outbreak of Yellow Fever.[52]

As we already saw in Boston, African Masonic Lodges became important organizing spaces for Black Christians. Unsurprisingly then, Jones and Allen solicited help from Prince Hall in 1797 to organize an African Lodge for Black Masons in Philadelphia. In 1799, Allen helped Jones with a petition that asserted Black citizenship, protested the clandestine slave trade in West Africa, condemned kidnappings in border states, and called for gradual abolition.[53] In 1809, the two men worked together to establish the African Society for the Suppression of Vice and Immorality.[54] Finally, the two collaborated in mediating between Philadelphia's Black community and the American Colonization Society in 1817. At the time of his death in 1818, Absalom Jones had a portrait of Allen hanging next to his own in his rear parlor.[55] What could have been an acrimonious clerical rivalry was, in fact, a highly effective activist alliance.

Similar patterns emerged among Black ministers and activists beyond Philadelphia. The African Masonic Lodge in Boston sprouted both the African

Society in 1796 and the First African Baptist Church in 1805, plus a national network of African Masonic Lodges that organized local reform activities in all of their many locations.[56] In New York, the New York African Society held together a coalition of both Methodists and Episcopalians. Much like in Philadelphia, where Richard Allen's AME Church continued to collaborate with Absalom Jones's Episcopal parish, so too did the AME Zion Church collaborate with Black Episcopalians at St. Phillips African Church in New York. This collaboration endured for decades. In 1827, Peter Williams Jr., the first priest of St. Phillips, teamed up with William Hamilton, a founding member of the AME-Zion denomination, to launch *Freedom's Journal,* the first independent Black newspaper in the nation. The ecumenism extended even further when Williams and Hamilton recruited Samuel Cornish, a Presbyterian, and John Brown Russwurm, who was not yet particularly religious.[57]

Societies run by women and Black Americans often maintained impressive levels of ecumenism. White, male reform organizations, however, continued to draw heavily on denominational networks even as their organizing expanded from conversion to reform. And so as denominationally driven nationalisms directed the benevolent empire, denominational authority continued to direct the United States. But debates about slavery always threatened to undo denominational unity.

Denominations and the Problem of Abolitionism

As denominations slowly pieced themselves together, they remained ever vigilant to avoid the divisiveness of slavery. Eventually the issue boiled over and divided the nation's denominations, but for the first two decades of the nineteenth century, denominational leaders took quick, decisive action to eliminate any disruptive abolitionist agitators. Previous purificationist campaigns to expel enslavers morphed into purificationist campaigns to remove abolitionists. The vast majority of denominational leaders, even in the South, had not yet fully succumbed to a proslavery gospel, yet the reliance on conversionism and a desire to maintain national organizational unity led the overwhelming majority of religious leaders to treat abolitionism somewhere between suspicion and abhorrence.

Denominations were not alone in this process. As the first party system crumbled in the aftermath of the War of 1812, national coalitions of all kinds deployed strategic silences on slavery and abolition.[58] In pursuing national missions of salvation, Methodists, Presbyterians, and Baptists all suppressed even the mere discussion of slavery. Slaveholders maintained the silent status quo by threatening to withdraw from the national commitment to salvation that bound denominations together and promised to transform the world. The experience of two abolitionist ministers are illustrative. Both the Baptist David Barrow and the Presbyterian George Bourne believed that the nation could not experience the providential outpouring of salvation until it first purged itself of slavery. Denominational leaders disagreed and instead purged their denominations of these troublemaking abolitionists.

David Barrow offered the most aggressive antislavery message of any white southerner in the first decade of the nineteenth century.[59] As a result, he was forced to abandon his denominational connection. Barrow dreamed of a Baptist church purified of the sin of slavery, and he believed that only that untainted church could fulfill the divine mission of bringing salvation throughout the nation. Denominational leaders disagreed, and Barrow suffered the consequences of opposing conversionism.

Born in Brunswick County, Virginia, in 1753, David Barrow began his ministry, at the age of eighteen, itinerating between Baptist congregations in Virginia and North Carolina. Soon thereafter he earned a reputation as a courageous minister who openly and dramatically confronted persecution. During a 1778 church service, held at the invitation of a gentleman in the Virginia tidewater, a gang of twenty men seized Barrow and a fellow traveling minister, and after beating them for nearly a half mile, forcibly dunked the two—mocking the Baptist practice of immersion.[60] The arrival of disestablishment put an end to persecutions along these lines, but Barrow found other ways to provoke.

In 1797 Barrow moved west to Kentucky and immediately gained a reputation as an obdurate opponent of slavery. Thirteen years earlier, he had freed his enslaved laborers and had spent the ensuing years pressuring others to do the same. Other Baptists did not share his convictions and attempted to purge him from the ministry. In 1805 the Elkhorn Association of Baptists in central Kentucky resolved "it improper for Ministers, Churches or Associations, to meddle with emancipation from slavery."[61]

In condemning Barrow, the Bracken Association issued a circular letter to all of the local churches that, among other things, included a condemnation of antislavery ministries. The letter read, "Some are so far deluded that their printing, preaching and private conversation, go to encourage disobedience in servants, and a revolution in our Civil Government, contrary to the wholesome words of our Lord Jesus Christ." The authors then appealed to the discourse of conversionism, writing to local churches, "we beseech you to flee from these evils; contend earnestly for the power of the gospel, and for the effect and evidences of union with Christ." Southern churches had to purify themselves of abolitionism in order to protect "the power of the gospel" and ensure "the effect and evidences of union with Christ." American salvation, for these Baptists, depended on silencing abolitionism.[62]

Barrow was unmoved, even as the next year began with renewed chastisement. He was vilified in both the annual association meeting and in the networks of correspondence that held together the Baptist churches in northern Kentucky.[63] When his congregation rallied to his side in 1807, the association reversed itself, restored Barrow, and tried to ignore the issue by avoiding even disguised references to Barrow's ordeal in the annual circular letter.[64] The following year, however, Barrow's church at Mount Sterling purified itself of sinful connection with the enablers of slavery by removing itself from the North-District Association. Barrow then avoided further conflict with proslavery Baptist denominational authorities, at least for a while.[65]

The same year that Barrow removed his church from the North-District, he also published his antislavery thoughts in one of the more remarkable evangelical antislavery statements of the era.[66] Had he not removed himself from the ministerial association already, these incendiary remarks would surely have resulted in his permanent expulsion. Barrow worked hard to avoid offending enslavers, adopting a civil, if uncompromising, tone. He dreamed of unity; in a previous publication he had attacked "unhappy divisions, animosities, janglings, groundless criticisms, heart-burnings, evil- speaking," while praying for the expected day when "all party names may be lost in oblivion, and that an indissolvable union may take place among all true Christians, upon the old apostolic plan." In short, he expected "Heaven-borne truth" to prevail.[67] For Barrow, heaven-borne truth required that Christians abandon slavery.

Barrow believed that the body of Christ would put aside a disgraceful past and unite in eternal holiness through emancipation. And when the church embraced emancipation, purification would result in a greater outpouring of conversion. This was his work, and under these expectations, he attacked the sin of slavery. Baptist leaders could not tolerate this attempt at purificationist abolitionism and Barrow was forced to pursue his ministry isolated from the denomination that originally ordained him. Instead, Barrow and ten other Baptist ministers formed their own network called the Baptized Licking-Locust Association, Friends of Humanity.[68]

George Bourne experienced an even more contentious eviction from his Presbyterian church in 1817. In 1805, Bourne migrated to Baltimore from England at the age of twenty-five. After working as a newspaper editor for six years, Bourne joined the Presbyterian Church and accepted a position as a teaching elder in Port Republic, Virginia. He was a skilled preacher and a committed denominationalist, representing his local Lexington Presbytery at the national General Assembly in both 1813 and 1814.[69] His denominational service quickly turned to encouraging reform. In 1812, for instance, Bourne helped form the Virginia Tract Society, drawing on his prior experience in publishing to help establish a printing house in Harrisonburg, Virginia, while the next year he helped to form the Virginia Bible Society.[70]

Around this time, however, Bourne first took action against enslavers, seeking to rid his church of their sin. He began by denying sacraments to anyone who did not emancipate their enslaved laborers. Bourne's isolated location in the Shenandoah Valley allowed his purificationist actions to escape notice of denominational authorities for awhile. But Bourne was not content to rest in personal pious purificationism; he wanted the rest of his denomination to join him in denouncing both slavery and enslavers.

So in 1815, Bourne again represented the Lexington Presbytery at the General Assembly in Philadelphia, this time with his vocal abolitionism in tow. Bourne attempted to speak with a committee formed to consider whether slavery violated Presbyterian law. The Westminster Confession of Faith had long prohibited "theft, robbery, man-stealing, and receiving anything that is stolen." Bourne argued that this meant Presbyterians had always banned slaving, and it was time finally to enforce this church law. When the committee refused to meet with him, Bourne took his question to the floor of the entire General Assembly. He began by citing the Westminster Confession's prohibition on "man-stealing" and discussing the scriptural foundations on which this portion was drawn. He then launched into a detailed account of slavery's brutality in Virginia, including highlighting abuses committed by Presbyterian ministers. Bourne hoped that his firsthand account of slavery would be sufficient to rally pious Presbyterians in condemning the practice and purging slavers from all Presbyterian churches. In this, he was disappointed.[71]

Bourne returned home after the General Assembly committed to amplifying his abolitionism. He began by attacking local Presbyterian enslavers, sparking a rebellion among his own parishioners, who applied to the local Presbytery for a new minister.[72] By the end of 1815, Bourne's abolitionism caught up with him, and the local Lexington Presbytery began a trial.[73] Robert Herron provided the crucial testimony, relaying that at the General Assembly Bourne accused a local minister of whipping an enslaved woman, leaving her tied up to preach, returning to whip her again, and then ordering the execution of the enslaved woman's husband after he attempted to interfere. When the General Assembly asked Bourne to name the minister who committed the barbaric act, he refused.

Herron also claimed that Bourne had earlier attested that he "believed it to be impossible that anyone could be a Christian and a Slave holder."[74] A letter was then presented where Bourne had written to a local minister that "a Christian slaveholder is an everlasting liar, and thief, and deceiver." Bourne continued "that a man could be a Christian or a democrat and a slaveholder was quite a jest among northern and eastern and western brethren in the Assembly—it is absolutely impossible."[75] Bourne was convicted of "making injurious impressions in the Assembly against the Presbyterian Clergy in Virginia" and immediately removed from his ministry.[76]

But he would not stop. Bourne appealed the conviction at the next national General Assembly while continuing to act on his abolitionist convictions. No longer able to influence his local congregation, he took his purificationism to a larger, national stage. In 1816 Bourne wrote and published the incendiary *The Book and Slavery Irreconcilable*.[77] According to historian David Brion Davis, this work was "the most radical abolitionist tract yet to appear in America."[78] Bourne did not pull any punches, claiming that slavery destroyed "all capacity for the fulfillment of terrestrial duties [and] nullifies the evangelical law of love and equity"; anyone who supported such an institution could not call themselves a Christian.[79] For Bourne, guilt extended beyond enslavers, as he claimed all Americans "participate in its corruption."[80]

After his removal from ministry in Virginia, Bourne accepted a new position with a Presbyterian church in Germantown, Pennsylvania, a fitting location given the famed 1688 Germantown Protest against slavery.[81] At the 1817 General Assembly, Bourne's appeal was granted, and the assembly found "that the charges were not fully substantiated, and if they had been, the sentence was too severe." However, this favorable decision was not final. Bourne would again have to face trial from the Lexington Presbytery in Virginia. Trying him in absentia, the Lexington Presbytery now advanced the same two charges with four more added, including a new accusation that Bourne purchased a horse on the Sabbath. All four charges were confirmed, and these Virginia Presbyterians again stripped Bourne of his ministerial credentials.[82]

Bourne once again appealed to the General Assembly, but this time to no avail. The denomination had turned against him, likely as a result of Bourne's abolitionist pamphlet. With no additional explanation, the 1818 General Assembly declared Bourne "deposed from the Gospel ministry."[83] By 1818, Presbyterians were nearly unanimous in condemning abolitionism. In order to maintain church unity and fulfill its mission of expanding salvation, Presbyterians would now accept only one alternative to the slaving status quo, an alternative that emerged largely from Presbyterian denominational networks: the relocation of Black Americans to Africa.

The 1818 decision to expel Bourne was made by a small committee of ministers including Ashbel Green, Dyer Burgess, and George Baxter. Baxter was from the Lexington Presbytery and had led the charge against Bourne's abolitionism on the ground in Virginia. As editor of the General Assembly's missionary magazine, Ashbel Green had ten years earlier circulated the reports of Robert Finley's revival that opened this chapter. By 1818, however, he was six years into his presidency of the College of New Jersey at Princeton (later Princeton University), an important site for Presbyterian networking and organizing.

In addition to convicting Bourne, this committee of Presbyterians issued a statement on slavery and abolition. They began by echoing the denomination's 1793 declaration by calling slavery a "gross violation" of the "sacred rights of human nature" and "incompatible with the spirit and principles of the gospel of Christ."[84] However, also like the 1793 declaration, they refused to endorse abolitionism. Instead, they called on all Presbyterians "to patronize and encourage the [American Colonization Society], lately formed, for colonizing in Africa, the land of their ancestors, the free people of color in our country." Moreover, in an appeal directed at Bourne and other Presbyterian abolitionists, they demanded that Presbyterians "forebear harsh censures, and uncharitable reflections on their brethren, who unhappily live among slaves, whom they cannot immediately set free; but who, at the same time, are really using all their influence, and all their endeavors, to bring them into a state of freedom, as soon as a door for it can safely be opened."[85] Presbyterians were at work creating a national institution that would save the world. They could not risk the loss of unity in that effort. Moreover, God was bringing emancipation through the denomination's ministry. Salvation was coming, and nothing, including abolitionism, could be allowed to interfere with God's plan.

Denominationalism and the Benevolent Empire

Another hazard to national salvation emerged when the United States Post Office threatened the sanctity of the Sabbath. Potential converts had to be in church on Sunday if they were to hear the gospel. Economic transformations triggered anxieties of a backsliding populace and a pernicious, immoral market crowding out the concerns of Christianity. The opening of post offices on Sundays proved a flashpoint for conflict. Historians have noted the relationship between Sabbatarianism and political culture, following Bertram Wyatt-Brown in understanding Sabbatarianism as a "Prelude to Abolitionism" in the way it led to political confrontation and accelerated the second party system.[86] Richard S. John went further in tracking the religious motivations of the movement, but historians of the benevolent empire have missed how Sabbatarianism became a crossroads in the reform culture of the Presbyterian Church, and accordingly a crossroads in the history of American social reform.[87] Sabbatarianism taught religious leaders that their denominations would not guide national policy directly but that their real power would come in encouraging grass-roots activism.

The issue first came to a head in 1809 when Hugh Wylie, postmaster and active Presbyterian in Washington, Pennsylvania, opened his local post office on Sunday.[88] Local church leaders referred the matter to the Ohio and then to the Pittsburgh Synod to determine whether Wylie should be excluded from membership. During the 1809 annual meeting, the Pittsburgh Synod deliberated over the matter, concluding that "Mr. Wylie's officiating as Postmaster on the Sabbath day, in existing circumstances, is a sufficient reason to exclude him from the special privileges of the church."[89] Wylie appealed the decision to the General Assembly, but the 1810 meeting upheld the ruling of the Pittsburgh Synod.[90] When a number of local Presbyterians in Washington, Pennsylvania, submitted an 1812 petition asking the General Assembly to reverse its decision, they were denied, and Wylie remained excluded from fellowship.[91]

The case became more than a matter of church discipline, however, when on April 30, 1810, the United States Congress passed "An Act regulating the Post-office Establishment." Section Nine of the law required "that every postmaster shall keep an office in which one or more persons shall attend on every day on which a mail, or bag, or other packet or parcel of letters shall arrive by land or water."[92] Five months after the passage of the law, the Synod of Pittsburgh held its annual conference. The synod approved a petition to the United States Congress, calling the law "glaring violations of the laws of God, and therefore an infringement on the rules of conscience." Furthermore, it mustered its best jeremiad to warn Congress that a national policy desecrating the Sabbath gave "reason to fear it may provoke God to inflict upon us, grievous judgments and calamities."[93] The Pittsburgh Synod's was not the only petition, but it was the most radical. Other protests came from Philadelphia, Boston, and New York.[94]

The Presbyterian protest did not go unnoticed, and in 1811, Postmaster General Gideon Granger attempted to compromise by opening post offices for only one hour after the conclusion of weekly worship.[95] Granger's new policy only fueled the uproar, as the controversy extended beyond western Pennsylvania. In 1811 the Presbyterian Synod of New York and New Jersey felt that the desecration of the Sabbath had reached disastrous levels. The synod believed "it to be their duty to do whatever may be in their power to check this growing iniquity." The synod appointed committees from each state in the synod to examine Sabbath laws and then to "apply to the Legislatures to make any alterations which may be thought advisable."[96]

The General Assembly was under great pressure to address the issue. The 1811 General Assembly lamented "the prevalence of Sabbath-breaking" but did not take action directly. Instead the delegates rested in the hope "that associations for the suppression of vice and the promotion of morals, will be generally established, so as to arrest the wicked, and support faithful magistrates in enforcing the laws."[97] The success of the Synod of Pittsburgh in handling the problem proved to the General Assembly that this was a matter that could be handled locally.

One year later, the arrival of open war with Britain changed the mood of both the nation and the General Assembly. In July, the General Assembly declared a national fast day to ensure divine aid in the war effort. This fast day inspired a national reflection on the godliness of the United States and provided a window for Sabbatarians to again agitate against the policies of the federal government. Congregations across the United States experienced the fast day as a rallying cry against the desecration of the Sabbath. With this momentum, the 1812 General Assembly petitioned Congress to cease opening and carrying the mail on Sundays. The national Presbyterian body echoed the Pittsburgh synod in employing the language of the jeremiad, blaming the outbreak of war on American impiety.[98] But the petition had no impact. The Presbyterian Church had spoken with all of its self-claimed authority as keepers of the national faith. And they were ignored.

The failure of the 1812 petition marked a turning point in the tactics of the General Assembly and American denominational activism as a whole. The General Assembly issued the 1812 petition in its own name but found that it held little sway in the halls of government. In 1814 the delegates tried a new tactic, this time drafting two thousand petitions from each of the towns represented by the General Assembly. Instead of receiving one petition from the representatives of America's Presbyterians, Congress would now hear directly from the people at the local-church level. Where centralized attempts at reform had failed, the General Assembly hoped perhaps a groundswell of public opinion could succeed.

For this public relations campaign, the General Assembly delegates solicited the support of their Reformed brethren in New England, earning the allegiance of the general associations of Connecticut and Massachusetts. By January 1816 over one hundred petitions had reached the floors of Congress, and a new mode of grassroots national denominational political protest was born.[99] Reformers could not wield a national church, nor could they invoke its authority in directing policy. Appeals from formal denominational bodies to the legislature could be dismissed as sectarian clerical power plays. But denominational networks could be leveraged to create a groundswell of support. Social reform would result from the chorus and cacophony of American democracy. And yet American democracy still relied heavily on denominational identities. It is not surprising then to find that American reform emerged out of denominational bodies.

Historians of reform have not recognized the denominational origins of many of the most influential reform organizations of the early nineteenth century. The men who staffed the benevolent empire created careers for themselves, stability for their families, and discourses justifying the authority of their denominations. The age of reform both drew on and then further fueled the power of denominational bodies. The importance of denominational networks in creating the benevolent empire can be illustrated in several brief case studies. Tract societies, Bible societies, Temperance societies, and the American Colonization Society all drew on denominational networks.

Tract societies sought to extend the mission of conversion beyond the physical churches of the denomination. Anyone who could read could experience conversion as a result of these tracts. Yet, both in content and in structure, tract societies mirrored denominational structures. The New England Tract Society (NETS) formed in 1814 promised to produce tracts "calculated to receive the approbation of serious Christians of all denominations," but these Calvinist Congregationalists generally believed that only theologically similar members of their own denomination deserved to be considered "serious." Conservative Congregationalist ministers affiliated with Andover Seminary devised the NETS, and until the highly connected reformer Justin Edwards took the reins from the orthodox war horse Jedediah Morse, the society distributed tracts predominately to their codenominationalists.[100]

Tract societies in New York were even more denominationally fractured. The Protestant Episcopal Tract Society was formed in 1810 and distributed a handful of tracts to Episcopal churches in the region. All the key founders of the New York Religious Tract Society were strict Calvinists of either the Associate Reformed tradition or the Dutch Reformed Church.[101] The New York Methodist Tract Society joined the market in 1817.[102] Eventually, the New York Religious Tract Society attracted Baptists and Episcopalians and inched toward ecumenism, but in the early days, members from the Reformed tradition dominated. Tract societies were nearly all directly tied to denominational bodies.

The American Bible Society eventually emerged out of a network of state societies, all designed to copy the British and Foreign Bible Society (BFBS), formed in 1804. The Philadelphia Bible Society materialized first in 1808, but state societies followed the very next year in Connecticut, Massachusetts, New York, and New Jersey. This phenomenon was not confined to the North. In 1810 Charleston, South Carolina, formed a Bible society and three years later Christians in Richmond, Virginia, followed. In 1809 the Connecticut Bible Society requested support from "young ladies desirous of contributing a mite towards promoting the important object for which the Connecticut Bible Society was instituted." Women appeared eager to help; the Connecticut Bible Society advertisement concluded by listing the current membership already well established at 152.[103] Efforts to consolidate these local organizations stalled until the explosion of nationalism surrounding War of 1812 encouraged reformers to link these state societies.[104]

The Presbyterian General Assembly called for the formation of "a general Bible Society" at its annual meeting in May 1814. When the denominational body stalled, the elderly but deeply respected Presbyterian and former states-man Elias Boudinot took matters into his own hands. Boudinot appealed to two national networks: Presbyterians and Federalists, the latter of whom rec-ognized the benevolent empire as an opportunity to continue shaping national policy as their party crumbled.[105] Four months after the General Assembly adjourned, Boudinot sent a proclamation to Bible societies throughout the na-tion to meet the following May in New York City to create "a well organized constituted Body, to be called 'The General Association of the Bible Societ-ies in the United States.'"[106] Presbyterians in the mid-Atlantic dominated the meeting, but orthodox Congregationalist and Federalist powerbroker Jedidiah Morse of Charlestown, Massachusetts, made his presence felt. Other societies soon followed the path of the Bible Society, including the vastly influential American Temperance Society.

The campaign for temperance progressed through two stages. The spirit of religious purification influenced the first phase as reformers excluded the intemperate from the flock. The second wave employed the politics of reform, attempting to prohibit the sale and consumption of alcohol. This transition from temperance (exclusion) to prohibition (reform) mirrors the distinction between purificationist antislavery and abolitionism. Denominational bodies directed each shift in the temperance movement. Studies of temperance have dwelt extensively on the social, economic, and political motivations of reform, often considering religious motivations as epiphenomenal.[107] Other histori-ans who do take religion seriously overemphasize the functions of revivalism, obscuring the ways in which the development of temperance was intimately bound up in denominational structures.[108]

Accounts of the temperance movement often begin with Benjamin Rush's pamphlet "An Inquiry into the Effects of Ardent Spirits upon the Human Body and Mind," but historians usually elide the connections between Rush's research and Presbyterian denominational action. In 1811 Rush donated a thou-sand copies of this pamphlet to the Presbyterian General Assembly. The na-tional Presbyterian body accepted this gift with gratitude, for that same year the General Assembly reported that they "have heard of the sin of drunkness prevailing—prevailing to a great degree—prevailing even amongst some of the visible members of the household of faith." One year later, the situation worsened as the General Assembly declared "profane swearing, drunkenness, and Sabbath-breaking" to be "sins of our land." To combat the supposedly in-creasing sin of drinking, the assembly "recommended to all the ministers of the

Presbyterian church in the United States to deliver public discourses, as often as circumstances may render it expedient, on the sin and mischiefs of intemperate drinking."[109]

In June 1811 the General Association of Massachusetts appointed a committee of four ministers and four laymen to cooperate with the committee of the General Assembly of the Presbyterian Church and the General Association of Connecticut in devising measures for the promotion of temperance. Two years later this very same committee organized the Massachusetts Society for the Suppression of Intemperance. The three key founders of the Massachusetts Society—Justin Edwards, Lyman Beecher, and Leonard Woods— would become the most influential proponents of temperance organizing, and all three committed to the cause under the direction of denominational bodies. Denominational leadership blended smoothly with leadership in the benevolent empire, enabling ministers to eventually approach the problem of slavery with new moral authority and new institutional influence.

The American Colonization Society (ACS), the national organization designed to confront slavery while protecting white supremacy, similarly drew from denominational networks and mimicked the organizational structures and procedures of other elements of the benevolent empire. The idea of colonizing Black Americans in Africa dated back to the late eighteenth century, and in 1815 the Black Quaker Paul Cuffee successfully organized an expatriation of several dozen Black Americans to the British colony of Sierra Leone. But the formal origins of the ACS began with collaborations spawned through Presbyterian connections born at Princeton. Charles Fenton Mercer, a Presbyterian and Princeton graduate serving in the Virginia House of Delegates, was stunned when he learned that Thomas Jefferson had earlier considered colonization.[110] After reading Jefferson's colonization thoughts, Mercer immediately began to dream of schemes that would be directed by the Virginia House of Delegates and the president of the United States. But American reform would not be driven by government. Denominational networks and the benevolent societies spawned by those denominational networks would direct American reform.[111]

Presbyterians, particularly Presbyterians associated with Princeton, would take colonization from a speculative conversation among friends to a massive national movement. Mercer's Princeton contacts included Elias B. Caldwell, the adopted son of the benevolent leader Elias Boudinot, who was a long-term trustee at Princeton and helped found the American Bible Society before serving as its first president. His adopted son, Elias Caldwell preached from time to time in Washington as an ordained Presbyterian minister while also serving as a clerk of the Supreme Court. Mercer shared his colonization dreams with his former Princeton classmate. Caldwell was converted to the cause and reached out to his brother-in-law, the Presbyterian minister Robert Finley.[112]

Finley had long dreamed of bringing salvation to Africa and saw the colonization effort as a perfect vehicle in accomplishing that goal. From these Presbyterian roots, the American Colonization Society blossomed into a curious collection of abolitionists, philanthropists, enslavers, and Americans of nearly every religious and political persuasion. The ACS presented their ambitions as offering seemingly innumerable benefits, including the uplift and then elimination of American free Black communities, the erosion of slavery, the destruction of the illicit slave trade, the expansion of American commerce, and the conversion of Africa. This last ambition came to dominate the public discourse around colonization, and for decades, public conversations around slavery centered around the increasingly contentious colonizationist movement.

IN THE FIRST FEW decades of the nation's history, American reformers lacked the national religious imagination required to pursue national reform. By the 1810s, however, leading clergymen enlarged their understanding of ministerial spaces from congregations or regional associations to the new republic in its entirety. Denominations became the mechanisms for clergymen to define the nation and direct its destiny. The spatial expansion of clerical duty enabled the leaders of these new national religious cultures to plot the purge of the great sins of the republic. But denominational formation also connected coreligionists across sectional lines. These often intensely personal connections discouraged denominationalists from engaging in increasingly vitriolic sectionalist discourse. For northerners, denominational connections created a window in the world of the South and made it more difficult to ignore the reality of slavery, but these same connections also restrained antislavery northerners from condemning the men and women with whom they collaborated in the missions of their churches.

Historians have lauded the antebellum revolutions in transportation and communication. Indeed, technological advances collapsed space, but long before the railroad or telegraph knit together the continent, denominational affiliation created connections across great distances. Americans created and deployed religious discourse to discover themselves and to pursue spiritual errands—errands that always involved ambitions both personal and political. As the nation began to recognize itself as a unified body, the sins of the day took on a greater threat. From their foundations in denominational bodies, national reform societies began to combat the great sin of slavery. But the obsession over religions conversion again exerted itself in the process, as the most powerful national movement designed to alleviate the problem of slavery owed its origins to dreams of an American-led global expansion of salvation.

◇◇◇◇ 3 ◇◇◇◇

Saving Africa and Redeeming the United States, 1815–1825

O N FEBRUARY 13, 1820, several dozen white and Black Christians huddled around a flickering flame. Samuel Bacon's voice filled the crowded cabin of the *Elizabeth* with tales of missionaries, past and present. Eighty-six emigrants rocked with the swells of the Atlantic as they drifted farther from their families in America and closer to their new home along the western coast of Africa. Daniel Coker, born enslaved, now a free man, a husband, a father, and a missionary, reflected on the evening devotional. Bacon's words left him "refreshed much," and Coker reported that all on board "felt encouraged in our work, in the conversion of the heathen." Coker and the eighty-five other emigrants risked everything they had in traveling across the ocean, and they did so for many reasons, but "the conversion of the heathen" excited Coker more than anything else.[1]

Historians have focused studies of colonization on its relation to slavery, most recently emphasizing how the movement sought to weaken slavery and how later abolitionists arose in opposition to the American Colonization Society.[2] By making it easier for benevolent masters to manumit their slaves, colonization promised a gradual solution to the problem of slavery, but a later generation of abolitionists did indeed first take action by opposing colonization. Other historians see the movement as a desire to strengthen slavery by removing free people of color, whose existence questioned the logics of slavery and provided a constant opposition to American slaving.[3] Still others stress the ambitions of Black nationalists in creating African American identities independent of white Americans.[4] Colonization certainly influenced slavery debates, and the movement accelerated the development of African identities, but colonizationists—white and Black—invoked another motivation with far greater frequency and intensity than the explanations emphasized in the historiography.

Conversionism led colonizationists to frame their movement as fulfilling the millennial promise of Psalm 68, "Ethiopia shall soon stretch forth her hands to God."[5] In the minds of early nineteenth-century white conversionist Christians, colonization promised to do more good than abolition, as the salvation of a continent weighed heavier than the emancipation of several million. Despite the consistently prophetic, liberationist critique against slavery from Black Christians, many white and Black Christians shared the belief that Africa required salvation. Vibrant millennial imaginations convinced Americans that the wildly impractical goal of extending salvation through African colonization was all but assured and that these conversions would begin a global process of Christian triumph.

Both white and Black Christians shared an evangelical soteriology, the theology of salvation, and believed that without a transformative Christian conversion, eternal damnation awaited all sinful souls. Both Black and white Christians also relied on millennial imaginations. The millennium envisioned by African Americans often proved more capacious, including racial equality and powerful Black nationalism, but both white and Black Americans privileged Africa in their providential expectations.

Conversionist Christianity provided a powerful biracial discourse that colonizationists briefly wielded with surprising success. Both white and Black Christians also sought to rewrite the history of the slave trade, transforming it from a horrific act of torture into an agent of global Christianization. The impending conversion of Africa would repay the wounded continent with the gift of Christianity and transform enslaved men and women into exalted soldiers for salvation. For white Americans, colonization promised salvation for Africa and moral redemption for the United States. Black Americans were less interested in redeeming their former enslavers, but they shared the desire of extending Christian salvation to the African continent. Tracing conversionist ideologies among early colonizationists reveals the goals and expectations of the men and women who invested so much capital, human and otherwise, in this ambitious venture as well as illuminates the powerful conversionist ideology shared by both colonizationists and their opponents.

BRITISH COLONIZATION IN West Africa began in 1787 when a small group of impoverished Black Londoners relocated to Sierra Leone. Once again, we find Americans racing to catch up with the activities of British Christians. Shortly after these Black Londoners arrived in West Africa, the Sierra Leone Company formed to resettle 1,196 African American refugees who had escaped from slavery during the Revolutionary War.[6] Americans had discussed the prospects of bringing salvation to Africa since at least 1774 when Samuel Hopkins and Ezra Stiles attempted to organize Black Americans to missionize West Africa. Thomas Jefferson considered colonization in his 1783 *Notes on the State of Virginia,* but no serious attempt emerged from Americans until Paul Cuffee and thirty-eight African Americans sailed for Sierra Leone in late 1815. Cuffee, a deeply pious Black Quaker and wealthy maritime entrepreneur, paid for the expedition himself, but he passed away before he could organize another.[7] By that time, white Americans had taken up the cause and the American effort began in earnest.

The ACS held its first meeting in Washington, DC's Davis Hotel on December 21, 1816, and incorporated shortly thereafter. Many Black Americans almost immediately mobilized in opposition of the white-led effort, but white Christians overwhelmingly ignored this opposition and trumpeted the few Black Americans who were willing to relocate. Immediate efforts to secure funding from the national government finally came to fruition in 1819. One year later, Daniel Coker and eighty-five other Black Americans joined three white ACS agents in boarding the *Elizabeth.* Unable to procure land on the mainland, these first emigrants settled on the uninhabited Sherbro Island, just south of the British settlement of Freetown, Sierra Leone. A year later, in late 1821, Lieutenant Robert Stockton of the US Navy forcefully acquired land for the ACS on Cape Mesurado, just over one hundred miles south of the British colony. Over the next decade more than 2,500 American settlers arrived in what would come to be called Liberia, including several white and Black missionaries. Colonists suffered terribly from disease and conflicts with the Indigenous people they displaced as the venture proved shockingly costly in both dollars and lives.[8]

This study does not chronicle the establishment or struggle of these African colonies but rather restricts itself to questions of what Americans sought to accomplish and how colonization influenced the later abolitionist movement. The on-the-ground reality of colonization involved tremendous suffering and all the violence of conquest and settler colonialism, but the motivations for these actions repeatedly circled back to extending salvation. Colonization held together men and women, North and South, Black and white, in an unprecedentedly widespread effort. A stunning roster of influential Americans voiced their support. Bushrod Washington, Supreme Court justice and nephew of the venerated first president, served as the society's first president. Major contributions were made by Henry Clay, the speaker of the House; William Crawford, secretary of the Treasury; and the legendary Senator Daniel Webster, then a representative in Congress.

It would be difficult, if not impossible, to find another contemporary group that claimed so wide a mandate or spectrum of supporters as the American Colonization Society. The only societies that perhaps could have rivaled the ACS include other conversionist groups like the American Tract Society or the American Bible Society. Cutting across the major political and geographic divisions of white society in the early republic, the ACS coalition was wide and unwieldy but tremendously influential. The ability to transcend these divisions resulted from the ACS's use of the great unifying force of the era: conversionist Christianity. The vast majority of free Black Americans remained skeptical and, beginning in Philadelphia, almost immediately turned against the white-led society despite largely sharing the belief that the world should and would receive Christian salvation.

Colonizationist pamphlets extolled a lengthy list of blessings to result from African colonization, including the removal of free Black communities, the development of an American empire, the enervation of American slavery, the destruction of the Atlantic slave trade, and economic growth resulting from new markets and trading networks. But the promise of salvation was mentioned more often and with greater rhetorical intensity. Throughout the antebellum era, colonizationists almost constantly reprinted Robert Finley's 1816 tract *Thoughts on the Colonization of Free Blacks*.[9] Finley's words set a template for American colonizationists that endured for decades.

Finley's brief eight-page essay laid out a rhetorical pattern shared by nearly all colonizationist tracts. After promising that colonization would mount an assault on illegal slave trading, lead to a decline in domestic slavery, edify free people of color, decrease the risk of slave revolt, and advance American commerce, the most intense emotional rhetoric came in the final paragraphs with the promise of African conversion and American moral redemption. In the final paragraph he proclaimed, "Nor shall Africa be forgotten. Her bosom begins to warm with hope and her heart to beat with expectation and desire." He later continued by rejoicing that through colonization the United States would surpass other nations, "exceed[ing] them in the great cause of humanity which has begun its never-ending course."[10] This "great cause of humanity" was the expectation of global salvation that promised to hasten the millennium so craved by American conversionist Christians. A review of the annual reports of the ACS reveals the generation of essayists who copied Finley's style, overwhelming readers with a lengthy catalog of the seemingly innumerable benefits of colonization before concluding with an emotionally heightened plea to save African souls and absolve American sins.

Finley's work posed and answered a series of queries that guided colonizationists. The remainder of this chapter explores five of these questions. The very first sentence of the tract asked, "What shall we do with the free people of color?"[11] The answer was simple: transform them from a loathed, dangerous threat to white democracy into a blessed agent of international salvation. He also asked why Africa should be the location for a colony. Finley and others considered a number of potential sites, but they ultimately chose West Africa because they believed doing so answered an additional question: How can the United States redeem itself from the sins of the slave trade and compete with the moral work of Great Britain? Kidnapping and trafficking were heavy crimes, but the moral ledger would be more than balanced by bringing eternal life to millions.

But American redemption hinged on bringing mass conversions across the ocean. The British colony in Sierra Leone could begin this process, but Americans knew that God wanted to work through their nation, not through the old despotism-ridden European powers. Finley and other colonizationists had to answer how this plan would work. Again, their answer looked to the heavens. By reading scripture as well as the signs of the times, colonizationists were convinced that God was behind their effort. The Black community, however, was not so convinced. In the response to Black opposition, we again see the reliance on conversionism in attempting to achieve the impossible.

"What Shall We Do with the Free People of Color?"

The early American republic held together partly through shared commitments to white supremacy and dreams of Christian salvation. Conversionism united white Americans with a widespread intensity rivaled only by pervasive racist fears of Black people. St. George Tucker composed his early colonizationist tract shortly after Gabriel's 1800 conspiracy in Richmond, Virginia. Tucker and others interpreted the attempt at rebellion as proof of the danger of the free Black population in the Old Dominion, and Tucker pointed to religion as the connection between potentially violent Black Americans and the laboring classes of poor white Virginians. He lamented, "Fanaticism is spreading fast among the negroes of this country, and may form in time the connecting link between the black religionists and the white."[12] As Tucker well knew, evangelical religion was powerful, and unless white leaders harnessed this power, it threatened to undo the fabric of slave societies. His solution was to purchase land from the Spanish on the North American continent on which to colonize free people of color.

In 1805, Thomas Branagan, a former slave trader turned antislavery writer, created an elaborate metaphor describing the problem of slavery in the United States and the role colonization could play in its amelioration. Just five years after Gabriel's aborted rebellion, Branagan wrote that slavery was "a large tree planted in the South, whose spreading branches extends to the North; the poisonous fruit of that tree when ripe fall upon these states." This poisonous fruit represented the formerly enslaved people who became free people of color. His solution was to "lop off the branches that drop their untimely fruit in our states, and transport them in a land more congenial to themselves, where they may grow and flourish without annoying any person, and become in process of time in Africa, a flourishing tree which may be beneficial to the union in a commercial and agricultural point of view."[13]

For the majority of Americans who despised the existence of Black people in their country, colonization provided an attractive solution. Robert Finley shared these views, beginning his colonizationist tract with the very question "What shall we do with the free people of color?"[14] Finley, however, fretted more over the religious health of the nation than over the threat of slave revolt.[15] He felt that free people of color damaged the virtue of white Christians because religion required industry, and the presence of Black Americans gave whites a feeling of entitlement and a dangerous enjoyment of luxury. But "the gradual withdrawing of the blacks would insensibly and from an easy necessity induce habits of industry and along with it a love of order and religion."[16]

This transformation would facilitate conversions of both African American emigrants and the white Americans who remained behind. Sending African American missionaries across the ocean would not only hasten the conversion of Africa but facilitate the conversion of the white Americans who had yet to join the church. Colonization would yield conversion abroad and conversion at home. These were potent promises for the many Americans eager to seek and save the lost.

White missionaries signed up to bring the gospel across the ocean, but many Americans came to believe that only African Americans could truly bring salvation to Africa. James S. Green, the Presbyterian who was vice president of the New Jersey Colonization Society, agreed. He feared that "it seems almost impossible without a miracle, which we have no reason to expect, that it ever should be Christianized except by Africans." The climate and the customs of Africans would supposedly prohibit successful white missionary efforts, but "native missionaries, moreover, when well qualified, are, on various accounts, more acceptable to their brethren than strangers, and can address them with more advantage from a knowledge of their customs and their feelings."[17]

Fears of tropical climates and racist anxieties of supposed African barbarism joined with a practical awareness that many Africans understandably equated white skin with fears of slave trading, fears that would certainly impinge on missionary activities. As Anthony Benezet mourned in his antislavery tract, European Christians spoiled their opportunity to evangelize the continent.[18] Henry Clay feared the same but believed that Americans could yet still make a difference in claiming that "the African Colonists, whom we send to convert the heathen . . . will be received as long lost brethren."[19] Imagining the encounter between an African and an African American missionary left white American colonizationists swelling with paternalist pride. Even the sin of slavery could be transformed into a powerful agent of God's divine plan for salvation.

Despite the desires of proslavery Americans, the ACS program involved much more than rounding up free people of color and deporting them across the ocean. Finley wanted only those migrants to go who would be well prepared, those who upon arrival would "be the great instruments of spreading peace and happiness." He dreamed of assembling an army of "thousands and tens of thousands" of Black men and women to make the voyage. Surely "in a land of civil liberty and religious knowledge" there would be no trouble finding such an army.[20]

Colonization promised to transform Black Americans as well as their African brethren. Training African American missionaries would turn a class of reviled, feared, and pitied Black Americans into pious servants of Christ. In the minds of white colonizationists, dangerous enslaved and free Black people would become disciplined missionaries. In 1817, Newark Presbyterian minister Edward Dorr Griffin, preaching on behalf of the African School, a Presbyterian training ground for African American missionaries, proclaimed that "it can no longer be made a question whether the elevation of the African race is a part of the new order of things. The providence of God has declared it."[21] The Christian College at Clapham in England, the African Seminary in Philadelphia, and the African School in New York all promised to furnish well-educated, passionate missionaries. Through the benevolence of American colonizationists, African Americans would take their place as trusted servants of God, and Africans would be brought into the kingdom of Christ. The concerns of Christian nationalism, both regarding competition with Europe and the fears of rising American sectarianism, further fueled the movement.

Why Africa?

Africa was not the only site considered for colonization. Finley contemplated a colony west of the Mississippi and even concluded that "Africa would be a much more arduous undertaking" than establishing a community on the North American continent.[22] But Finley was not looking for expediency. He was after souls. Other possible locations were similarly vetoed for their lack of missionary potential. Prince Saunders, a New England Black educator, pressed the case for Haiti, claiming that Christians had a duty to help the infant republic. Saunders himself arrived in Haiti in 1815 and worked as an agent for the administration of Henri Christophe.[23] Christophe's political rival, President Jean Pierre Boyer, also encouraged American migration, sending a representative named Jonathas Granville to the United States in 1824.[24]

Richard Allen, the widely respected founder of African American Methodism, greeted Granville and aided the Haitian agent in finding emigrants. Haiti continued to compete with Africa for Black American emigrants. Loring Daniel Dewey, a Presbyterian minister and agent for the ACS in New York, had grown frustrated in attempting to attract migrants to West Africa and instead arranged a migration to Haiti. The ACS fired Dewey, but Dewey persisted, corresponding directly with President Boyer. Eventually over two hundred Black Americans relocated to Haiti, but the plan never generated nearly as much political or economic support as African colonization.

Boosters billed the two migrations differently. Haiti was sold as a refuge, Africa as a mission field. President Boyer wrote of Haiti as "a sure asylum to unfortunate men."[25] Boyer wrote that African Americans, "debased by ignorance and exasperated by misfortune, have become turbulent and dangerous." While white colonizationists often held the same opinion of Black Americans, ACS materials sparingly invoked this discourse, opting instead to focus on the positive potential of colonization for both Africa and the United States. Both before and after the founding of the ACS, Americans looked to migration as a means of liberation, but white colonizationists could not divorce African American migration from the mission of Christianization.

James S. Green dismissed the possibility of facilitating Haitian migration in his address at the 1824 inaugural meeting of the New Jersey State Colonization Society. According to the rules established by President Boyer, immigrants to Haiti enjoyed religious liberty but were restricted from proselytizing. Supporters of African colonization knew this restriction would make Haitian emigration a nonstarter for many philanthropically inclined Christians. How could any true Christian hold their tongue and allow their neighbor to pass through life on their way to an eternity of torment? How could any pious American, Black or white, watch the Catholic Haitians suffer under papist idolatry and not share the truth of the Protestant gospel? According to Green, any true Christian would not be able to "never say or do anything to save them from 'the wrath to come!'" In his words, "It is impossible."[26] By prohibiting conversionist activity, Haiti nullified its candidacy as a major site for colonization.

Americans had to convert, both at home and abroad. Africa needed conversion, but the United States needed redemption. African colonization promised both. Theodore Frelinghuysen similarly appreciated the offer from Haiti but told the same New Jersey Colonization Society, six months later, that "the trespass was committed against the continent—and to the continent, let retribution be made." Speaking for the United States, he claimed that "we have injured, and we must make reparation." Frelinghuysen framed the need for redemption as a millennial imperative, for what would happen "when America beholds, flaming from the eternal throne, 'The blood of injured Africa calls for judgment.' What must be our plea?" He concluded that the United States would be found "guilty before God."[27] The injury of the slave trade required reparation, and colonization promised not only eternal life for Africans but also absolution for the nation's sinful slave trading.

According to many white antislavery Americans, slavery had corrupted a continent. Africa held a curious place in the American mind. Despite its being understood as a den of pagan idolatry, American and British Christians also shared a religious imagination of Africa as blessed with a rich and often mythic Christian past. This imagination often transcended time and space, holding places of prominence for white Christians in the eighteenth and nineteenth centuries on both sides of the Atlantic. Benjamin Rush took for granted that his readers would be well aware of African Christianity, asking "Who has not heard of the Christian Church in Africa?"[28]

Ezra Stiles pored over the travel accounts of James Bruce looking for remnants of ancient Christianity. Stiles even wrote Bruce, correcting the Scottish explorer's claims regarding the travels of the early apostles and asking if "there may not be found some relics of oppressed Africans of St. Matthew, in lower Ethiopia?"[29] Granville Sharp's antislavery pamphlet *The Just Limitation of Slavery in the Laws of God* included an extensive history of Christianity in Africa, drawn mostly from William Cave's *Scriptorum Ecclesiasticorum Historia Literaria,* a widely reprinted literary history of early church writers. Sharp followed the interests of his grandfather in studying the major African church councils in Carthage and even provided a numerical count of 310 bishops in the West African City of Baga by 394 CE. According to Sharp, the continent had "lamentably, fallen back into gross ignorance" since the glory of the early African church, yet he and so many others determined "to restore the heathens to their lost privileges."[30] Restoring the heathen would return Africa to her glorious past, earning the United States the special approbation of heaven. But Americans had to act now.

Africa was both the location of a proud Christian past and an anticipated glorious Christian future, but in the minds of American and British Christians, it was also an unrivaled challenge for missionaries eager to win the world for Christ. Colonizationists drew on the deeply racist understandings of Africa held by Anglo-Christians for centuries.[31] In an 1820 funeral sermon honoring two fallen ACS agents, William Augustus Muhlenberg called Africa "the strong hold of Satan," a land "enveloped in a moral night of tenfold darkness."[32] This imagery of Satan's strongholds and tenfold darkness directly contributed to imperialist ends, but when first articulated, they represented earnest missionary pleas of conversionist Christians fretting over the souls of unreached Africans. It would be a mistake to overemphasize the imperial ambitions of the earliest American colonizationists, but the seeds of what would bear troubling fruit sprouted in even the earliest colonizationist rhetoric. Historians have recently focused attention on the relationship between religious conversion, antislavery enforcement, and the development of Western imperialism. The best of these studies resist the tendency to caricature missionary zeal and antislave trade enforcement as nothing more than justifications for empire, instead illustrating how the two motivations fused over the course of the nineteenth century.[33]

Why America?

American Christians paid close attention to British colonization, but an American colony, Finley assured, would have a far easier time than a British colony. British action proved the viability of colonization, but according to the spiritual father of American colonization, "toward this land of liberty [Africa] turns her eyes." Edward Dorr Griffin also implored Americans to "no longer look to Europe for the redemption of Africans: the work is laid on ourselves by the plain direction of heaven."[34] Robert Finley never doubted that Africa would return to Christian glory.[35] The settlers at Sierra Leone were refugees battered about the Atlantic World. American colonists, by contrast, "could carry with them property, the useful arts of life, and above all, the knowledge of the benign religion of Christ."[36] The British proved it could be done, but Americans would do it right.

Elias B. Caldwell, Finley's brother-in-law and clerk of the United States Supreme Court, understood the millennial promise of colonization as a unifying program that would unite an increasingly fractured American Christianity, soothing tensions within and between American denominations. While Caldwell acknowledged differences of opinion among American believers, he stood confident in the knowledge that all Americans shared "the belief that the scriptures predict a time, when the gospel of Jesus Christ shall be spread over every part of the world." An increasing number of Americans came to believe "this glorious and happy day is near at hand," and by emphasizing this shared belief, American Christians could overcome their contentious economic, social, and theological divisions.[37]

Caldwell pointed to "great movements and mighty efforts in the moral and religious world" as evidence of an approaching international wave of conversions that would transcend geographic and denominational lines.[38] Colonization offered a message of unity that not only cut across political and sectional divides but also transcended denominational and theological barriers. Christians of nearly every theological and denominational persuasion shared the dream of a converted Africa. Calvinists and Arminians, Baptists, Presbyterians, Methodists, and Episcopalians all labored together. The promise of global conversion appealed to a wide array of Americans, and through the promise of Psalm 68 that Ethiopia would stretch forth her hands unto God, Africa took center stage in the great millennial drama about to unfold.

By the second decade of the nineteenth century a clear majority of Americans believed the Atlantic slave trade was evil, and although it had been abolished, a moral scar endured. Finley believed that the United States had committed a grave sin, but colonization offered "the atoning sacrifice." The slave trade robbed Africa of millions of children, encouraged violence between African nations, and hindered the progress of missionaries by linking Christianity to slavery. Finley wrote, "If wrong has been done to Africa in forcing away her weeping children, the wrong can be best redressed by that power which did the injury." By bringing the gospel to Africa, the United States would earn the praise and honor of all of Europe and "exceed them in the great cause of humanity, which has begun its never ending course."[39]

William Augustus Muhlenberg praised American attempts to weaken the Atlantic slave trade but regretted that the nation still owed a debt to the sons and daughters of those taken into captivity. In an 1820 sermon he proclaimed that if by the labors of the American Colonization Society, "we can transmit to Africa the blessings of our arts, our civilization and our religion, perhaps we may extinguish a part of the great moral debt."[40] Colonizationists repeated the theme of debt. Edward Dorr Griffin claimed that Americans "owe a greater atonement than any other nation to bleeding Africa."[41] This debt mocked American claims to greatness. For Americans to regain their moral capital, they must repay Africa.

The impending wave of conversions had begun. God was calling the United States to lead the charge. By doing so, Americans would erase the sins of their slave-trading past and establish themselves as the preeminent moral authority among the nations of the world. James Patterson, in a July 4 sermon in 1825 told his ecumenical audience that "we cannot conceive how this country would make a reparation to Africa for the wrongs done her." But Patterson and others wanted to do more than make reparation. They wanted to assert American righteousness. Patterson asked, "Would this government give a Christian education to her slaves, which she is bound to do, and then return them to their native country, what greater favor under heaven could they possibly confer on Africa?" What greater favor could there be than providing "60,000,000 of souls, sunk in the most cruel heathenism, with the most efficient missionaries."[42]

The successful conversion of Africa would recast the tragedy of the slave trade as a divine step in the workings of Providence. In a curious late eighteenth-century tract, James Beattie lampooned the work of proslavery writer Richard Nisbet, mocking the claim that the slave trade "has been the principal means of heaping wealth and honors on Europeans and Americans and rescuing many millions of wretched Africans as *brands from the fire.*"[43] By the early nineteenth century, however, proslavery Americans made these same points without a tinge of irony.

As the nineteenth century progressed, the conflict between proslavery and antislavery thought accelerated. Both sides drew arguments from an earlier conversionist consensus. The proslavery assurance that the slave trade bore a positive good in saving African heathens from a life of barbarism and an eternity of torment received a major boost from colonizationists, many of whom carried antislavery convictions. By tracing the anticipated millennial revival back to the slave trade, antislavery colonizationists loaded one of the most potent weapons in the proslavery arsenal, a weapon that would be wielded repeatedly in the pamphlet wars of the mid-nineteenth century.

Absalom Jones, the first African American Episcopal bishop, made this very point. In an 1808 sermon he asked, "Why the impartial Father of the human race should have permitted the transportation of so many millions of our fellow creatures to this country, to endure all the miseries of slavery." His answer was that God allowed this great evil to happen in order to raise up a generation of African American missionaries. He mused, "Perhaps his design was, that a knowledge of the gospel might be acquired by some of their descendants, in order that they might become qualified to be the messengers of it, to the land of their fathers."[44] *Poulson's American Daily Advertiser*, in its account of the very first ACS meeting, remarked how colonization might "become in the hands of Divine Providence, the instrument of introducing amongst savage brethren, the blessings of civilization."[45]

The white colonizationist James Green wrote in 1824 that the fault for the great injustice of the slave trade fell exclusively on Christian nations. But he took comfort from the belief that "when Christians shall repent of their crime, and seek to repair the injury they have inflicted by restoring to Africa her enslaved children, these freemen and Christians will be the instruments in the hands of God, to civilize, and Christianize." Even the horrors of the slave trade "shall eventually be made productive of the richest blessings, which the inhabitants of that quarter of the globe have ever received from the Father of Mercies." Green searched the scriptures and human history to find "the usual order of the divine dispensations" and determined that God always worked in ways contrary to the nefarious intentions of mankind. Since "from the sure word of prophecy, we know that 'Ethiopia shall stretch forth her hands unto God,'" it was clear that "Africa shall yet be Christianized."[46]

The rhetoric of national redemption emerged in surprising places. In its immediate attempt to secure funding from Congress, the ACS proclaimed in a memorial, "it may be reserved for our government . . . to become the honorable instrument, under Divine Providence, of conferring, a still higher blessing upon the large and interesting portion of mankind." The United States was still struggling to establish a national identity by distinguishing herself from Great Britain, and members of the ACS believed that by bringing the gospel to Africa, Americans would earn a "glory with which the most splendid achievements of human force or power must sink in the competition and appear insignificant and vulgar in the comparison."[47]

The House of Representatives responded with a report read before the whole body on February 11, 1817. Even the national legislature recognized the continent as "a wide field for the improvements in civilization, morals, and religion" and expected Christianity "in process of time, to spread over that great continent."[48] The initial proposal suggested following the mission of Paul Cuffee in sending Black Americans to the British colony of Sierra Leone. But the possibility of sending a great mass of colonists to a British territory caused pause. Congress did not want Britain to accumulate all of the expected glories from the colony, nor were they comfortable with the prospect of Americans becoming permanent subjects of British tyranny. These concerns delayed Congressional action, but only temporarily.

The removal of the threatening free Black population and the expected boon to American commerce certainly enticed legislators, but the Congressional report focused on the "humane and enlightened" policy of African conversion and the ensuing moral redemption of the United States. In 1823 Samuel Miller, preaching on behalf of the African School in New Jersey, declared that by training African American missionaries "we may thus most effectually repair the multiplied wrongs we have done to *Africa*."[49] But this mission would ultimately depend on the willingness of the pious African American colonists expected to inaugurate the continental revival.

The ACS chapter in Loudoun, Virginia, exhibited a great interest in both the conversion of Africa and the resulting redemption of America. A well-placed colony would spread the gospel across the continent, restoring Africa to her lost greatness. The United States would benefit as well, of course. These northern Virginians quaked at the thought of a slave revolt and feared the "greater evils [that] have been apprehended, from the existence of such a population amongst us." But emphasis placed on the increased safety of draining off a dangerous population was dwarfed by the rhetoric placed on national moral redemption. By fulfilling the colonizationist mission, the Loudoun chapter rejoiced that "our national character will cease to wear its most marring blemish."[50]

Will They Convert?

The anticipated moral redemption of the United States required the successful conversion of Africa, and so colonizationists had to convince their countrymen that Africa was ripe for salvation. To do so they relied on racist perceptions of African pliability and confidence that God ordained the United States as his agent for international salvation. When Anthony Benezet reflected on Christian atrocities committed in Africa, he mourned a missed opportunity, lamenting how Christendom failed to deploy her maritime prowess in the cause of Christ and instead enriched herself through war and plunder. Hope remained for the continent of Africa, but slavery posed a great obstacle to missionary ambitions. Benezet and others feared how "the slave trade must necessarily raise in the minds of the thoughtful and well-disposed negroes the utmost scorn and detestation of the Christian name."[51]

Benezet cited the German explorer of South Africa Peter Kolb, who wrote that "numbers of these people have given it as reason for their not harkening to Christianity."[52] The greatly influential early eighteenth-century Anglican divine William Law shared Benezet's concern for the salvation of Africans, warning that the slave trade nullified the Christian witness.[53] Kolb, Benezet, Law, and numerous others feared that the slave trade had damaged the cause of conversion by linking Christ with slavery in the minds of Africans. For many reformers, the legacy of slavery was seen as an insurmountable obstacle to missionary activity in Africa. The colonization movement had the solution. Black missionaries would be greeted as lost kin, and a nation shrouded in darkness would turn toward the light.

Colonizationists undercut many arguments of inherent African inferiority while also reinforcing the widespread belief that a stable, biracial America could never exist.[54] Benjamin Rush repeated racist tropes by claiming that Africans were known for "idleness, treachery, theft and the like," but he found these vices to be "the genuine offspring of slavery and serve as an argument to prove that they were not intended for it." Polygamy, however, he found to be an inevitable vice among Africans, given "the heat of the climate, the early maturity and speedy decay of the women, [and] the peculiar fertility of the soil."[55]

Other sins, such as an absence of friendship and gratitude, were the temporary result of their lack of Christian civilization. Despite these temporary problems, Rush did not doubt the capacity of Africans for religious improvement, and he used Anthony Benezet's citations of distinguished European thinkers, including Michael Adanson and William Bosman, who similarly asserted the intelligence of Africans.[56]

After researching African colonial history and observing African culture firsthand, Carl Bernard Wadström, a Swedish geographer in the service of the Sierra Leone Company, declared Africans to be "already predisposed by their natural dispositions and principles to receive Christianity."[57] Catholic missionary success in Congo, Angola, and several other Portuguese African possessions illustrated just how fertile African soil could be if the gospel was sown with care.

This faith was shared by many Black American Christians, as well. The African American poet Phillis Wheatley understood Africa as ready for harvest and praised the early colonizationist scheme of Samuel Hopkins and Ezra Stiles. In a 1774 letter to Hopkins, Wheatley assured him that Africans would zealously turn to Christianity, and she rejoiced that she could see "the thick cloud of ignorance dispersing from the face of my benighted country." Wheatley declared that African "minds are unprejudiced against the truth," and accordingly believed Hopkins's missionaries would enjoy great success.[58] Minds unprejudiced against truth and ingrained yearnings for Christianity portended a thorough triumph for suitable missionaries willing to voyage across the Atlantic.

A half-century after Wheatley reflected on Africa's missionary potential, racist understandings of the continent as a religious blank slate persisted among British and American Christians. Ralph Randolph Gurley, addressing a Fourth of July crowd in 1825, described Africa as a land without any "formidable systems of superstition consecrated by age and authority." He dismissed Indigenous beliefs as "shadowy conceptions [that] cannot fortify their minds against the arguments and appeals of the word of God." Nowhere in the world was a missionary field "more easy for cultivation, or rich in promise." He claimed that African chiefs had found Christians morally and intellectually superior and accordingly would aggressively work to help missionaries convert their people.[59] The alleged vapidity of Africans and their eagerness for Christian instruction promised great success for a concerted conversionist enterprise. Evangelical Christianity and racist assurances of Anglo-American supremacy combined to create expectations of a smooth and speedy African conversion.

Conversionists had to present Africans as desperately needing the gospel yet not so horribly depraved as to be unreachable. A gathering of abolitionists in 1818 opposed colonization partially because the "bold and martial race, entirely addicted to war, many of them a large size, strong and well proportioned" that occupied the African coastline was ill-suited for religious conversion.[60] This line of argumentation got nowhere. Conversionists largely agreed that Christ could and would redeem everyone, and abolitionists would later learn that their best hope in defeating colonization lay in distinguishing between colonists and missionaries, not questioning whether Africans were capable of salvation.

The ACS easily swept aside this attack, condemning the licentiousness of Africans while praising the power of salvation. Everyone could be saved, even the despised population of Black Americans. Colonization advanced the belief that African Americans, if they were removed from the exploitative relationships of American society, could elevate themselves to at least near equality with whites, and if exposed to the light of the true gospel, even the supposedly war-hungry pagans of the African coast could repent and join the kingdom of God.

Reports of conversionist advances in Africa and elsewhere assured colonizationists of missionary success. In the late eighteenth century, four years prior to his election as bishop of London, Beilby Porteus preached before the Society for the Propagation of the Gospel. For him and many others "a real, and general conversion of the negroes is no romantic project, but a thing perfectly practicable."[61] He praised Moravian missionary successes in the Caribbean and expected them to be replicated in Africa. Robert Finley looked to the missionaries in New Holland (Australia) and others in Africa who had "already been so successful in teaching the Cassre, the Hottentot, the Boshemen, the means of present happiness and the way of eternal life."[62] Christians anticipated the advance of the gospel with eager zeal and sought to join the glorious cause as it swept the globe. The international march of conversions foretold a transformative, historic advance in the history of the church. The millennium loomed, and Americans had only to ask themselves if they would serve their Lord by advancing His cause. Many responded affirmatively and contributed their money and support to colonization.

In 1817 the ACS ignored Black opposition to colonization and proclaimed that "there exists an unusual sensibility and desire to aid the cause of humanity and religion. The tone of public feeling is elevated."[63] The local branch of the Pennsylvania Abolition Society in Columbia contemplated the character of their age as "marked as it is with a concurrence (unexampled in history) of events of striking import in the physical, political, and religious worlds" and "exertions that are making in different sections of the globe for the melioration of the condition of man." These great advances occurred because of "the footsteps of deity in the mighty revolution," but they were only precursors to something far greater. A rise in conversions was on the horizon and "the time is nevertheless approaching when through the blessings of Providence upon human exertions, justice and mercy shall become respected in the earth and this much injured and long degraded race be raised to their proper grade in the scale of being."[64]

Robert Finley was thrilled to be living in a period when "the voice of justice and humanity begins to be listened to with attention."[65] He rejoiced that "the time at last is come when not a few are imbibing the spirit of Him who came from Heaven 'to seek and save the lost.'" Americans understood the missionizing spirit to be strongest in the new republic but spreading rapidly across the globe. "Europe begins slowly, but sensibly, to reform her governments. The gloomy and dread superstitions of Asia begin to totter before the Gospel of Christ. Nor shall Africa be forgotten."[66] In 1774 Phillis Wheatley rejoiced "that which the divine royal Psalmist says by inspiration is now on the point of being accomplished, namely, Ethiopia shall soon stretch forth her hands unto God."[67] William Augustus Muhlenberg agreed and thundered in 1820, "The heathen are demanding the gospel. On us hang the fulfillment of the promises. The time is come. The church is on her march to victory."[68]

As Americans looked to the millennium, their eyes turned to Africa. The conversion of Africa had become an essential requirement for the fulfillment of millennial prophecy. For most Americans, and nearly all colonizationists, millennialism had little to do with precise understandings of eschatological theology but rather manifested itself as a component of the versatile, nonspecific Protestantism that dominated the early republic. Millennialism became a venue for imperial ambitions, fantasies of racial homogeneity, and the enduring optimism of messianic American nationalism. While a few painstakingly searched the scriptures for a prophetic checklist, the vast majority of Americans went about their lives with hearts and eyes directed heavenward in assurance of impending radical improvement. Colonizationists harnessed millennial faith as a unifying force and read current events as signs of the times portending African conversion.

Early reports of British activity in Sierra Leone offered encouragement and illustrated the potential power of nonwhite missionaries. The story of one

African prince circulated on both sides of the Atlantic as evidence of African religious potential. King Naimbanna, an African chief who ceded land for the Sierra Leone settlement in 1787, sent his son John to England where he experienced a dramatic religious conversion.[69] John drew the attention of England's elite and became a celebrity among evangelicals opposed to the slave trade. The prince evinced all the characteristics of pious Christianity. After his conversion, he stopped dressing in the ostentatious manner of African royalty and refused to drink more than one glass of wine per day.[70] After several years in England, Prince John returned to Africa. His departure inspired the English playwright, philanthropist, and moral reformer Hannah More to wistfully reflect that "such instances of fine affections—such generous sentiments—such aptitude to receive religious truth—and have every reason to believe, that instances of this kind are to be found, more or less, in all parts of this unhappy country."[71]

Through the work of the Sierra Leone Company and the influence of the Christian prince's return, Britons expected to convert the continent. The vessel that carried the Christian African prince back to his homeland took the name of *Naimbanna* in honor of its prized passenger. Tragically, John Naimbanna grew ill as he drew nearer to Africa and he died almost immediately after reaching shore, unable to fulfill his missionary dreams. Information on John Naimbanna stems exclusively from the 1791 annual report of the Sierra Leone Company. Zachary Macaulay, an influential booster for the company, popularized the tale in his 1796 publication *The African Prince*. American printings of the story began in 1799 when Thomas Dobson of Philadelphia printed a summary of several reports from the Sierra Leone Company and then again in 1800 with Hannah More's *The* Black *Prince*.[72] All of these writings reveal far less about the actual thoughts of John Naimbanna and more about the preoccupations of the English and American men and women who used his tale as evidence of Africa's potential for salvation.

Conversionist goals not only motivated colonizationists but also directed the creation and governance of the colony. Robert Goodloe Harper, a former Federalist candidate for the nation's vice presidency, considered the missionary purpose of the colony when he offered advice on establishing a settlement. In a private letter to the ACS secretary, Harper emphasized the importance of maintaining goodwill with locals. Friendly relations would offer practical benefits, but most importantly they would enable the colonists "to communicate to them the knowledge and habits of civilized life." He suggested that the colony find a location near the Niger River as it would most effectively offer "the extension of civilization."[73] For Harper, the extension of civilization was intimately bound up with the extension of Christianity, because one was impossible without the other. Other colonizationists had divergent opinions regarding the relationship between these two ideas; as some believed that civilization must precede conversion, and others took the opposite stand.

Theological questions surrounding the nature of conversion threatened colonizationists' unity. Evangelicals who saw conversion as a discrete, emotional experience privileged its occurrence over the process of civilization, while Episcopalians and other more liturgically inclined missionaries believed that civilization must come prior. William Augustus Muhlenberg, as a self-described Catholic evangelical Episcopalian, bridged the gap between the liturgical conversionists who emphasized a slow moral development and evangelicals who called for a radical immediate conversion experience.[74] While eulogizing two ACS agents who died in Sierra Leone, Muhlenberg claimed that "to induce the untutored mind to submit to the labor of acquiring [civilization], some great motive is necessary." For Muhlenberg, religious conversion would catalyze civilization.[75]

G. A. Robertson, a British explorer writing a study of Africa for Britain's Board of Trade and Plantations, took the opposite view and accordingly criticized the optimistic reports of African conversions. Robertson shared the goal of converting Africa but attacked British missionaries for failing to generate genuine conversions. Whereas missionaries aimed for mass conversions, Robertson espoused a slower process that would privilege cultural development as its own goal. Unchecked enthusiasm on the part of Protestant evangelists would only send undisciplined Africans into the arms of Catholic missionaries. Robertson dreamed of a Christian Africa, but he hated the "attempt to convert them to Christianity before they have acquired a knowledge of the most useful arts and conveniences of life."[76]

Most Americans or Britons did not parse the difference between Christianity and civilization. James S. Green said it the most clearly by writing that "civilization and Christianity will go together, and mutually assist each other. They are indeed all but inseparable."[77] Conflicts over the meaning of conversion endured, but the ACS subsumed most debates under a banner of generic Protestantism. As the nineteenth century progressed, however, conversion became increasingly linked to education. Conversionist leaders formed schools to facilitate conversion both at home and abroad.

Muhlenberg connected schooling to the missions of conversion and civilization, writing, "Christian missionaries are the most successful civilizers. The very methods by which they teach religion necessarily conduce to the habits of society. The natives are assembled for worship, their children are formed into schools, and they are instructed in the arts of domestic economy as Christian virtues."[78] Schools for free people of color were seen as models for future African academies. Finley predicted that "there might soon be fixed a seat of liberal learning in Africa from which the rays of knowledge might dart across those benighted regions."[79] All of these plans, however, hinged on the cooperation of Black Americans, which did not materialize as expected.

How to Overcome Black Opposition?

African Americans largely shared the conversionist mission, but an overwhelming majority of free Black Americans had no desire to leave the land of their birth for foreign soil. Moreover, most of the Black Christians who attended the new seminaries and missionary training grounds felt a call to minister in North America, rather than across the Atlantic. Panic swept through free Black communities as terrifying rumors spread of forced removal and deportation. Free Black Christians found themselves in a difficult situation. Many yearned for the conversion of Africa but, like white Christians, most believed it to be a task best suited for someone else. Moreover, Black Americans understandably mistrusted the ACS's white leadership, many of whom were enslavers. Tenuous Black freedoms were already under attack, and Black Americans recognized how the ACS would be mobilized against their liberties.

In response to the panic, over three thousand Black Philadelphians gathered at Mother Bethel African Methodist Episcopal Church to draft a response. Richard Allen, pastor of Mother Bethel; Absalom Jones, priest at the African Episcopal Church of St. Thomas; and James Forten, wealthy and respected business owner, took the lead. Russell Parrott, also in attendance, had earlier published an oration celebrating the anniversary of the abolition of the slave trade that included a millennial cry for Africa. Parrott had rejoiced, "Religion has unfolded [Africa's] sacred page; and while she holds the heavenly volume to the eye, by her enlivening presence she dispels the clouds of paganism and error, which had so long overshadowed her." Parrott's very last line proclaimed that recent African conversions illustrate that religion "with her divine associates, Knowledge and Liberty, shall pervade and humanize the whole habitable portion of the world!"[80] Absalom Jones, the abolitionist minister of the

African Episcopal Church of St. Thomas, had frequently shared his commitment to African conversion, including in an 1808 sermon where he mustered nearly every millennial trope possible in proclaiming,

> May *Ethiopia soon stretch out her hands unto thee,* and lay hold of the gracious promise of thy everlasting covenant. Destroy, we beseech thee, all the false religions which now prevail among them; and grant, that they may soon *cast* their *idols, to the moles and the bats* of the wilderness. O, hasten that glorious time, when the knowledge of the gospel of Jesus Christ, shall cover the *earth, as the waters cover the sea;* when *the wolf shall dwell with the lamb, and the leopard shall lie down with the kid, and the calf and the young lion and the fatling together, and a little child shall lead them;* and, *when, instead of the thorn, shall come up the fir tree, and, instead of the brier, shall come up the myrtle tree: and it shall be to the Lord for a name and for an everlasting sign that shall not be cut off.*[81]

Jones connected the conversion of Africa to the imminent millennium and the peaceful paradise that would come along with it. The case with Richard Allen is more complicated. The founder of African American Methodism became a supporter of Haitian emigration and even advocated for a colony to be placed in Canada. But in the early years, Allen was a major booster for African colonization, holding meetings in his home and laboring to support Paul Cuffee's early attempts to settle African Americans in Sierra Leone.[82]

Despite the earlier views of these influential leaders, the three thousand Black Philadelphians responded to colonization with overwhelming opposition. White ACS leaders clearly had a difficult task in earning the trust of potential emigrants. The language of conversionism proved to be the most effective means of forging and maintaining connections across the racial divide. But many African Americans who shared conversionist goals nonetheless opposed colonization. James Forten and Russell Parrott issued a statement on behalf of the three thousand African Americans who met at Mother Bethel. In evaluating this statement, historians emphasize the African American sense of ownership of the nation where they lived. Julie Winch, in her excellent biography of James Forten, for example, provides the following quote from the document: "Whereas our ancestors (not of choice) were the first successful cultivators of America, we . . . feel ourselves entitled to participate in the blessings of her luxuriant soil, which their blood and sweat manured."[83]

Another portion of the same message, however, reveals another reason for opposition that has not received scholarly attention. The authors proclaimed their support for the conversionist mission and shared the ACS's optimism regarding the religious fate of Africa. They feared, however, that an insufficient number of well-educated free people of color would voluntarily emigrate. The intense resistance of the Mother Bethel crowd illustrated the hesitance of settled free Black people to emigrate. They remarked that if the new colony was populated solely by uneducated former slaves, "the light of Christianity, which now dawns among that section of our species, [would] be shut out by the clouds of ignorance, and their day of life be closed without the illuminations of the gospel."[84] Philadelphia's free Black community framed their opposition around the importance of African conversion but distrusted the ACS to provide the training necessary to fulfill the glorious mission. Black Philadelphians either shared the conversionist, millennial convictions of the ACS or at least recognized the potency of the discourse, and they framed their opposition accordingly.

Fifty years earlier Phillis Wheatley had similarly worried about the prospect of sending unqualified missionaries. Writing to the English Christian philanthropist John Thornton, she weighed the possibility of traveling to Africa as a missionary herself. Wheatley yearned for the conversion of Africa and enthusiastically supported missionary efforts to the continent, but she ultimately declined the invitation to participate. This early mission never got off the ground, but Wheatley's excuse for standing on the sidelines again reinforced her support for the project. She wrote that she did not speak the language, so she would only be a drain on the African American missionaries who were slated to lead the expedition. She nonetheless gave her support to the mission and prayed for its success.[85]

Baptists provided the strongest base of African American support for colonization, as Black Virginians Lott Cary and Collin Teague dreamed of "spreading through the land of Ham, the knowledge of the Redeemer." These two African American ministers successfully transmitted their dream to the First African Baptist Church in Philadelphia, and ultimately persuaded both the northern and the southern white leaders of the Baptist General Convention to support the movement.[86] The two sailed for Africa in 1821, and in 1822, Cary established Providence Baptist Church in Monrovia. Men and women like Daniel Coker, Lott Cary, and Collin Teague, who were willing to risk their lives in the pursuit of expanding African salvation, represented a very small minority. Coker, Cary, and Teague, however, gave ACS officials symbols to trumpet in their publications. White colonizationists gladly read tales of these devoted Black missionaries, and colonization continued to hold greater currency in white populations who could piously praise the conversionist mission without having to risk their lives across the ocean.

The ACS fretted over the lack of African American support but ultimately ignored the overwhelming opposition of the free Black community, pointing to the small number of emigrants and the missionaries who joined them. The ACS also claimed the mantle of Paul Cuffee and used his image in its advertising campaign. Before the ACS had formed, Cuffee and thirty-eight other Black Americans arrived in Sierra Leone in February 1816. This mission proved terribly expensive, and Cuffee passed away before he could lead another group of emigrants. Before his passing, however, Cuffee grew more ambivalent about African colonization, and he became suspicious of the ACS. Despite his conflicted relationship with the ACS, the society exploited his image and reputation.

In 1818 Robert Finley published an imaginary dialogue between the ghosts of Cuffee, William Penn, and Absalom Jones. In the dialogue, Finley had Cuffee begin by praising the benevolence of the movement, assuring that the plan was "calculated to restore the race of Africa all the losses they have sustained, heal their wounds and make reparation for their injuries, reinstate them in the honors of their nature, retrieve their sullied glory, and convert their greatest curse into the most signal blessing to themselves and to the world."[87] Cuffee promised that colonization would bring Christianity to Africa and would purge the national guilt of the United States.

Jones stood in as a representative of African American resistance to colonization. Cuffee and Jones turned to Penn to adjudicate their disagreement, and after discussing the issue with the ghost of George Washington and other "illustrious shades of Paradise," Penn sided with Cuffee in support of colonization. After a long discussion of other prospects for emancipation, Cuffee and Penn made their final arguments in attempts to sway Jones, leaning heavily on the rhetoric of African conversion and American redemption. Penn emphasized the prospect of American redemption by proclaiming, "How rich will be the return, and how noble the reparation, which America will make to Africa, for all the injuries she has done her!" By transmitting the gifts of the gospel to Africa, "that which was the greatest curse of mankind is unexpectedly, under the direction of Heaven, transmuted in to their most signal blessing!"

This fictional Cuffee was less concerned with America's fate and was more moved by the prospect of African conversion. Finley imagined Cuffee weeping over the prospect of the ACS "erecting the structure of pure religion upon the ruins of the gloomy doctrines and idolatrous rites of paganism." Cuffee's ghost parroted the imperial and anti-Islamic rhetoric that folded into the colonizationist movement by envisioning that "the Crescent is again made to bow to the Cross, and Christian nations, nations friendly to civilized man, take possession of those capitals now occupied by pirates and robbers."[88] Before these twin arguments, Jones buckled and retracted his opposition. In Finley's imagination, all American Christians would unite under the promise of a converted African continent. Finley's fantasies aside, Christianity did prove to be the most potent force in forging biracial ties in the early republic, and both African Americans and many enslavers shared the conversionist obsession.

EARLY REPORTS FROM AFRICA encouraged Americans that the continental conversion was already underway. Ephraim Bacon sailed from Norfolk on the brig *Nautilus* in January 1821. On their very first evening in Sierra Leone, the ACS agents attended a worship service, followed by another service less than twelve hours later. The colonists stared intently at their Bibles, closely following the sermon. "Such cheering fruits" told Bacon that "surely Christians ought to feel themselves encouraged in the support of missions." He emphasized the order and cleanliness of the parishioners, a striking instance of "a Christian congregation in a heathen land." On a single Sunday, he recorded services attended at six and ten in the morning and then two more at three and six in the evening. At the primary service in the morning, he recorded four hundred Christians receiving communion.[89]

Encouragement came from Black colonists as well, many who were strongly encouraged to extoll the virtues of living in West Africa in epistles and public writings. Samuel Wilson wrote from Sierra Leone in 1818 to free people of color in America, "Your fathers were carried into that land to increase strangers treasures, but God has turned it all to good, that you may bring the gospel into your country."[90] A joint letter crafted three days later by eleven Black emigrants echoed this idea, claiming that "all that has befallen us is of God for our good, that we may bring the gospel into our country."[91]

By 1825 a few things had changed. Optimism for a world breaking free from generations of tyranny slowed, and confidence in the missionary abilities of Black Americans waned. Despite the attempts by the ACS to encourage only glowing reports of life in Africa, additional information revealed a more realistic portrait of the challenges that lay ahead. James S. Green had anticipated in 1824 that African conversion would take as long as one hundred years, but was still convinced that "a century hence civilization may exist and Christian churches may be planted in every part of the African continent."[92]

Ralph Randolph Gurley, the two-time chaplain for the House of Representatives, editor for *The African Repository and Colonial Journal,* and an active officer for the ACS, addressed the American Colonization Society in 1825 and delivered a far drearier portrait of the world, asking, "Is not the iron rod of despotism stretched out over a hundred nations? Bleed not a hundred nations under superstition's scourge?"[93] The faith in imminent global transformation that rang throughout the early nineteenth century gave way to a more somber interpretation of world events.

Earlier encomiums to African American piety waned, as many white Americans grew increasingly intolerant of the expanding population of free Black Americans. Gurley criticized the Christianity of Black northerners by writing that "even religion their sole benefactress seldom rouses them for their insensibility to her motives and rescues them from their captivity to the lowest indulgencies of sense. Her light shines around, but penetrates not the darkness of their minds." Despite the negative portrait of Black spirituality, Gurley on the very same page asserted that the ACS would send free Black Americans "to the soil of their ancestors and assist them there in founding the institutions of freedom, civilization, and Christianity."[94] Gurley believed that the free Black population had tremendous potential, but for now he saw them as only a degraded, licentious nuisance.

The dream of African conversion endured, and Gurley's rhetoric matched the soaring heights of earlier colonizationists. In his 1824 Fourth of July oration, he told the audience "Africa appeals to us this day!" Still deploying the language of national guilt, he claimed that Africa "stretches out her hands, and implores us in the name of justice as well as of mercy and religion to remember the unparalleled wrongs which, for centuries, she has endured from Christian nations." Burned villages, stolen children, and lost property "bear testimony to the validity of her claims," and America stood in need of redemption. By bringing the gospel to Africa, the current generation would surpass even the honored revolutionaries who earned national independence. Through their mission to Africa, Americans would "erect to our national honor a monument more durable than granite, inscribed to charity, the queen of the virtues."[95]

It was one thing to harbor these dreams in 1819, before the American settlements had struggled to gain traction, but by 1825 it was quite another to pursue the conversion of Africans with the same enthusiasm. In that year, the ACS's Petersburg auxiliary society in Virginia composed a circular letter to local ministers with some of the most elevated conversionist rhetoric in all of colonizationist literature. In telling their own history, the society claimed they were "instituted, principally through the instrumentality of a devoted soldier of the cross," and that the prayers of pious Christians "have never yet ceased to ascend on its behalf." It had been nearly a decade since the movement began, but now the prayers of faithful Americans were joined with "the humble but ardent *Amen*" of the infant churches in Liberia, churches that were already saving souls in Africa and honoring the United States for her benevolence. To these local ministers to whom the circular was addressed, the authors asked, "Will you not be on the Lord's side?"[96] Virginians had a choice. They could either join the patriotic Christian mission of saving Africa and redeeming their nation, or they could stand with Satan, allow Africans to perish for eternity, leave America sullied by the sins of the slave trade, and expose their neighbors to the horror of slave revolt.

Despite these remarks, the conversionist consensus began to erode as sectional tensions heightened. Colonizationists continued to frame their mission as an agent of Christianization, but it became increasingly difficult to maintain the millennial faith of African conversion as Liberia struggled to remain viable. The reality of Liberian struggles extinguished the fiery confidence earlier held by so many. Furthermore, national tensions over slavery shortened the reach of the ACS, transforming the society from a national force for unity to a refuge for moderates uncomfortable with the growing militancy of pro- and antislavery factions. Conversionism could no longer hold together its national coalition and colonization suffered accordingly.

As Daniel Coker sailed across the Atlantic in 1820, he called to the heavens, "Oh! my soul, what is God about to do for Africa? Surely something great." Only a few days before arriving, he rejoiced, "Has not the day of African's salvation already began to dawn? I imagine I behold the uplifted hands of thousands, in prayer, that it may shine more and more to the perfect day."[97] Historians have understandably assessed colonizationist movements in relation to slavery. The debate will continue as to how the movement weakened and strengthened the institution, but colonization, apart from how it influenced slavery or African identity, is worthy of attention.

Daniel Coker, Samuel Bacon, and hundreds of others dreamed of restoring Africa to the church and expunging the national sins of the slave trade. Ethiopia would stretch forth her hands to God, and as she did, millions of saved Africans would look with gratitude on the United States for transforming the horrid slave trade into a blessed agent of evangelism. Africa would be saved. America would be redeemed. Religious conviction cannot be understood solely as a ruse for political ambitions, but it is ultimately irrelevant whether the conversionist emphasis flowed from genuine sentiment or a pragmatic attempt to hold together a fractious coalition. Either way, conversionism united colonizationists in a way nothing else could.

Opponents of colonization eventually learned this lesson. By the 1830s a new generation of anticolonizationists, Black and white, abolitionist and proslavery, again assailed the ACS by attacking the conversionist ideology at the heart of the colonizationist movement. If colonization could be portrayed as an opponent of conversion, rather than as its great facilitator, Americans would slowly surrender their support. For abolitionists, the movement against colonization followed Black Americans' opposition to removal from their homeland. Despite a shared commitment to missionary work, Black Americans refused to be swept across the ocean and instead pressed the United States to make real its purported founding ideals. As increasing numbers of Black activists prophetically preached against the hypocrisies of white Christianity, the growth of American slavery proved that Africa was not the only idolatrous land needing salvation.

✧✧✧ 4 ✧✧✧

Missionary Dreams and Anti-Colonization
Movements, 1825–1830

D ENOMINATIONAL BODIES RALLIED around colonization's promise to
expand salvation and solve the problem of slavery without upending
white supremacy. While colonizationists trained their eyes heavenward
during the 1820s, the dreams and realities of their movement drifted farther
and farther apart. Very few Africans converted to Christianity, disease killed
scores of colonists, and new opposition from both enslavers and abolitionists
assailed the ACS. Despite these realities, colonizationists kept the faith, and
the absence of mass conversions did not limit the soaring millennial rhetoric.
Hollow, symbolic events distracted members eager to see the fulfillment of
prophecy and the conversion of the African continent. Denominational support, organizational alliances, international partnerships, educational institutions, and the lack of organized domestic opposition buoyed colonizationists
at home even as colonists across the Atlantic failed to generate meaningful
missionary success.

Opposition soon arose, however, from both proslavery polemicists and abolitionist agitators, and by the early 1830s, the conversionist consensus was under siege from both sides. Ascendant proslavery sentiments among southern
religious leaders began to oppose even oblique references to emancipation, no
matter how grounded they were in promises of salvation. Tensions over slavery
had grown so explosive that proslavery Christians came to revile even the white
supremacist colonization scheme. Evangelism could no longer justify the mere
suggestion of emancipation. Attempts to secure more federal funds in support
of colonization attracted the ire of southerners. The promise of expanding salvation failed to protect colonization from the political maelstrom over slavery.
Meanwhile abolitionist radicals followed Black activists in decrying colonization as a proslavery ploy. Conversionism no longer held its unifying power.
The strains of sectionalism weakened the American Colonization Society and

soon after tore apart the national bodies of American Protestantism. But as the 1820s began, colonizationists had good reasons for optimism.

Colonization, Denominationalism, and American Missions

Colonization appeared to answer countless prayers. Since at least the American Revolution, conversionism had promised that the problem of slavery would be solved through a millennial expansion of salvation. Many white Christians interpreted the rise of the ACS as the fulfillment of this very prophecy, and powerful religious authorities trumpeted the cause in the early 1820s. Denominational leaders saw many advantages in colonization, as the ACS offered to eliminate the dangerous divisiveness of slavery debates, secure white supremacy, and confirm the role of the United States as an international harbinger of salvation.

The very first edition of the ACS's magazine boasted in 1825 about supportive resolutions that state legislatures had issued in Virginia, Maryland, Tennessee, Georgia, Ohio, New Hampshire, and New Jersey. Yet before bragging about the sanction given to their cause by these state governments, the ACS recognized the larger, more influential bodies whose blessings carried greater weight than that of state legislatures. As the magazine gloated, the Presbyterian General Assembly, Methodist General Conference, Baptist General Convention, and the General Convention of the Protestant Episcopal Church had all given their formal denominational blessing on the work of colonization.[1] The work of Robert Finley had succeeded. American denominations appeared united in the goal of expanding salvation through colonization. Americans recognized the power of national denominational bodies, and denominational support for colonization buoyed the movement.

Eventually, every major Protestant denomination expressed support for the missionary labors of the American Colonization Society. In 1819 the Presbyterian General Assembly resolved that the mission of the ACS was "benevolent in its design, and, if properly supported and judiciously and vigorously prosecuted, calculated to be extensively useful to this country and to Africa." This resolution argued that intractable racism against Black Americans formed "an insurmountable bar [that] has been placed against the execution of any plan for elevating their character." But these Presbyterians also rejoiced that the ACS was "introducing civilization and the gospel to the benighted nations of Africa."[2]

That same year, the Presbyterian Synod of Virginia decreed that colonization "will produce the happiest effects, particularly in aiding to communicate the glad tidings of the gospel to an interesting quarter of the globe."[3] Episcopalians responded with similar speed and similar support for the missionary potential of the movement. The convention of the Protestant Episcopal Church, gathered in Petersburg, Virginia, resolved in May 1919 "that this convention highly approves of the objects of the American Colonization Society." These leaders of the Episcopal Church in America formed a committee to share this resolution throughout the nation.[4]

Methodists were more circumspect. In 1820 the Methodist General Conference instructed the Committee on Slavery to consider whether the Methodist Church should express support for the American Colonization Society.[5] This charge eventually fell to the Committee on the Affairs of the People of Colour, yet they too were relieved of the task in 1824 when a new committee was formed to consider how to interact with the ACS. This new committee reported back to the General Conference that they could not make a recommendation as to whether the General Conference should express official support for the ACS. However, they advised that the national Methodist missionary society should recognize the work of the ACS as creating "a suitable mission field for sowing seed of the Kingdom of God."[6] Methodists were unsure if the ACS would solve the problem of slavery, but they were confident that it could expand salvation, and that was enough to earn their approval.

The General Conference resolved to begin budgeting for "a missionary or missionaries to the colony in Africa."[7] One year later a Methodist man wrote the ACS offering to support himself for a few years in Liberia. He considered this commitment as a sort of suicide mission, writing, "In that fatal climate I need not calculate upon long life." However, he was willing to donate his life and personal library of about three hundred books for the purpose of "raising up a few young African preachers to carry the Gospel into the interior." The first official missionary from the Methodist Church would not arrive until 1833, but the 1824 interest in the missionary potential of colonization was enough for the ACS to begin asserting that they had received Methodist support.[8]

Smaller religious and fraternal organizations also added their names to the list of devotees. A July 1825 edition of the *Masonic Mirror* congratulated the Presbyterian Synod for being the first religious body to formally contribute toward the society. In the following month, according to the newspaper, "the Reformed Dutch Church, the Convention of the Episcopal Church in Virginia, the Baptist Foreign and Domestic Missionary Society, and several other highly respectable bodies" likewise offered support. The Masons sent their best wishes as well, claiming that the ACS could "not be employed in a more glorious or humane cause."[9]

The 1826 Baptist General Convention expressed its favor for the ACS, proclaiming that "the enlargement and support of this colony is intimately connected with the progress of missions in that part of the world." The General Convention encouraged Baptists to do more than simply voice their support; it called on Baptists across the nation to donate to the ACS. Ministers were implored "to take collections on the 4th of July, and at any other proper seasons, in aid of the funds of the Colonization Society."[10]

Baptists were not alone in using the Fourth of July as a fundraising opportunity for the ACS. Similar plans were put in place by Connecticut Congregationalists, Maryland Methodists, Ohio Baptists, Virginia Presbyterians, Dutch Reformed New Yorkers, and Pennsylvania Lutherans—all of these white Christians expressed their nationalism and celebrated American independence by taking up donations to support the conversionist mission of the ACS.[11] In the late 1820s, nearly all denominations linked their nationalism with the international expansion of salvation. American independence, they believed, inaugurated a process of global salvation that was finally being fulfilled by colonization.[12]

Despite the support from national denominations, the ACS still faced very serious challenges, including competing benevolent institutions, fundraising shortfalls, and a lack of properly trained missionaries. The American Board of Commissioners for Foreign Missions (ABCFM), the nation's largest and most influential missionary organization, shared the ACS's dream of converting Africa and closely monitored the progress of the ACS. Reports from the ACS filled the pages of the ABCFM's *Missionary Herald,* and the missionary Samuel Mills worked to coordinate the efforts of the two societies.[13]

Members of the ACS likewise recognized the importance of the ABCFM, yet occasionally expressed resentment at the latter's resources. In 1823, the Washington-based *Daily National Intelligencer* complained that "thousands upon thousands of dollars annually are absolutely wasted in vain expensive missions to Christianize the heathen." If New Englanders truly cared about converting the world, they would recognize that simply focusing on establishing a colony in Africa would "spread Christianity more extensively and more surely than it has ever before been spread."[14]

Two years later, the *African Repository and Colonial Journal* asserted that, "were the income of the Colonization Society to equal that of the American

Board of Commissioners for foreign missions, the belief in its efficacy to accomplish ends of the highest movement would yield to more correct opinions."[15] Earlier that year, the same publication had praised the ABCFM, but claimed that the benevolence of American Christians would always be insufficient for the great task of colonization. In fact, "no private association can accomplish more than a very small portion. The State Legislatures and the National Government can alone consummate the proposed design."[16] Challenges of funding and the quest for governmental support continued to preoccupy the society throughout the 1820s, and request for government funds eventually triggered a southern backlash.

Colonization was wildly expensive, and the ACS was constantly on the verge of financial crisis. But the need for qualified missionaries was nearly as pressing. The ACS rejoiced in 1825 when the ABCFM resolved to admit Black Americans into its missionary school, promising that "no part of the world promises a better reward to missionary exertions" than Africa.[17] Again in 1827, the ACS rejoiced in the news of the ABCFM's support of colonization, and hoped "their intentions may be fulfilled without delay" with the training and arrival of new missionaries.[18] When colonists failed to produce the expected conversions, ACS officials redirected attention toward the next generation of missionaries receiving training in missionary schools like that of the ABCFM. For ACS officials and other Americans supportive of missions, these Black Americans would soon become a vanguard of salvation. Yet exactly what made a qualified missionary remained up for debate, and soon, some Americans would come to question the relationship between colonization and conversion.

The ACS was also heartened by an appeal from Swiss Pietists to send missionaries to West Africa in 1827. The Rev. Christian G. Blumhardt of Basel, Switzerland, wrote to Jehudi Ashmun, the ACS's agent in Liberia, inquiring as to the needs of the colony and the strategy for conversion. The ACS and other missionary supporters widely circulated Ashmun's revealing reply. By the time he wrote to Blumhardt in 1827, Ashmun had spent almost four frustrating years in West Africa. He indicated how much work was to be done, admitting that they had contact with only a small number of Indigenous societies. He believed that African languages, or at least that of the Vai and Dey, were "not worth the labour of reducing it [their languages] to a grammatical or graphical form." He dismissed the Bassa dialects [of the south] as "a jargon so rude in its structure and pronunciation" that it could not "exist as the medium of communication among rational beings." So instead of learning local languages, Ashmun advocated teaching English to all of the African peoples near the colony.[19]

Blumhardt also inquired whether the first missionaries should be skilled in trades or trained to teach. Ashmun emphatically suggested that skills could wait and teachers should focus on "the higher principles of religious truth." According to Ashmun, missionaries "must first teach them to think, to reflect, to inquire, before they can hope to see their doctrine take root."[20] Despite several years of struggle with little success at converting more than a few locals, Ashmun remained optimistic. He believed that local elites in Grand Bassa would welcome "good white men to come and reside with them and teach them the book of God."[21] For the ACS, the promised expansion of salvation always appeared to be just over the horizon.

The ACS, however, diverged from Ashmun's characterization of qualified missionaries as "good white men" by stressing their belief in 1825 that "to employ colored men in this enterprise is certainly desirable."[22] Fears of the African climate and assumptions that white skin would be linked to slaving motivated missionary leaders to recruit trained Black evangelists.[23] Moreover, they knew how hard it was to recruit anyone to travel across the Atlantic and face the deadly climate and harsh living conditions in the colony.

Colonizationists closely charted and loudly trumpeted the progress of the African School in Parsippany, New Jersey, established in 1816, the same year as the ACS, for the purpose of training Black missionaries that would serve both in the United States and in Africa. Presbyterian colonizationists in the mid-Atlantic paid particular attention to the school. In a report to the Presbyterian Synod of New York and New Jersey, the directors rejoiced that "our Synods originated the first proposition for an organized system and elevation of the free people of color."[24] In March 1824, the New Haven–based *Religious Intelligencer* shared a report from the school that "numbers of the African students have expressed great readiness to embark for their shores of their ancestral inheritance, to aid in the illumination and salvation of their countrymen."[25] Recounting the piety of a handful of aspiring Black missionaries enabled colonizationists to elide both the struggles on the ground in West Africa and the overwhelming opposition of Black Americans.

Educating Black Americans was an essential aspect of missionary preparation. Robert Goodloe Harper, for example, spearheaded a particularly ambitious education plan. In 1824, Harper wrote to Leonard Bacon, a Yale theologian and eventual anti-abolitionist stalwart, and Leonard Woods, the active reformer-theologian at Andover Seminary who trained many missionaries. Harper wrote out his vision to educate Black Americans through "a seminary farm, which may serve as a pattern for similar institutions throughout the Union, and especially in those states where slavery exists."[26] Harper died shortly after his attempt to solicit support from Woods, and dreams of the seminary farm never materialized.[27]

A pattern of free Black education did develop, however, with the help of national denominations, as seen by an 1827 survey of US African Free Schools published in the *African Repository and Colonial Journal*. Yet, from the beginning these schools were utilized not to encourage a multiracial democracy but rather to encourage emigration. Portland, Maine, had one school and Boston three (two primary and one grammar). A school had recently formed in Salem, Massachusetts, but it closed after only six months, due to a lack of financial support. New Haven had two schools, Philadelphia three, and New York two.[28] From these institutions, colonizationists expected a generation of well-trained missionaries to cross the Atlantic and extend the blessings of salvation. Much hope hinged on the development of these institutions and the missionaries they were training. However, very few ever reached the colony, much less evangelized the local population.

Although built for the education of Black Americans, most of these free Black schools, like the wider colonization movement, did not believe that Black people could live as equals with white Americans. An extract from the African School's directors, which appeared in a November 1825 edition of the *Genius of Universal Emancipation,* discussed the school's challenges as a way of undergirding the impracticability of immediate emancipation, even equating the act with "the tender mercies of the wicked." The article claimed that Black Americans could not govern themselves. It would take years of intense education, for, the white directors claimed, every black American "needs a guardianship more than infancy."[29]

White supremacy and segregation were ingrained in the very logic of this institution, as its managers claimed "no system of amelioration for them can possess any energy unless it be exclusive. They are emphatically a separate people." As this article made clear, colonization, with all its missionary zeal, was also a radical extension of white supremacist logic. In the words of the directors of the African School, "we are instructing them not for our society . . . but preparing them to go home."[30] Colonizationists, North and South, continually upheld racial divisions. As the managers of the Colonization Society of

Connecticut asserted, there was "a broad and impassible line of demarcation between every man who has one drop of African blood in his veins and every other class in the community."[31] This segregationist logic damaged the already weak support for colonization among Black Christians and fueled the Black nationalist impulses for those who nonetheless participated in colonization.

Lott Cary, a formerly enslaved man who became a Liberian minister, acutely felt the sting of white supremacy. Before he left for Africa, Cary reflected, "I wish to go to a country where I shall be estimated by my merits, not by my complexion."[32] However, Cary also cared deeply about converting the continent. In fact, he believed he cared much more than the white leaders of the ACS. In an 1822 sermon to his Liberian congregation at Providence Baptist Church, Cary encouraged his congregation to prioritize missionary work and not to trust the ACS or the new government for that purpose.[33] Cary and Jehudi Ashmun, the white ACS agent, both labored intently to convert West Africans. Both largely failed, and by the fall of 1828, both were dead. Death rates were tragically high in the colony. According to historian Eric Burin, 29 percent of colonists died in the 1820s.[34]

The brutal reality of life in the colony contrasted sharply with glowing reports from the ACS. Even though colonization failed to gain many real converts, supporters in America touted "success" and continued to contribute their support. In May 1823, for example, the *Evangelical and Literary Magazine* reprinted reports of mass conversions and rapid transformations in Sierra Leone.[35] In the white American mind, success in Sierra Leone would surely mean that success was imminent in Liberia.

These outlandish reports ranged from small exaggerations to outright lies. Yet, for advocates of colonization, the accuracy of the claims was less important than what the claims could demonstrate about the broader colonization effort. So, unlike the *Evangelical and Literary Magazine,* the ACS advocated a different tactic the following year. Instead of focusing on specific successes, the ACS implored Americans to evaluate "not its history and details only, but its purposes and principles, not the failures which it may have suffered from accidents or inexperience, but the motives by which it is actuated."[36] This way, even if colonizationists never achieved any measurable missionary success, the purity of their motives would still merit great celebration and support. For most white American Christians and their denominational bodies, colonization was a moral triumph regardless of setbacks, and benevolent providence would ultimately ensure the mission's success. Salvation could not be stopped.[37]

Denominationalism and Anti-Abolitionism

Despite denominational support for colonization, many powerful white southerners became increasingly suspicious of the ACS during the 1820s, fearing that
government support for colonization could lead to government support for
emancipation. Denominationalists continued to try to maintain unity through
dreams of salvation, yet the paranoia of enslavers as well as the unwavering activism of Black Americans and their few white allies confronted colonizationists and their denominationalist leaders. Eventually, denominational leadership
required ministers to take positions on slavery and abolition, and southerners slowly turned away from colonization in favor of full-throated proslavery
religion.

Historians have acknowledged the integral role of African Americans in
catalyzing American abolitionism, but it should also be noted that the actions
of Black Americans worked to radicalize southerners into ever-more-aggressive
proslavery positions. Rebellions and conspiracies challenged the paternalist status quo and prompted discussions of slavery. We have already seen how this
occurred in the aftermath of Gabriel's 1800 rebellion in Virginia. It would happen again in South Carolina in 1822 with the resistance of Denmark Vesey. The
aftermath of slave rebellions amplified proslavery commitments in the South.
We see this process in the life and ministry of the Baptist Richard Furman,
the Episcopalian Frederick Dalcho, and the Presbyterian John Holt Rice. The
activism of these southern denominational leaders led southern Christians in
turning against colonization.

The collision of Black resistance and denominational leadership pressed
the Baptist denominational leader Richard Furman into his vocal proslavery
positions. In many ways, Furman was an unlikely candidate for the proslavery
pulpit. Though he owned enslaved laborers and was even willing to sell them
with little regard to family ties as a means of covering debts, he nevertheless
characterized the violence of slavery as "undoubtedly an evil" and lamented its
growth.[38] Furman's journey from a self-reported reluctant enslaver to a loud
proponent of human bondage mirrored his rise as a major Baptist leader.

Richard Furman was an essential advocate for national Baptist denominational formation and the president of the first two meetings of the national
General Convention. He also worked to organize at the city, district, and state
levels. An emphasis on conversion and education infused all his denominational activities. As early as 1792 he pressured the Charleston Baptist Association (CBA) to set aside funds for the education of ministers. A year later, he

succeeded in convincing William Staughton to leave England for the United States, and with encouragement from Furman, Staughton began a ministerial education program that eventually grew into Columbian College in Washington, DC, fulfilling Furman's dream of creating a national Baptist college.

In 1802 Furman began promoting missionary societies through the CBA, and in 1813 he partnered with Luther Rice, a former missionary turned fundraiser, in establishing the national framework to support the American Baptist mission in Burma. In 1821, Furman used his role as president of the South Carolina Baptist Association to offer his first public pronouncement on slavery. He began his address by thanking God for the "protection afforded [South Carolinians] from the horrors of an intended Insurrection."[39] Just five months earlier, Furman's neighbor Denmark Vesey and thirty-four other Black men were convicted and hanged for attempted insurrection in what would have been the largest slave revolt in American history.[40]

Because of the seriousness of the conspiracy, Furman's role as a denominational leader required him to respond. He did so with a definitively proslavery statement, pushing him further from his previous position as a moderate nationalist and establishing his reputation as a proslavery sectionalist. Furman framed his address as a defense against an unnamed army of abolitionists who were allegedly working "indirectly, to deprive the slaves of religious privileges, by awakening in the minds of their masters a fear, that acquaintance with the Scriptures, and the enjoyment of these privileges would naturally produce the aforementioned effects."[41] Furman claimed to hate abolitionists primarily for making it harder to convert enslaved southerners.

After this initial attack rooted in protecting opportunities for the enslaved to receive salvation, Furman outlined the biblical sanction for slavery, a process that would be repeated with greater clarity decades later by another South Carolina Baptist minister, Richard Fuller, in a debate with Brown University president and Baptist minister Francis Wayland.[42] The address concluded with Furman's solution to prevent future rebellions. With great pride he noted "there were very few of those who were, as members attached to regular churches, (even within the sphere of its operations) who appear to have taken a part in the wicked plot."[43] Members of the African Church (later known as Mother Emanuel African Methodist Episcopal Church), however, he demonized as potential rebels. Vesey and his conspirators were, in fact, actively involved in the African Church. For white southerners this fact demonstrated the need for their denominational bodies. Americans, white and Black, must remain under the care and authority of godly churches which would uphold the white supremacist social order.

To prevent rebellion, Furman unsurprisingly called for masters to send their slaves to Baptist churches. According to him, Christianity not only sanctioned slavery; it ensured that the system functioned properly. At the very next annual meeting, the South Carolina Baptist Convention reprinted the speech and circulated it throughout the state. The convention also requested that it be published in the *Southern Intelligencer* and the *Columbian Star*. The later publication's national reach would ensure that Furman's words reached northern audiences. According to Furman, southern churches offered to save souls and ensure domestic tranquility. Abolitionists, on the other hand, hindered the work of salvation and promoted violent insurrection.

Furman was not alone in these charges. Others, like Frederick Dalcho, emerged as prominent proslavery voices by using their positions as denominational leaders. Dalcho's story begins outside the church, when in 1801 he pushed to bring the Supreme Council of the Scottish Rite, a Masonic organization, to the American South. Beginning in the early 1820s, Dalcho resigned this Masonic leadership post and took a more active role in the Episcopal Church. This transition, coupled with the actions of Vesey, led him to make a public pronouncement on slavery. Writing as "a South Carolinian," Dalcho cited Furman's earlier work as an authoritative account of the origin of slavery but differed from Furman in describing the present practice of American slavery as "not in accordance with all our feelings. We deprecate the evil which attends it." But to absolve slaveholders from guilt, Dalcho claimed, "it has descended to us; we have not produced it. We would most willingly apply the remedy, if we knew what it was."[44]

Dalcho's primary argument claimed that the only injustice brought about by American slavery was the failure to "giv[e] religious instruction to our Negroes."[45] But the burden to expand salvation among the enslaved must fall on southerners, not invasive northern missionaries. For only southerners could be trusted with exercising "the measure of prudence, which is necessary to improve their moral and spiritual condition, without deranging the existing order of society." Conversion would both save Black souls and white lives. Both colonization and proslavery drew on the same expectations of salvation, yet while the ACS trained its eyes across the ocean, southerners focused their attention on the potential enslaved insurgents in their neighborhoods and the abolitionists who they feared would incite rebellion.

In his last major point, Dalcho, like Furman, asserted his denominational allegiance in a comment on the Denmark Vesey conspiracy. As he told his audience, *"None of the Negroes belonging to the Protestant Episcopal Church were concerned in the late conspiracy."*[46] His Episcopalian denominational leadership and the threat posed by men involved in the Vesey conspiracy inspired Dalcho to take action on the problem of slavery, but his denominational allegiance also framed the way he understood the problem. Too many wild evangelicals had filled "improvident and depraved" Black Americans with the dangerous intoxication of religious enthusiasm.

Furman praised the proslavery gospel found in Baptist churches, and Dalcho proclaimed that the Episcopal Church alone could bring true conversion and social stability, the only guarantee for safety in the Black majority Palmetto state. Denominational leadership required an active voice on the great issues of the day, and after the Missouri Crisis, slavery increasingly became that great issue. Denominational leadership pressed southerners like Furman and Dalcho into proslavery pronouncements. Other southern Christians avoided committing to proslavery, but nearly all denominational leaders actively denounced abolitionists as opponents of American salvation.

John Holt Rice feared that abolitionists within his Presbyterian denomination hampered his attempts to gain converts in his home of Richmond, Virginia. Writing to his close friend and denominational colleague Archibald Alexander, the head of Princeton Theological Seminary, in 1827, Rice shared his apprehension that the Ohio Synod of the Presbyterian Church was leading Presbyterianism down an abolitionist road he dared not follow. His alarm was compounded by the election of John Quincy Adams, causing him to predict "a violent collision between the north and the south; that the subject of slavery would be brought into party politics and religion; and that Presbyterians were to be greatly embarrassed by it."[47]

Rice felt that if the Presbyterian Church followed the abolitionist leanings of the Ohio Synod, "they may just as well bid us abandon the Southern country." Ignoring the spiritual needs of half of the country was absolutely out of the question for conversionists, North and South. By stymieing the expansion of conversions with inflammatory rhetoric, Rice feared that abolitionists were not only endangering souls but also hindering the expansion of holiness that he believed would eventually prove the most powerful driver of emancipation.

Conversionism became the core of proslavery Christianity, enabling southerners to oppose colonization without surrendering the discursive weapon of salvation in their defenses of slavery. In 1825, the Presbytery of Lexington, Virginia, called George A. Baxter to deliver the installation sermon honoring the appointment of Thomas Caldwell as minister over the churches of Lebanon and Windy Cove. Baxter took the opportunity to consider the question of slavery and relied on the logic of conversionism, telling his audience of Virginia Presbyterians, "The achievements of heroes or politicians; the liberty or slavery; the rise or the fall of empires, are little matters compared with the conversion of sinners, or the evangelizing of the heathen."[48]

Converting sinners and evangelizing the heathen were essential components of proslavery activism. As proslavery thought developed, conversionism increasingly became more than a defensive justification for slavery; it also became a weapon to preemptively attack the alleged idolatry of abolitionism. We see this most clearly in the Methodist mission to the slaves that began in 1829. Since at least the 1770s, Methodist missionaries in North America had targeted slaves for conversion, but the nineteenth century brought a more deliberate organization to the effort. But despite the efforts of Francis Asbury, and other leaders, Methodist missionary outreach to Black southerners remained a spotty affair, particularly in the Deep South. Enslavers often remained hesitant to expose their enslaved laborers to Christian teachers unless the gospel was clothed in proslavery paternalism.

As abolitionist attacks on slavery accelerated, both southern churchmen and elite planters recognized the power of conversion as a potential proslavery weapon. Historian Donald Mathews illustrates how Methodist ministers adapted their ministry to meet the needs of slaveholders, presenting slave conversion as a means of maintaining plantation discipline. And indeed, in South Carolina, a number of elite non-Methodist enslavers prompted the renewed commitment to evangelizing the enslaved when other state leaders sought legislation to ban Black literacy entirely. It was the South Carolina slavocracy, rather than the clergy, that led this most consequential antebellum conversionist effort.[49]

Many evangelical enslavers worried over the souls of their enslaved laborers while ignoring the physical and emotional toll of their actions. Paternalist fantasies and fear of rebellion pressed others to ensure that their slaves heard a version of the gospel that defended slavery and white supremacy. If abolitionists would distort the message of Christianity into antislavery propaganda, then enslavers would take the initiative to combat these lies by ensuring that their enslaved laborers had a strong foundation in the true proslavery gospel.

Toward that end, the wealthy and politically well-connected enslaver Charles Cotesworth Pinckney traveled to the Charleston home of William Capers in 1829. Capers was among the most respected southern Methodist ministers, a leader in the denomination, editor of the *Wesleyan Journal,* and delegate to the international gathering of Methodist ministers in England. When Capers returned to South Carolina after this international meeting, Pinckney asked the minister to serve as a missionary on his expansive plantation.

Pinckney believed that Christianity served as an essential tool in managing enslaved laborers, proclaiming to the Agricultural Society of South Carolina that same year, "Nothing is better calculated to render man satisfied with his destiny in this world than a conviction that its hardships and trials are as transitory as its honors and enjoyments." But Pinckney also drew on the rhetoric of conversion to offer the strongest defense against "Abolitionists and others, who are striving, against experience, to keep up that farce of Philanthropy." Pinckney deployed conversionism against the "lubrations of these visionaries," telling his fellow Charleston planters that converting slaves "would give us the advantage in argument over our Northern Brethren."[50] Salvation could support slavery.

Several other enslavers followed Pinckney, and an Episcopalian parish even offered to finance the work of a missionary from the South Carolina Methodist missionary conference. Capers declined to accept the role himself but, having long worked to convert enslaved South Carolinians, he delighted in the opportunity presented by these requests. Capers arranged to have other Methodist missionaries sent to a number of plantations throughout the South. From these humble origins came the largest organized attempt in all of American history to Christianize enslaved men and women. Over three hundred missionaries would labor until the Civil War, growing the body of southern Black Methodists from 65,000 in 1835 to 217,000 in 1860.[51] The missions to the slaves bent conversionist discourse directly toward the proslavery agenda. Southerners built a wall of Christian conversion to defend against encroaching abolitionists and to provide moral cover for the opposition to colonization.

Southern Opposition to Colonization

Opposition to colonization developed as the specter of abolitionism grew even more haunting after the threat of Denmark Vesey and the very real political turmoil of the Missouri Crisis. This process happened first and most intensely in the South. In the late 1810s and early 1820s, colonization enjoyed considerable support from white southerners, especially in Virginia and North Carolina. But this support began to wane in the latter half of the 1820s. The conversionist implications of colonization remained the movement's greatest asset, but commitments to slavery and white supremacy slowly began to crowd out visions of a converted Africa.

Some opponents grounded their criticism in the belief that there were others closer by who deserved the Christianizing influence of colonization. A North Carolinian wrote to the *Genius of Universal Emancipation* in January of 1822 proposing a colonization scheme in North America. The man supported the ACS's ambitions mostly "for the purpose of promoting civilization among the natives" in Africa. However, this writer claimed, African colonization was too difficult to simultaneously solve the "national evil" of slavery and expand salvation to other needed corners. To accomplish both, the man suggested that the United States create a colony in the west of the continent, a plan which Robert Finley himself acknowledged to likely be more expedient than planting a colony in Africa. Finley, of course, preferred Africa primarily because he was tantalized by the prospect of bringing salvation to the continent wounded by the slave trade. But this Carolinian suggested that Africans were not the only people in need of salvation. By setting up a colony in the West, he felt "far more would be done towards civilizing and christianizing the Indians, than has ever been or ever can be done by the zeal and labor of all the missionaries that can be sent amongst them."[52] For this man and many white Christians, conversion required colonization, and the West needed converting.

Some southerners opposed colonization from the very formation of the ACS, refusing to see the movement as anything but a Trojan horse for abolitionism. Interestingly, these critics almost never acknowledged missionary discourse in their critiques, knowing that too many Americans supported the idea of converting Africa. The success of these critics, then, hinged on their ability to change the nature of the conversation. When considering the role of religion, these opponents of colonization adopted the tactics of antirevivalists, dismissing the entire enterprise as the result of "enthusiasm," a term derisively used for centuries to question revivals. If the supposed conversions generated by colonization were merely the expressions of enthusiasm, as opposed to genuine, sober repentance, anticolonizationists could retain the high ground of conversionist Christianity.

A Georgian writing under the pseudonym of Limner recognized the relationship between the ACS and conversionism. Mirroring earlier attacks against religious revivals, he lambasted the project in such terms, arguing that "enthusiasm, in the onset, may design no evil, yet the experience of ages proves, that the passion knows no bounds."[53] Another Georgian, inspired by Limner, claimed that "the same spirit which possesses the fanatic in religion, animates the enthusiast in this cause."[54] An anonymous supporter of colonization from South Carolina responded to Limner by trying to strip the word "enthusiast" of its pejorative connotation. The South Carolinian wrote that the ACS and Limner were both enthusiasts. However, "the enthusiasm of the former attempts to restore the husband to the widow and the parent to the orphan; but the latter, to separate them."[55]

Historian Matthew Mason has shown how proslavery defenders attacked the antislavery spirit of humanitarian reform as misguided enthusiasm.[56] Again and again, proslavery critiques mirrored the rhetoric of antirevivalists in their challenges to colonizationist schemes, which they saw as latent attempts to attack slavery, promote equality, and increase the likelihood of race war. However, revivalists and antirevivalists, reformers and antireformers, did not always neatly align. Discourses of conversion, reform, and slavery blended into one another in ways that shaped all three.[57]

The timing of the growing opposition to colonization was no coincidence; a number of political and social issues arose in the 1820s to help fuse the burgeoning proslavery movement to anti-colonization. A new generation of proslavery Christians began to attack the ACS after the Missouri debates, the terror of the Vesey conspiracy, and bolder attempts to secure federal funds for colonization. This last event deserves particular attention. Historian Douglas Egerton claims that in the 1830s "only when too many Northern benevolent reformers threatened to make common cause with the Society ... that proslavery theorists began to take a second and harder look at the movement's goals."[58] However, the tide had already been turning a half-decade earlier when the movement solicited additional federal funds without emphasizing how those funds would extend salvation.

Southern antipathy to colonization accelerated after New York senator Rufus King introduced a bill to earmark funds generated by federal land sales for emancipating and colonizing enslaved Americans in 1825.[59] King's bill represented the first widely publicized call for colonization that did not mention the expected conversion of Africa. King's role as a northern partisan in the

Missouri debates guaranteed that his proposal would engender suspicion. By failing to wield the unifying discourse of conversion, he all but guaranteed major southern opposition.

Instead of emphasizing conversion, King paired colonization with emancipation. The southern rebukes were intense. The most vitriolic came from wealthy South Carolinian enslaver Whitemarsh Seabrook, whose critique of colonization defended slavery as fiercely as any secessionist fire eater would a generation later. While Seabrook ignored the question of converting Africa, he did take special aim at colonizing ministers, claiming that "clergy have in all ages exercised an almost boundless sway over the minds and actions of mankind."[60]

Reactions were similarly shrill in Georgia. Governor George Troup predicted that "soon, very soon, therefore, the United States' Government, discarding the mask, will openly lend itself to a combination of fanatics for the destruction of everything valuable in the Southern country." The state legislature similarly passed a resolution asserting that the federal government had "no constitutional power to appropriate moneys to aid the American Colonization Society."[61] The rising politicization of slavery blasted the conversionist consensus, and the resulting ruptures threatened denominational bodies and eventually the nation itself.[62]

King's bill inspired a debate over colonization that filled the pages of the *Richmond Enquirer* from August 1825 until August 1826. John White Nash, a slaveholding representative of the eastern Piedmont in the Virginia House of Delegates, wrote a sharp critique of colonization under the pseudonym Caius Gracchus. William Henry Fitzhugh, an ACS officer and enslaver, replied as Opimius. The exchange was later reprinted at the request of opponents of colonization. The firestorm began when Nash asserted that colonization was impractical and would require unconstitutional levels of government involvement. Worse, he claimed, the movement was merely a step toward abolition. Nash never directly acknowledged the missionary cause but given his dogged opposition to all other aims of the society, one can assume that he was referring to African salvation when discussing the "good motivations" animating what he nonetheless considered a foolish enterprise.[63]

The ACS's official rejoinder dismissed the fears of federal interference by citing the unanimous supportive resolution of the Virginia legislature. Virginians largely shared the goal of using colonization as a means of extending the gospel, and so the ACS promised that there was nothing to fear if the federal government acted in concert with the wishes of the Old Dominion. As for fears over abolition, the ACS responded by claiming, "the slaveholders were the first friends of the Society: the abolitionists, its only enemies."[64]

Fitzhugh took up the cause of the ACS thereafter under the name of Opimius. He began by identifying himself as an enslaver from Fairfax County, Virginia. He then critiqued his opponent by distinguishing the imperialism of European nations from the "Christian benevolence" of the ACS and promising "the sympathies of mankind."[65] The editorialist blamed the sufferings of Africa on "the cupidity and inhumanity of our own countrymen." While he was not willing to spend national resources solely in service of "civilizing and improving the conditions of foreign nations," he believed that all Americans would rejoice at the thought of the nation bringing "civilization and religion to those who have hitherto received at its hand, nothing but stripes and chains and death."[66] Again, in a later piece, Fitzhugh invoked the "obligation to carry to Africa, whom we have injured, the healing balm of the religion in which we believe."[67]

Nash recognized the centrality of religious arguments to the ACS and sought to differentiate between southern Christians and northern clerics. He ended his first pamphlet and began his second with attacks against the union of "church and state," an appeal particularly effective to southern Baptists who continued to remember their persecution prior to disestablishment. After two articles asserting the limitations of the federal government, Nash turned to a direct consideration of the humanitarian aims of colonization. He mocked the dreams of converting Africa as ravings "in such strains of rhapsody as almost to drive reason from her throne."[68] Instead of a mission of conversion, Nash predicted a mission of extermination. Presaging future attacks from abolitionists, Nash considered the colonization of North America and subsequent slaughter of Native Americans.

Fitzhugh roared back comparing Nash's dismissal of missionary potential to the British defense of slave trading, as both asserted a "hopeful degradation of Africa, its incapacity for improvement, and its fitness only for ministering to the wants of civilized man." More seriously, Fitzhugh indicted the tendency to dismiss religious imperatives and instead obsess over practical detail. He wrote, "Details are certain fields of triumph to county court ingenuity; and religion and philanthropy are ever fruitful themes of sarcasm and invective to the thoughtless and licentious." The exchange continued but Nash never again addressed the issue of converting Africa and only obliquely mocked the society as consumed by "the rage of religious enthusiasm."[69] Instead, he repeatedly accused the ACS of advocating for abolition. Fitzhugh struggled to parse the ACS's stance on slavery and the debate quickly descended into ad hominem attacks.

The ACS later reviewed the printing of the entire exchange, framing opposition to colonization as "ignorance of the purposes of Providence," or at least suspicion that anything so noble and grand would naturally "appear chimerical" to those without faith. Anyone who would "admit the authority of Christianity" and acknowledge that "the laws of the Deity extend to every department of human affairs" would automatically support colonization. The problem then was simply that of an unfaithful nation. God's plan was clear and "the only obstacle which can prevent the entire fulfilment of the design of the American Colonization Society, lies in the will of the American people." American sin, not the challenges of colonization, was the only true barrier. Only after this preface did the author dig into the arguments, claiming that Nash was "more familiar with the doctrines of political expediency than with the ethical system of Christianity." To Nash's accusation that private charity was unreliable and insufficient for such an aim, the ACS responded by citing the vast sums raised by the ABCFM in support of their multiple foreign missions.[70]

The exchange remained in the minds of colonizationists for at least one additional year. Stephen Foster, the pastor of Second Presbyterian church in Knoxville, Tennessee, began his 1826 Fourth of July essay on the ACS by turning to history, claiming that never had a colonization effort survived so many hardships and enjoyed so many successes. He added that the colony's "infant fortunes seems to have been woven by the finger of God." Foster then quoted Fitzhugh's comments about the legal propriety of colonization, but his most intense rhetoric was reserved for praising the "spirit of American missions to spread into Africa's deepest interior the deepest joys of the great salvation." He then credited this yearning shared by Americans to spread salvation as animating the rapid growth of colonization as well as the ABCFM, American Bible Society, and American Education Society. Foster catalogued this growth and labeled it as "the precursor of the reign of God over his revolted children."[71] Yet the colonizationist conversionist consensus that supported these religious arguments was unraveling. Colonizationists could no longer rely on the support of white southerners, many of whom began to oppose the movement by the end of the 1820s. And they were not alone.

Abolitionist Opposition to Colonization

White abolitionist opposition to colonization took much longer to solidify than the attacks emanating from proslavery southerners. Even the Quaker abolitionist Benjamin Lundy supported colonization in the 1820s. Through his *Genius of Emancipation* newspaper and his own organizing, he aided the American Colonization Society as well as organized his own colonization schemes. Despite Lundy's support, abolitionists would turn against the ACS by the 1830s.[72]

The Quaker minister and editor Elisha Bates raised some of the earliest white abolitionist objections in 1822. Bates accused the ACS of illogical duplicity. How could Black Americans be both "the pests of society, corrupted, and corrupting" and then also be the agent of mass evangelism? Radicals like Bates increasingly mocked colonizationists who claimed that Black Americans were both depraved dangers to society and the ordained agents of African salvation.[73]

Most colonizationists ignored the obvious logical inconsistency in their rhetoric, while others argued that education was a means of transforming dangerous dregs into enlightened evangelists. Bates himself was concerned with transforming sinful souls into pious saints, as he spent most of his ministry working with troubled members of his monthly meeting rather than seeking to expand his local Quaker flock. For Bates, however, there was no purifying element to colonization. It is not a surprise that his attack on colonization concluded with the fear that the purifying opportunity to end American slavery was slipping away due to conversionist fantasy.[74]

The most serious challenge to colonization, however, came not from white radicals like Bates, but rather from Black Christians, who pushed back against the missionary logic of colonization from the very beginning. Ever since thousands of Black Philadelphians expressed their disapproval in early 1817, Black Americans had questioned whether the ACS would succeed in their promise of extending salvation. The pages of the Black newspaper *Freedom's Journal* were rife with debate over colonization. John Russwurm, one of the paper's founders and editors, eventually became a prominent Black colonizationist and emigrated to Liberia in 1829.[75] But the paper mostly communicated the Black community's dual position of opposition to the ACS yet support for the missionary effort.

A June 1827 article claimed that the paper was "opposed to colonization in any shape, unless it be merely considered as a missionary establishment." The article framed its critique primarily as a manner of missionary expediency. The author advocated sending missionaries to Africa, not colonists: "Let a single nation be converted through the instrumentality of a mission family, and they will become far better pioneers, in effecting the work of civilization, and salvation through the vast regions of Africa, than any colonists that are likely to emigrate to that country."[76]

Some critics even blamed colonizationists for the death of missionaries. A March 1837 edition of the *Colored American* relayed explorers' reports from South Africa that distinguished "the sickly shores of Liberia" from "the healthy interior." The magazine blamed "the colonization humbug" for "the blood of all the devoted missionaries" who died from disease.[77] If missionaries were sent individually, they might move into the salubrious interior rather than being stranded on coastal colonies. According to these Black Christians, colonization was crippling the spread of the gospel.

The most important opponent of the ACS was Richard Allen, the bishop of the African Methodist Episcopal Church. Allen's reputation extended across the nation, and inaccurate rumors of his early support of the ACS generated considerable energy. As a result, the *Freedom's Journal* asked him to clarify his views of colonization. The result ran in late 1827 and anchored anticolonizationist abolitionism for decades. Allen began by admitting that he had spent "several years trying to reconcile" the colonization of Liberia.[78]

Allen was originally sympathetic to the movement. He eagerly supported Paul Cuffee's attempts to settle Black Americans in Sierra Leone and remained entranced by the prospect of converting Africa. He also actively supported emigration to Haiti.[79] A decade after the formation of the ACS, Allen still foregrounded the conversionist implications of colonization, opening his anticolonizationist letter by claiming that Black Americans lacked the training "to be sent into a far country, among heathens, to convert or civilize them."[80] From his years in the ministry, Allen knew that it took training to serve as an effective agent of salvation, and the ACS was not doing nearly enough to ensure that colonists would have that training.

Allen also recognized the desire of enslavers and many white northerners to eliminate all vestiges of Black freedom in North America and their attempt to use the missionary authority of the ACS in pursuing their vision of white supremacy. In the absence of widespread missionary training, the bishop understood colonization merely as a proslavery ploy dressed up in missionary language. His final appeal drew on his experience and interests as a denominational leader, as he praised the United States as a land "where wisdom abounds and the gospel is free."[81] Ministers under Allen's leadership were busy sharing the gospel among American Black communities. Siphoning off leaders from his flock in a misguided missionary scheme would only hamper his quest to build a unified Black American church.

Richard Allen's anticolonizationist message swayed countless Black Americans, none more influential than David Walker. David Walker's 1829 *Appeal to the Colored Citizens of the World* shook white Americans across the nation. Never before had such a widespread publication included a call for slave rebellion. Walker had a lot to say on a variety of issues, but white readers were understandably preoccupied with his message to Black Americans that it was "no more harm for you to kill a man who is trying to kill you, than it is for you to take a drink of water when thirsty." This language marked a turning point in the abolitionist movement. Walker invoked the hymn of William Cowper that historian Stephen Marini calls "the most printed classical providence hymn," to publicly frame "the destruction of the oppressors" as God's "wonders to perform."[82] Walker's apocalyptic prophecy of divine wrath jarred white antislavery Christians who had been content to rest on the promise of conversionist emancipation.

Walker's appeal did more than invoke violence. His biting wit took direct aim at the missionary arguments of colonizationists. In recounting the history of colonization, Walker quoted statesman, slaveholder, and colonizationist Henry Clay, who claimed that Africa was the ideal site for colonization because it offered the greatest chance of expanding Christianity. Walker retorted, "Here I ask Mr. Clay, what kind of Christianity? Did he mean such as they have among the Americans—distinction, whip, blood and oppression? I pray the Lord Jesus Christ to forbid it."[83]

Walker published three editions of his *Appeal* and an increased reliance on religious argumentation formed the most important difference among the three.[84] By the third edition, Walker attacked the binary between Christian America and heathen Africa by questioning the Christianity of white Americans. Walker, like most Black activists, was nurtured in radical Black Christianity. The powerful spirituality of the Black protest tradition nurtured Walker, first at the African Church in Charleston, South Carolina, the same church where Denmark Vesey worshiped, and then as an active member of the biracial May Street Methodist Church in Boston. Christian imagery suffused all of his work.[85]

In a speech delivered a year before the publication of his *Appeal,* Walker claimed that "a hungering and thirsting after religion" would, in part, "ultimately result in rescuing us from an oppression, unparalleled." In the same address, Walker praised "the truly patriotic and lamented Mr. Ashmun, late Colonial Agent of Liberia." Despite Walker's committed anticolonizationist convictions, he nonetheless claimed that Ashmun, "with a zeal which was only equaled by the good of his heart, has lost his life in our cause." Walker concluded by exclaiming, "I verily believe that God has something in reserve for us, which, when he shall have parceled it out upon us will repay us for all our sufferings and miseries."[86] Writers like Walker worked hard to uncouple dreams of salvation from plans for colonization. By the end of the 1830s, they had largely succeeded.

In his *Appeal,* Walker went beyond noting the beam of slavery in the eye of the nation, and he even pushed past the radical purificationists who sought to purge slaveholders from the church. Instead, by his third edition in 1830, Walker spent his very first sentence dismissing "white Christians, who hold us in slavery" as "pretenders to Christianity." Walker knew the importance of millennial rhetoric to American Christianity and even acknowledged that slaveholders were "looking for the Millennial day."[87]

Conversionist millennialism was not enough for Walker. His study of history led him to believe that slavery was worse than the manner that "devils themselves ever treated a set of men, women and children on this earth." The depth of this evil harkened millennial action, but it would neither be a wave of salvation nor a sifting of wheat from chaff. Christ's return would mean fire and blood. Walker invoked Psalm 68 and encouraged his Black readers to "stretch forth our hands to the Lord our God," and he believed that when they did, white Americans would be in grave danger.[88]

In one of the few moments where Walker addressed white readers, he proclaimed, "your destruction is at hand, and will be speedily consummated unless you repent!"[89] The move to relabel slaving Christians as, in fact, not Christians at all was replicated in Black communities throughout the North. Black residents of Hartford, Connecticut, for instance, gathered at the African Church and resolved that anyone behind a pulpit who supported colonization should be seen as a "pretended minister of the gospel, who is in league with those conspirators against our rights." The gathering in Hartford equated colonizationists to the evil prophet Balaam, who cast "a stumbling block in the way of the children of Israel."[90] To protect true religion and enable the extension of salvation, these Black Christians called for the defeat of colonization.

* * *

COLONIZATION AND THE CONVERSIONISM that enabled it would not die easily. For white Americans who dreamed of international salvation, white supremacy, and national unity, colonization continued to offer unparalleled promise. But theological changes and new strategies brought new allies to the movement against both slavery and colonization. Revival was soon to come, and this new outpouring of salvation inspired new modes of activism. From the fires of these revivals, new activists came to see slavery as an unparalleled evil that must be eradicated immediately by human hands. No longer content to wait on God, a new generation of white abolitionists followed the example of Black activists and demanded an immediate end to slavery. In pursuing this mission, white Christian abolitionists came to see Christian enslavers as incapable of spreading American salvation. A new birth of purificationism arose, conversionism weakened, and a national crisis loomed.

◇◇◇◇ **5** ◇◇◇◇

Shattering the Conversionist Consensus, 1830–1837

HE 1830S TRANSFORMATION OF American abolitionism would have been impossible without concurrent transformations in American salvation. A new revivalism called white Christians to fuse the pursuit of salvation with the crusade for immediate abolitionism. These new abolitionists followed Black activists in attacking the American Colonization Society. The ACS fought back with increasingly desperate pleas for national unity through their entwined visions of salvation and white supremacy. This growing rancor over colonization and the untiring resistance of Black Americans, enslaved and free, forced denominational leaders to take stands on the new abolitionism.

Debates over slavery could no longer be contained, nor could Black and white abolitionists who refused to acquiesce to conversionist appeals. The Southampton Rebellion led by Nat Turner in 1831 inspired a fierce backlash against abolitionists, and denominational leaders spoke up aggressively, just as they had done nearly a decade earlier following Denmark Vesey's planned rebellion. Religious leaders, North and South, continued to lambast abolitionists as allies of race war and enemies of salvation. Yet abolitionists captured enough antislavery ground to prevent the creation of new, moderate conversionist antislavery organizations.

For the remaining decades of the antebellum era, more Americans felt compelled to support slavery or abolition. The weakening of conversionism and the marginalization of moderates would come to destroy national denominations. But before sectional schism, there was a theological revolution rooted in new understandings of salvation. To understand this revolution in revivalism, we have to begin nearly a century earlier with what scholars now call the First Great Awakening and track the theological transformations that gave birth to radical abolitionism.

Theology and Immediate Abolitionism

The congregants dutifully slid into the pews of the hot and stuffy First Church of Enfield, Connecticut, on a July evening. As the sun slowly set, yellow light pierced through the narrow windows, filling the chapel with an eerie glow. By 1741 New England was several years into what came to be known as the Great Awakening, yet this congregation had remained stubbornly resistant to earlier attempts at revival and now appeared hopeless. As the service began, the congregation chattered among themselves, paying little attention to the proceedings.

As the small man at the pulpit quietly and deliberately extolled divine agency and berated human sinfulness, the tenor in the room shifted from lighthearted sociability to grave unease. Pauses in the sermon were no longer greeted with causal whispers but with heavy silence as nervous souls contemplated their deserved damnation. Slowly, gasps and muffled cries filled the warm air. These sounds increased until mournful moans and piercing screams forced the minister to close the service without finishing the sermon. Revival had reached Enfield as Jonathan Edwards identified all of humankind as sinners in the hands of an angry God.[1]

Ninety years later, descendants of the New Englanders who experienced this "great and general awakening" had made their way west over the Catskill and Adirondack Mountains into the upper portions of New York State, populating the new cities that sprang up after the completion of the Erie Canal in 1825. In a winter evening in 1830, recently repentant souls and several fence-sitters crowded into the Brick Church in Rochester. At the very beginning of the service, Charles Grandison Finney—a tall, thin man with sharp, fiery eyes—welcomed congregants who felt troubled, convicted, or otherwise in need of special prayer to a bench at the front of the church. To these unsettled souls he aimed the loudest, most intense and pointed appeals of his sermon. With the eyes of the congregation on their backs, the eyes of the revivalist boring into their own, and the eyes of God penetrating their very souls, those seated upon this anxious bench eagerly obeyed the call to publicly confess their sins, accept the grace of God, and live a life free of the sinful excesses so common in this economically booming corner of the republic.[2]

These two moments of revival embody the sea change in American Protestantism that occurred during the ninety years that separated them. A key passage in Jonathan Edwards's sermon terrified his listeners, insisting, "There is nothing that keeps wicked men, at any moment, out of hell, but the mere pleasure of God."[3] Finney's sermon, on the other hand, reached its pinnacle when he called those on the front seat to "come out and avow your determination to be on the Lord's side."[4] The years between the two revivals brought a shift in popular theological understanding of human agency. Where the congregants in 1740s New England passively hoped for God to spare them from their deserved punishment, those in 1830s New York were told that they could made a conscious choice to renounce their sin and accept the gift of salvation.

Moreover, immediately after choosing salvation, Finney's converts were enlisted in a host of reform crusades. An emphasis on religious conversion united the two eras, but the public ethos had changed. The old Calvinist model of human incapacity had been replaced by a model of individual agency rooted in Arminian theology and Jacksonian democracy. Americans could choose salvation, both for themselves and for their world. Instead of waiting on God, Americans could take the first step themselves, confident that God's power would flow through their actions. Concurrently, a new coercive politics of reform harnessed and directed these democratic, individualistic currents in an attempt to fulfill the nation's destiny as a world-redeeming republic of righteousness.

In the first three decades of the nineteenth century, missionary efforts successfully brought the gospel to the frontier, and religious leaders entrenched themselves at the very center of American life and national identity. Fears of an un-Christian frontier were joined by concerns over the righteousness of the converted republic. Conversionists began to construct institutions capable of nurturing the Christian republic into righteous maturity, while new abolitionists and other reformers demanded immediate change through the transformation of laws. Conservative antislavery voices and proslavery apologists both marshaled the old conversionist consensus against the new abolitionists, but during the 1830s, the center would no longer hold. New theologies of reform worked around the emphasis on conversion, but ultimately the uncompromising insistence of radical abolitionists shattered the conversionist consensus, setting the stage for decades of tense sectionalist animosity and eventually civil war.

Throughout the antebellum era, many white Christians continued to place significant faith in the power of conversion to solve the problems of the nation, including slavery and its attendant vices. However, theological changes, particularly the turn away from Calvinism toward Arminianism, shifted the agency of salvation away from an inscrutable deity in favor of individual repentant sinners. These trends sometimes enervated the millennial confidence in conversion as an antislavery strategy. In other cases, they shifted the agent of millennial action from God to His people. Reformers increasingly believed that they could bring the millennium by remaking institutions themselves, rather than waiting on God for systemic change.[5] One need to look no further than the most successful revivalist of the 1820s and 1830s to see how the routinization of revivalism encouraged a new assault on American slaving.

Charles Grandison Finney replaced the formerly mysterious saving act of God with a predictable, almost mechanical process infused with human agency. Edwards's sermon described "Sinners in the Hands of an Angry God" as hell-bound if not for the grace of God. Finney's aptly titled 1834 essay "Sinners Bound to Change Their Own Hearts" gave listeners more agency, offering a clear plan of action through which they could conquer damnation. The revivalist presented a staunchly Arminian account of salvation, undercutting an already declining American Calvinism.[6] Just as sinners were bound to change their own hearts, so too ministers were bound to change their world through an efficient, rational course of action, certain to yield predictable results. Finney claimed that spiritually attuned ministers could create revivals "with the same expectation as the farmer has of a crop when he sows his grain."[7]

Imagined as a sort of manual for sowing the gospel, Finney's *Lectures on Revivals of Religion*, first published in 1835, was intended as a guide for the harvest of souls. The volume was widely successful, selling over twelve thousand copies in the first three months.[8] A new message of national salvation emphasized human agency in the pages of Finney's lectures. Similar messages echoed through Finney's teaching at Oberlin College, a nursery for both revivalism and abolitionism, and in the testimonies of thousands of Americans who experienced personal regeneration at his revivals. This rising emphasis on human agency had great consequence for American moral reform.

Rather than expecting religious conversions to inevitably yield to the disappearance of sins like slavery, Finney encouraged his converts to work out their salvation in the great reform movements of the day, to take direct action in making themselves and their nation perfect.[9] In fact, he believed that the success of revivals depended at least in part on the ability of ministers to encourage social reform. He wrote, "Revivals are hindered when ministers and churches take wrong ground in regard to any question involving human rights." He then immediately followed this assertion with lengthy discussion of the church's duty to promulgate abolitionism.[10] Finney held onto a millennial expectation, claiming that God's kingdom could be inaugurated in less than ten years, but his understanding of causation differed from earlier conversionist millennialism, and this different understanding of causation yielded a more active and aggressive abolitionism.

Finney looked to an imminent millennium that would be inaugurated by a new generation of Christians achieving "higher and higher attainments" in bringing the kingdom of God into reality.[11] Finney encouraged individual salvation through his revivals and national salvation through reform. In his mind, both worked hand in hand to make real the kingdom of God, and both informed his preaching and his teaching at Oberlin.[12] Historian James Moorehead characterized Finney's conversionist ambitions as entirely in line with his expectations for social reform, writing, "So deep was Finney's commitment to the ideal of community based upon efficiency, function, and free choice that one might say without exaggeration that he refashioned the universe into a cosmic voluntary society." It is no surprise that, in the words of Moorehead again, abolitionists, "many of whom were converted in Finney's revivals . . . employed methods of mass persuasion patterned on those of the itinerant evangelist."[13]

Finney's ecumenism similarly fostered the kind of interdenominational cooperation necessary for a new age of abolitionism. Unlike the mission projects sponsored by denominational bodies, Finney cared little where the participants of his revivals went to church and even wrote that when settled pastors "begin to make efforts to get the converts to join their church, you see the last of the revival."[14] And so his revivals often functioned more like interdenominational reform meetings than conventional denominational church services. In fact, Finney mostly ignored the concerns of church governance that occupied the minds of denominational leaders. In his *Systematic Theology*, he reflected heavily on theological questions of divine sovereignty, but he did not devote any energy to a critical reflection on how churches should be organized or governed.[15]

Finney understood the church as having the identical function of reform organizations, and in fact he claimed that the purpose of the church was "to reform individuals, communities, and government." In his Twenty-third Letter on Revival, Finney wrote, "It is melancholy and amazing to see to what an extent the church treats the different branches of reform either with indifference, or with direct opposition." He went on, lamenting, "There is not, I venture to say upon the whole earth an inconsistency more monstrous, more God-dishonoring, and I must say more manifestly insane than the attitude which many of the churches take in respect to nearly every branch of reform which is needed among mankind."[16] Individual American churches could not rest complacently in attempts to generate converts. True Christians must seek both conversion and active social reform. Salvation required both.

While Finney inaugurated changes in American revivalism, a new generation of activists similarly remade American abolitionism. By the 1830s, abolitionists had diversified their tactics, drawing on petition campaigns, political pressure, pamphlet wars, and more. Yet religious discourse and religious networks remained essential to nearly all abolitionist organizing. Finney happily hosted the first organizational meeting for the American Antislavery Society in 1833 at his Chatham Street Chapel in lower Manhattan. This collection of reformers organized and amplified the thundering voices that unsettled the conversionist malaise with abrasive demands to end slavery immediately. The loudest of those voices belonged to the firebrand William Lloyd Garrison.

Garrison was raised by a deeply devout Baptist woman and internalized a veneration for righteous purity. His mother, Francis, instructed her children with rigid piety and leaned on other devout church members to survive after her alcoholic husband abandoned his family. The church saved her in more than one way and she in turn served its cause, founding the first female prayer meeting in Baltimore. Other Baptists similarly nurtured Garrison. When he first moved to Boston in 1826, Garrison lived with a William Collier, a Baptist missionary and temperance advocate. Collier's home became a waystation for missionaries, reformers, and revivalists, including Benjamin Lundy, the abolitionist editor of the *Genius of Universal Emancipation*. Lundy converted Garrison to the cause and hired him as coeditor of his antislavery newspaper. Garrison, however, quickly came to exert even greater influence than his mentor.[17]

William Lloyd Garrison burst onto the national scene with the same abrasive insistence on purity that his mother instilled in him as a child. It is difficult to overstate the impact of Garrison's rhetoric. The very first issue of his own abolitionist newspaper, the *Liberator*, set a clear tone attacking the heart of conversionist moderation. Rather than appealing to national religious commitments, Garrison offered outright threats, writing, "Let southern oppressors tremble—let their secret abettors tremble—let their northern apologists tremble—let all the enemies of the persecuted blacks tremble."[18]

Garrison knew exactly what he was doing. While admitting "that many object to the severity of my language," Garrison asked, "Is there not cause for severity?" For those, like Garrison, who did not believe that the church set the nation on a path to salvation and abolition, the truth became clear—change would require confrontation. Garrison clearly explained, "On this subject, I do not wish to think, or speak, or write, with moderation. No! no! Tell a man whose house is on fire, to give a moderate alarm; tell him to moderately rescue his wife from the hand of the ravisher; tell the mother to gradually extricate her babe from the fire into which it has fallen;—but urge me not to use moderation in a cause like the present." Garrison anticipated his critics, and indeed thousands of white antislavery Americans condemned his confrontational style. Yet he remained undaunted, as he wrote, "I am in earnest—I will not equivocate—I will not excuse—I will not retreat a single inch—AND I WILL BE HEARD."

Garrison's millennialism was one of wrath and judgment. In his only invocation of Christ's return, Garrison credits "the apathy of the people" as "enough to . . . hasten the resurrection of the dead." The end of days may be approaching, but for Garrison, it would come with fire and punishment as a result of the enduring sin of slavery. Garrison's threats were understood as a call to war, and his attempt to polarize his audience had its intended effect. The overwhelming majority of Americans loathed Garrison and the new abolitionism that he modeled. However, a small number of radical reformers, influenced by the religious changes of the age, boldly advanced a new abolitionist discourse. This new abolitionism drew on, while also modifying, the terms of conversionism.

In order to save the nation from the sin of slavery, this new generation of abolitionists sought to convert their countrymen to abolition. They called this plan "moral suasion." Black Americans had been adopting this tactic for years, but white abolitionists codified the strategy with the formation of the New England Antislavery Society in 1832 and extended it with the creation of the American Antislavery Society in 1833.[19] Arnold Buffum's presidential address to the New England Antislavery Society began by asserting "the only influence we can exert must be that of moral suasion, and not of coercion."[20]

Drawing on the legacy of Enlightenment optimism, Christian evangelism, and Jacksonian democracy, moral suasion served as a halfway point between conversionism and the coercive purificationist reform required to root out the entrenched system of American slaving. Moral suasion retained the millennial confidence of conversionism, as many abolitionists were confident that their countrymen would surely see the light and turn from the sin of slaving. However, moral suasion shifted the burden of this work from divine agency to human action. No longer content to focus solely on generating religious conversions, this new generation of abolitionists privileged purity on the issue of slavery and treated the liberation of the enslaved with at least the same passion as the salvation of souls from spiritual damnation. For these Christian abolitionists, national salvation required national purity.

Nothing better embodied the confidence and approach of moral suasion than Angelia Grimké's *Appeal to the Christian Women of the South*. This 1836 pamphlet called upon women in the South to petition their state governments to abolish slavery. Grimké herself was a southerner, born in Charleston, South Carolina, who had earlier moved to Philadelphia and defected from the Presbyterian Church to Quakerism. Despite frustrations with her home state, she remained confident that if she issued the right appeal with the right Christian framing, southern women would recognize the righteousness of abolition and enlist themselves in trying to save their states and their nation. She promised her readers that "there is something in the heart of man which will bend under moral suasion." In fact, it might only take "six signatures" to make a notable difference. Throughout the appeal, Grimké proclaimed that abolition would be best advanced "as a matter of morals and religion, not of expediency or politics."[21] Abolitionists could convert the nation to their cause, and Christianity would enable these essential conversions.

Black abolitionists rightly remained suspicious that white Americans might so easily be transformed into agents of liberation, yet many still drew hope from the tactics of moral suasion. In 1837, James Forten rejoiced at the inaugural meeting of the American Moral Reform Society, held in Philadelphia, claiming, "It is our fortune to live in an era, when the moral power of this nation is waking up to the evils of slavery and the cause of our oppressed brethren throughout this country."[22] The moral power of this new generation of abolitionists challenged the soothing charms of conversionism that had allowed many antislavery Christians to remain inactive in meaningful antislavery action. The American Colonization Society became one of the first casualties when abolitionists attacked conversionism.

Abolitionists, Colonizationists, and Conversion

The new generation of antislavery activists produced waves of pamphlets designed to convert colonizationists to abolitionism. Many of the most influential abolitionists had earlier been colonizationists, including Garrison himself, and leaders of the abolitionist movement came to believe that colonization had been siphoning off potential abolitionists by distorting Christian compassion. In 1839, Maria Weston Chapman claimed that "the natural and kindly tide of human sympathy for suffering, was turned away from the service of Freedom by the Colonization Society."[23] Real Christian compassion had to be redirected toward abolition and away from colonization. No middle ground could remain.

The abolitionist attack on colonization did not destroy the society, but it did succeed in drawing a sharp line between those who prioritized immediate Black freedom and those who did not. An anonymous woman asserted in an 1839 book exploring Christian motherhood that she was both "an abolitionist, glorying in the name" as well as "a friend of colonization." However, nearly a decade of untiring anticolonizationist activism among abolitionists and similarly dogged anti-abolitionist activism among colonizationists meant that by the late 1830s, this woman lamented, "I find that I am not considered by either party as belonging to their ranks, but am simply a mark for both to aim at."[24] The battle lines had been drawn, and abolitionists made sure that one could not identify as a member of their movement without opposing colonization, and colonizationists followed suit by condemning abolitionists as enemies of salvation.

In encouraging others to follow their path from colonization to abolitionism, these new radicals repeated three arguments, all designed to undercut the conversionist foundation that bolstered the colonization movement: first, they questioned the suitability of the colonists to serve as missionaries; second, they claimed that the commercial nature of the colony would prevent Christianization; and third, they questioned the underlying logic of colonizationist conversionism by redefining terms or appealing to other Christian imperatives. All of these tactics required tackling the conversionist logic at the heart of colonization. Garrison, for instance, opened his "Thoughts on Colonization" by calling the anticipated salvation of Africa "a hollow pretense for colonizing."[25] But Garrison recognized power in the pretense and had to rebut the claim before advancing his argument that colonization entrenched slavery and attacked tenuous Black freedoms.

Most American Christians were well willing to sacrifice Black lives in order to harvest souls, and so abolitionists had to do more than make Americans feel compassion for enslaved people: they had to argue that slavery and colonization threatened not only bodies but also souls. Garrison turned the majority of his volume over to dozens of messages from Black communities who likewise attacked the missionary argument.[26] James G. Birney, a former enslaver turned colonizationist and then abolitionist, knew firsthand the power of missionary discourse, as he wielded it effectively in his former post as an agent for the

ACS. After this defection to abolitionism, he shrewdly placed missionary considerations at the center of his anticolonizationist tract.[27]

In a letter to Birney, Theodore Dwight Weld, a prolific revivalist and abolitionist who worked for years alongside Charles Grandison Finney, maintained that colonization was in retreat but that its defenders "support it merely because they believe that it will convert Africa."[28] The previously discussed anonymous woman writing on motherhood began her explanation of why she remained supportive of colonization, despite her abolitionist sympathies, by writing, "I have looked to it as a star of hope for Africa."[29] Unlike Weld's claim, she did not support colonization solely because she expected it to yield salvation, but she did privilege that reason in her defense. For Weld, Birney, Garrison, and David Walker, revealing colonizationist missionary arguments as lies would enable Americans to see the ACS as hindrances to salvation, enablers of slavery, and opponents of the true millennium.

As Walker's *Appeal* and anticolonizationist pamphlets circulated in the 1830s, the relationship between the ACS and Black communities shifted from tense suspicion to outright hostility. Maria Stewart, the powerful Black orator, told a Black audience in Boston in 1833 that the ACS was an enemy to Black freedom, claiming "if they dared, like Pharaoh, king of Egypt, they would order every male child among us to be drowned."[30] But to defeat colonization, most abolitionists recognized that they must grapple with the issue of African conversion. And so, again and again, Black Americans questioned the logic of using uneducated colonists as missionaries. New York City–based African Episcopal priest Peter Williams Jr. protested the ACS in 1830 by expressing his support for the "civilizing and Christianizing of that vast continent." However, he claimed that "a few well-qualified missionaries" would "do more for the instruction and improvement of the natives" than colonization.[31]

Lewis Cork, writing for a group of Black Methodists gathered in Trenton at the Mount Zion Church, assured readers that "we highly approve of the evangelizing of Africa, but disapprove of the present measures." The New Haven–based Peace and Benevolent Society of Afric-Americans distinguished between colonists and missionaries, expressing an "earnest desire that Africa may speedily become civilized, and receive religious instruction; but not by the absurd and invidious plan of the Colonization Society."[32] The same feeling was held by "a numerous and respectable meeting" at African Hall in Brooklyn, which remarked that "we believe that a few men, well instructed and possessing a true missionary spirit, are calculated to do more good in that country, than a thousand on the colonization plan."[33] Some went so far as to declare that the ACS was sending murderers and rum peddlers who certainly would do little good in advancing the missionary agenda.[34]

Erastus Hopkins, a seminarian at Princeton, responded to these attacks with a widely circulated apology for the ACS. Hopkins began by asserting that conversion, or, as he put it, "the stupendous purpose of bringing the whole world under the renovating influence of Christian truth," was the one philanthropic aim that "rises above all others in magnitude and grandeur."[35] Colonizationist rhetoric hinged on romantic dreams for a converted Africa, and so Hopkins fired back, citing the annual report's claim that local chiefs ceded land to the colonists on the condition that they erect schools for local children. This report echoed earlier appeals that Africans were eager for Christian instruction.

Reports like these fueled assumptions of African passivity and so Hopkins rejoiced, "How different from the wild, intractable men whom the New England and Virginia colonists encountered!" Of course, seventeenth-century British missionaries used the same trope of the passive, eager Indigenous convert when describing the supposedly "intractable" potential converts of the seventeenth century. In some ways, little had changed in missionary discourse over the centuries, yet ACS-driven African conversion would ultimately depend on Black missionaries. And so, when Black and white anticolonizationists claimed that uneducated, formerly enslaved men and women would make shoddy missionaries, Hopkins highlighted recent fundraising to create a seminary to train ministers in Africa, rejoicing, "A flourishing seminary on the shores of that benighted continent, reared in the midst of its darkness is a proud monument of American philanthropy!"[36] Again, the ACS promised to transform loathed free people of color into agents of international salvation.

Hopkins devoted most of his apologetic to rebutting the argument of abolitionists. He divided abolitionist attacks into three categories: the principles of the Society, effect on Black Americans, and expected influence on Africa. When discussing the principles of the ACS, Hopkins highlighted the abolitionist accusation that slaveholders patronized the society, a point he acknowledged but deflected by claiming that their cooperation was required to achieve the abolitionists' ultimate goal of eliminating slavery. As to the effect of the ACS on Black Americans, Hopkins claimed that its only concern was to colonize, not uplift, so abolitionists were asking the society to do something it had no interest in. Moreover, he justified prejudice as the natural reaction to a "degraded" people and claimed "this prejudice is incurable." Of course, uplift was a key discourse among an earlier generation of colonizationists, yet conversion was always given greater prominence, and Hopkins was able to deflect this critique by hammering on his preferred theme of African conversion.[37]

Hopkins acknowledged the radicals' anticonversionist attacks on the ACS, but his response was simply apoplectic. He found it impossible to countenance any doubts to the ACS's conversion scheme. He asked, "Will not such a colony, we ask, thrown upon the shores of a benighted continent, spread light and blessings around it? If this is denied what can be asserted?" Hopkins refused to engage the conversionist arguments of anticolonizationists, and instead concluded his piece by pairing the promise of Psalms with the prophecy of Isaiah, proclaiming, "Let it [colonization] go till it causes the hundred millions of a benighted continent to rejoice in the blessings of civilization and religion; till that scripture is verified, which appears committed to our favored hands to fulfill, when Ethiopia shall stretch forth her hands, and the desert blossom as a rose!"[38]

In addition to claiming that colonizationists were ill-prepared to convert native Africans, anticolonizationists also claimed that the commercial nature of the colony proved it could never succeed as a missionary outpost. Black protesters from Brooklyn worried that "we well know that the examples of *traders* and traffickers are in no way calculated to induce heathens to embrace our religion."[39] While William Lloyd Garrison was careful not to impugn the particular character of Liberian settlers, he did claim that the capitalist spirit inherent in the colonization mission ensured that settlers could never make adequate missionaries, proclaiming that "the establishment of a colony of speculators, then, to evangelize Africa, does not discover much wisdom or promise much success."[40]

Ironically, Garrison made the same argument as John White Nash, the Virginia enslaver and proslavery critic of colonization, by claiming that history showed that colonizers—compelled by profit and inclined to wickedness—never Christianize, but either exterminate Indigenous people, descend into native licentiousness, or amalgamate.[41] Missionaries could and did succeed, according to Garrison's reading of efforts in Hawaii, Burma, and India. But only because of missionaries "who shall neither build forts nor trust in weapons of war." And yes, Garrison acknowledged, Africa was ripe for conversion, but not, he emphasized, from colonists.[42] According to Garrison, colonists were not missionaries. The latter were needed, but the former would only salt the mission fields of West Africa.

Colonization boosters took this claim head-on. In 1833, Cyril Pearl, a Congregationalist minister and ACS agent, sought to rebut Garrison by asserting that traders and merchants were, indeed, effective agents of Christianization. The year prior, Pearl held a procolonization rally in Augusta, Maine, only to see Garrison hijack the event and embarrass him in front of his own audience. Pearl's rebuttal to Garrison ignored the missionary critiques and leaned on millennial rhetoric, proclaiming that the ACS would continue its "grand experiment" and obey "the command of the Savior 'GO TEACH ALL NATIONS.'" The ACS was fulfilling prophecy. God was using the ACS in his plan to ensure that "the songs of salvation shall be heard wherever there are human beings."[43] Both colonizationists and their opponents claimed the high ground of supporting the salvation of the continent.

Perhaps the most important aspect of Pearl's reply to Garrison was his assertion that traders and merchants would prove effective agents of Christianization. While anticolonizationists claimed that traders were inhibiting the gospel, Pearl assured readers that "commercial intercourse of the colony with the native tribes is extending and the latter manifest an increasing desire to imitate the manners and customs of the former." This imitation included a rising demand for "schools and missionaries, that they may know and enjoy the blessings which civilization and Christianity can confer."[44] According to Pearl, demand for Western goods encouraged demand for Western values, including American education and American Christianity.

But opponents of colonization would not be moved by this procommercial perspective. James G. Birney, the former enslaver and ACS agent turned anticolonization polemicist, relayed a number of testimonies of colonist licentiousness rooted in the greed of commerce. According to Birney, religion, like agriculture, had to be planted not traded. Traders supplied "ardent spirits, fire-arms, powder and ball," But what, Birney asked, "is the first work of the missionary? Is it not to allure to peace, to *stationary* life and habits of settled industry?"[45] Commercially minded colonists would always place their self-interests first, and since agriculture, peace, and abstinence would undercut trading business, trade would ultimately harm the morals of the Africans. Attempting to appeal to the nation's long history of venerating agriculture and demonizing merchants, Birney lambasted colonization as a corrupt enterprise that threatened both American integrity and African souls.

When abolitionists could not succeed in sundering the conversionist argument by questioning the wisdom of sending untrained colonists as missionaries or framing commercial imperatives as inherently opposed to proselytization, they occasionally questioned the assumptions of the conversionist argument and the underlying racism of the movement. Most commonly, anticolonizationists summoned the spirit of Matthew 7:3 and used American slavery to contrast the mote in Africa's eye with the beam in the eye of the slaving United States. An 1830 address from the Colored Convention of Philadelphia proclaimed that if Africans knew how the United States attacked the freedom of Black Americans, they would "refuse to be civilized and eject our Christian missionaries."[46] The United States, it argued, could never send successful missionaries until the nation first purified itself of its original sins of slavery and white supremacy. If Americans truly cared about extending salvation, they must first create a godly witness by renouncing the sin of slaving.

For generations, Black Americans had espoused a counter-millennialism that advanced abolition and equality alongside international conversion. Protesters in Brooklyn concluded an address with a millennial vision that interpreted a future biracial republic as the fulfillment of divine prophecy: "We pray the Lord to hasten the day, when prejudice, inferiority, degradation and oppression shall be done away, and the kingdoms of this world become the kingdoms of God and his Christ."[47] White abolitionists grabbed onto this alternative millennial causation, arguing that washing away the sin of American slavery was more important, and thus should antecede, the missionary promise of colonization.

These new priorities that privileged purity as a necessary precursor to conversion are most clearly demonstrated through the writings of James G. Birney. Birney cast a long shadow throughout the 1830s and 1840s. This Kentucky-born Presbyterian attorney received enslaved laborers as a wedding gift, established a plantation in Madison County, Alabama, and rescued himself from financial strain by selling most of his enslaved laborers. Birney became an agent for the ACS until Theodore Dwight Weld, the apostle of Charles Grandison Finney, converted him to anticolonizationist immediate abolitionism. Birney's biography made him a powerful voice in the abolitionist movement and eventually elevated him to presidential candidate for the abolitionist Liberty Party in 1840 and 1844. But first Birney and other abolitionists trained their eyes on defeating his former employer, the American Colonizationist Society. To do that, they first had to counteract the ACS's claim to be an extender of salvation.

Birney expressed sincere belief that Black Americans would be powerful allies in missionary work, yet he also highlighted the impossibility of the ACS's goal. And indeed, the tone of his anticolonizationist pamphlet changed when he discussed African conversion. Birney pivoted from thunderous denunciations and instead used his skills as a meticulous attorney, picking apart logical flaws. He even conceded a central point, acknowledging that as the colony grew, it could provide footing for missionaries. However, he believed that the colony as it currently existed would "rather operate against their conversion." The case hinged on the belief that "nominally Christian colonies" would not yield converts.[48]

Birney went region by region in the Americas asking whether European colonization resulted in the Christianization of Indigenous peoples. He concluded that "the scorching spirit of colonial Christianity has utterly consumed them [Native peoples]."[49] Birney asserted that colonization had never worked as a means of converting. It did, however, work as a vehicle for genocide. If, however, American Christians wished to support colonization because of future hopes of effectiveness, Birney claimed that they will be "set down by the determined slaveholder of the South as full-blooded colonizationists endorsing his opinions, that slavery now, under existing circumstances is right."[50] Birney backed away from discussing conversion, confident that associating colonization with proslavery ideology would be sufficient to persuade the pious to oppose the ACS. Put another way, Birney briefly ceded conversionist discourse to colonizationists and trusted that antipathy to proslavery ideology would be enough to turn the tide against colonization. He was wrong. Other anticolonizationists knew better, including the Black Americans that remained the most reliable opponents to the ACS. Among these influential opponents were some of the very men and women who earlier had voluntarily emigrated to Liberia.

The AME missionary Daniel Coker traveled from the United States to Liberia in 1820 with joyful hope that he would convert the heathen. Thomas Brown, a free Black man, completed the reverse trip in 1834 with beleaguered relief that he had escaped a miserable death trap. Life in Liberia was wretched. Brown was a pious Methodist who had previously led classes in his Charleston, South Carolina, church; however, he, like the overwhelming majority of expatriates, did not travel to Liberia with the goal of converting Africans. He did so to pursue greater opportunities for himself and for his children. He failed.

Within the first three weeks, every member of his family grew terribly ill. Two of his three children died, as well as two of his siblings. The others survived but remained enfeebled until they escaped the colony fourteen months later. Brown had been a relatively successful carpenter in Charleston, and he immediately acquired land when he arrived in Liberia. However, land values depreciated dramatically, and Brown was unable to sell. He had two options. He could either seek to protect his land investment in the colony by obeying the ACS's injunctions to encourage additional emigration. Or he could tell the truth. Brown chose to tell the truth. Almost immediately after returning to the United States, he shared his tale of Liberian misery to any who would listen. In the growing number of anticolonizationists, he found a ready audience.[51]

In May of 1834, just as Birney defected from the ACS, Brown fielded questions from abolitionists and colonizationists in New York City. After fourteen months in Liberia, he returned to the United States and spent two days in New York discussing his experience at the invitation of the American Antislavery Society. According to Brown, progress with African conversion was at least partially offset by colonists losing their faith. He reported that two of the colonists took African wives and "adopted native customs," but he could not think of any locals who "put themselves under the protection of the colonists."[52]

The ACS recognized the danger in Brown's testimony and so ACS secretary and Presbyterian clergyman Ralph Randolph Gurley submitted his own series of questions. The ACS had attempted to control the narrative by strongly encouraging colonists to share only the blessings of life in West Africa. Yet instead of focusing on the material reality of life in West Africa, Gurley immediately invoked the conversion argument, asking, "Was it not professedly a great object with you for going to Liberia to do good to Africa?" Brown replied that he "did not go as a missionary." In fact, he reported, "my sole object was to get rid of the oppressive laws of South Carolina."[53] When asked the next day how many locals converted, Brown responded that he heard of only one man "said to be converted, but those acquainted do not think so." But Brown assured the audience that he was an enthusiastic proponent of the missionary aim. "I am glad the gentleman (Dr. Reese) interrogated me respecting the missionaries," he said, "I would not impeach their characters for all the world. They are as dear to me as to that gentleman."[54] Brown resisted the ACS's attempt to claim that only colonizationists supported African conversion.

His lofty assessment of the missionaries, however, did not extend to the colonists. When asked whether "the colonists often converse together about civilizing and Christianizing the natives," Brown replied in the negative. When asked if the colonists "act as if they considered themselves missionaries among the heathen," Brown likewise replied, "I cannot say they do." Instead, he claimed that ministers in the colony spent more of their time selling rum or engaging in party politics than planting the gospel. Again, he was asked, "What [are they] doing for the religious instruction in and near the colony?" Brown replied that churches were formed by and for those who are living in the colony, but as for other locals, "I know [the colonists] do not try to fetch them into the Christian faith." Again, he was asked, "Now tell us the actual influence of the colony at Liberia upon the native Africans?" Brown replied, "It has little or no effect."[55] The audience was incensed. The abolitionists attempted to solicit questions from the audience, but shouting made this impossible, and they closed the meeting before a riot could break out.[56]

Abolitionists continued to claim that colonists made ineffective missionaries, that a commercial colony could not Christianize the continent, and that colonization was built on a host of other mistaken assumptions. Yet throughout the 1830s and 1840s, colonizationists rebutted these critiques and trumpeted the few reports of African conversion as proof of colonization's efficacy. The lofty missionary visions of colonizationists collided with the harsh reality of reactions that ranged from ambivalence to hostility. A rapid expansion of salvation failed to sweep the continent, but colonizationists refused to temper their millennial rhetoric.

Missionary success was so ingrained in colonizationist arguments that the ACS soldiered on with millennial promises of African conversion even decades after previous promises proved false. In order to justify this duplicity, colonizationists began to focus on symbols of conversion rather than actual conversions themselves. The "devil's bush" became one of the most important of these symbols. In 1840, the *Baptist Missionary Magazine* reprinted an excerpt from the *Journal of Mr. Crocker,* a missionary in Liberia. Crocker wrote in June 1839, "At the age of about 16, the young men are permitted to go into what is called 'the devil's bush' (a patch of woods consecrated to this object)." According to Crocker, executions also took place at the devil's bush, so the space held considerable political and spiritual power.[57] The devil's bush became a common trope in colonizationist periodicals, and its eventual destruction served as proof of local conversions.

Methodist missionary George S. Brown reported that in 1840, when he went to build his home at the Heddington Mission, an Indigenous leader named King Thom fought off his carpenters and prevented them from cutting down the devil's bush. However, after conversions had taken place, King Thom was eager that lumber for the church be taken from the bush. Brown chronicled the event by writing, "'I can't pray God again,' said Thom, 'till all this Devil's Bush is cut down. Cut him down—cut him all down.'"[58] Archibald Alexander, in his history of colonization, similarly remarked that "Bob Grey, one of the principal chiefs at Bassa Cove, informed the missionaries that he had frequently sacrificed victims under a tree still standing near Edina, and celebrated "as the 'Devil's Bush.'" Alexander glowingly reported that "a Christian church is now sheltered beneath the branches of that tree."[59] The substitution of Christian churches for pagan spaces created a symbolic argument when conversions did not manifest. Colonization was always about conquering space and saving souls. When the latter did not occur, the former took on greater importance.

Still, many Black anticolonizationists continued to hold out hope for the conversion of the continent. The *Colored American* in December 1838 wished the colony "prosperity of every kind" and hoped "what wicked colonizationists meant for evil may be overruled for good." The Black newspaper distinguished missionaries from colonists, praying, "Let the American church send out her 'evangelists'. . . but let not these missionaries go out as secular colonists, as governors and as mercenary traffickers—if they do they will always be mercenary hypocrites, as we believe most who have been there, in these capacities have been."[60]

Not every Black American Christian shared this devotion to the cause of foreign missions, however. The Black activist Junius C. Morel published an open letter to the white Methodist missionary John Seys saying that "I could not, without a violation of fundamental principles, give one mite toward the support of foreign missions while millions of my own unhappy countrymen lay enshrouded in worse than heathen darkness in the land of whips and scourges."[61] For this Black man, slavery was worse than spiritual death. White Americans worried too much about an afterlife of torture when one existed in the here and how, destroying the lives of countless Black Christians.

Anticolonizationists were stricken by stories like that of Thomas Brown, the beleaguered former colonist who had testified in New York to the misery of life in the colony. By 1838 some anticolonizationists believed that they needed to outfit a rescue mission to save colonists by bringing them back to the United States. James Birney and Gerrit Smith, another colonizationist defector and abolitionist organizer, wrote a letter that was published in the *Colored American* explaining their plan and hoping to recruit an agent to go to Liberia and recruit any colonist who wanted "to escape from their present miserable circumstances." Smith and Birney were confident that they could bring back "not less than a fourth, to a half of the colonists."[62] The mission never got off the ground, but by the late 1830s, abolitionist agitation had succeeded in peeling off enough reform-minded Americans to seriously damage the movement.

Colonizationists fought back through the rhetoric of conversionism, and by the 1840s, conversionism became one of the most powerful weapons in the anti-abolitionist arsenal. The conversionist consensus had led most Americans to understand confrontational abolitionist tactics as antithetical to the progress of salvation. But the center was crumbling. Both abolitionists and proslavery agitators strained the bonds of conversionist unity. In the coming decades, these strains would split the major Protestant denominations and eventually pull apart the nation itself. But enslaved people refused to wait. Rebellion and resistance forced the issue and pressed white denominational leaders to take sides over slavery.

Rebellion and Reaction

Once again, radical Black Christianity nurtured an uncompromising and immediate insistence on emancipation. In the earliest hours of August 22, 1831, seven men sat around a small fire in the woods of Southampton County, Virginia. After six months of planning, Nat Turner and his six compatriots reviewed their plans. Turner had cultivated a charisma and seeming supernatural resolve after preaching countless sermons, testifying before both enslaved and free, and praying for God's deliverance and justice. Beyond Turner's leadership, however, a spirit of resistance had seeped through all levels of the enslaved community in Southampton, including many women and children. At two in the morning, the seven left the woods with their knives, hatchets, axes, and clubs. Creeping into the home of Turner's enslaver, Joshua Travis, the group of rebels killed the white man and his family. Traveling house to house, the band of seven grew to more than forty men and at least one woman. They eventually killed over fifty white men, women, and children. Within forty-eight hours the local militia, three artillery companies, and supporting sailors from the *USS Natchez* and *USS Warren* quelled the rebellion by killing over one hundred Black Americans, many more than were involved. Turner eluded capture for several weeks but was eventually found, tried, and hanged.[63]

Reports of what happened in Southampton echoed through every corner of the new nation, prompting scores of ministers to blame abolitionist agitation for the violence. Even in Boston, the horror and terror of the rebellion inspired an anti-abolitionist backlash. The most respected clergyman in the city and the leading figure in American Unitarianism, William Ellery Channing, wrote, "Massacre has resounded through the land"[64] and "there was never such an obligation to discuss slavery as at this moment, when recent events have done much to unsettle and obscure men's minds in regard to it."[65]

From his perch in Boston, Channing's primary goal was to consider the claim that abolitionism at least partly helped to "instigate the slave to insurrection." If true, he described this as "a crime for which no rebuke and no punishment can be too severe." Channing went further in claiming that "better were it for us to bare our own breast to the knife of the slave, than to arm him with it against his master."[66] While he opposed the violence of slavery, Channing reserved his sharpest condemnations for the Black men and women who resorted to violence and to the white abolitionists who justified these desperate attempts at securing freedom.

Always careful and quick to hedge his arguments, Channing asserted that the "charge of corrupt design, so vehemently brought against the Abolitionists, is groundless." However, he was not absolving the abolitionists completely as he affirmed that the "charge of fanaticism I have no desire to repel." According to Channing, abolitionists were not intentional instigators of rebellion, but they were dangerous fanatics whose irresponsible writings contributed to the catastrophe in Southampton County, Virginia.[67]

Resistance from the enslaved repeatedly forced white religious leaders to confront the problem of slavery throughout the antebellum era. Denominational leaders were required to comment on pressing issues of national concern, and enslaved resistance offered some of the most urgent issues in the era. We can see how the combination of slave rebellion and denominational leadership inspired William Ellery Channing, sage of American Unitarianism, to take a stand against slavery. In the age of David Walker and William Lloyd Garrison, Channing's lengthy 1835 treatise simply titled "Slavery" appeared conservative and even unoriginal, but Channing's essay created important space for anti-slavery Americans uncomfortable with the radicalism of Walker or Garrison. Understanding his turn to activism again reinforces the importance of denominational leadership to social activism.

Early Unitarians lacked the institutional structures or national reach of evangelical denominations, but the limited, informal leadership network of Unitarians followed patterns of larger, more cohesive denominations. All potential American reformers would have to develop an imagination that pushed them beyond their local context. For Channing, this was a unique struggle, as

Cambridge, Massachusetts, simultaneously possessed an unusual cosmopolitanism and a crushing insularity. This intensely literate religious community wracked itself over painstakingly nuanced theological squabbles and deeply provincial personal rivalries. A Cambridge minister could spend a lifetime of intense theological debate and professional intrigue without ever taking more than an afternoon's journey. Channing engaged deeply with the particular religious world of Cambridge and connected broadly with a network of sympathetic believers. But his emergence as a denominational leader pulled him across the Charles River and even out of New England. This expanded worldview enabled and advanced his antislavery work.

Our understanding of Channing is distorted by a tendency to emphasize the relationship between his Unitarianism and nascent transcendentalism. Conrad Wright pushes against this tendency by challenging our understanding of the mercurial divine as a romantic philosopher, arguing that "The Channing We Don't Know" is Channing as an evangelical, a Christian, and a man of affairs.[68] To this valuable contribution, we must add Channing the denominationalist. As John Lardas Modern has shown, the theological differences between evangelicals and Unitarians belie their shared commitment to their respective institutions. Despite the independence of spirit and sovereignty of conscience cherished by both evangelicals and Unitarians, religious leaders from the two traditions understood themselves as invested in institutions and their intuitional understandings framed their responses to the problem of slavery.[69]

Although rigidly independent in his thinking, Channing cared deeply about the Unitarian movement and worked intently to further its cause. In April 1819 Channing delivered his famed address "On Unitarian Christianity," the closest thing that antebellum American Unitarians would have to a founding text.[70] It is worth noting that he delivered this sermon at the ordination of Jared Sparks in Baltimore, far away from the Unitarian hearth of Cambridge. Channing veered from the usual explication of the duties of ministry, choosing instead to define Unitarian belief. The popularity of the address transformed Channing from a respected Cambridge minister into a nationally recognized denominational leader.

As he prepared this transformational sermon, Channing troubled over distant explosions of violence. In a letter fragment, probably written to Noah Worcester, Channing reflected on the threats of privateering in the Atlantic and Andrew Jackson's extralegal campaign against Seminoles. Against both he proposed sending memorials to Congress.[71] The preoccupation with distant political concerns was unusual for Channing at this stage in his career. It may very well be that his reflection on the nature of Christianity and the place of Unitarianism in the world led him to widen his field of vision beyond the Boston community, and even beyond the developing network of Unitarian churches stretching south to Baltimore from the stronghold in Cambridge.

Following his sermon, Channing showed a greater interest in fostering Unitarianism, both at home in Cambridge and in increasingly distant communities as well. In 1821 Channing founded the Berry Street Conference, which in 1825 would transform into the American Unitarian Association. By the 1820s Channing was driven less by the need to gain converts to Unitarianism and began to concern himself more with the internal purity of the movement. While preaching to Unitarians in New York City, a community in which he took particular interest, Channing wrote to Catherine Maria Sedgwick, the pious novelist with whom he maintained an active and mutually respectful correspondence. Channing reflected on the growth of Unitarianism with concern: "The numerical increase of my party is of very little object with me. Had I power, I would rather thin its ranks by dismissing not a few who call themselves Unitarians and have nothing but the name."[72] This quest for moral purity ultimately informed his denunciation of slavery.

By 1835 Channing felt that Unitarianism was strong enough to begin the process of social transformation. In earlier years, the fledgling movement had to defend itself against orthodoxy, but by 1835 Channing looked beyond Boston and saw Unitarian churches growing in New York and Baltimore. He developed correspondences with men in England, France, and Scotland and believed that the moment had come for Unitarians to purify the world they had begun to convert. The death of his former Harvard roommate Joseph Tuckerman also helped push him toward a new form of social activism.

By facilitating Tuckerman's ministry to the poor in Boston, Channing had for decades outsourced his reform energies. When his friend's health began to falter in the early 1830s, however, Channing could no longer vicariously claim the labor of his friend. In a July 1833 letter to the committee of the American Unitarian Association concerning Tuckerman's reduced duties, Channing declared that "the signs of the times point to a great approaching modification of society . . . the chief end of the social state is the elevation of all its members as intelligent and moral beings." He went on to say that "The present selfish, dis-social system must give way to Christianity" and that "the time is coming when religious bodies will be estimated by the good they do, when creeds are to be less and less the test of the Christian."[73] Unitarianism had grown sufficiently to begin seeking the transformation of the nation.

Channing's extended networks of correspondence pushed him to directly confront the problem of slavery. He wrote to his colleague Ezra Stiles Gannett that letters with friends in England had been "making me more ashamed of our country and more alive to its deep guilt, than I have ever been before."[74] Gannett and Channing exchanged numerous other letters in the fall of 1833 concerning slavery, and it was clear that Channing was growing increasingly agitated. While Channing had mentioned slavery briefly in earlier publications, his 1835 essay was his first direct discussion of the institution and the means for its removal.[75] What makes Channing's antislavery appeal so compelling is not its bold attack on the institution, for it was not bold, but rather the way in which Channing's position as a Unitarian leader inspired him to make this consequential public pronouncement.

Yet still, Channing began by condemning abolitionist attempts to incite slave revolt or violence. His call to action was restricted to elites. An issue of this great importance and emotional intensity could not be left to the mob but must be addressed exclusively in polite and educated circles. For Channing, it was not by "direct action on the mind of the slave that we can do him good."[76] In fact, northerners should be out in front in the effort "to discountenance a system of agitation on the subject of slavery, to frown on passionate appeals to the ignorant, and on indiscriminate and inflammatory vituperation of the slave-holder."[77] Antislavery action must be kept off the streets and confined to sanctuaries and parlors.

Unsurprisingly, Channing never involved himself in abolitionist organizations, preferring to work through denominational and intellectual channels. Many contemporary abolitionists criticized Channing's social reform as woefully moderate, and he, in turn, distrusted abolitionist groups, viewing them as intemperate bands of intellectual dependents. He praised individual action but looked down upon those who searched beyond their own conscience for answers, writing, "The enthusiasm of the Individual in a good cause is a mighty power. The forced, artificially excited enthusiasm of a multitude, kept together by an organization which makes them the instruments of a few leading minds, works superficially, and often injuriously."[78]

Channing was, of course, not the only religious leader to respond to the threat of slave rebellion. George Baxter, the president of the Presbyterian Hampden–Sydney College, offered his own discussion of slavery and religion a year after Channing. Comparing Channing and Baxter reveals how slave resistance pushed many denominational leaders, North and South, to oppose abolitionists. In *An Essay on the Abolition of Slavery*, Baxter sought to build a wide base of support for his anti-abolitionism, appealing to both northern and southern conversionists in claiming that slavery brought stability and salvation while abolitionism brought distraction, division, and violence.

Baxter accurately described the national reaction to abolitionists by writing that "northern people opposed the abolition doctrines as unreasonable in themselves, and as calculated to sever the union," Southerners, however, felt the threat more immediately and "considered them as a weapon aimed at the very vitals of society, as a spark thrown into a magazine whose explosion would bring instantaneous destruction on everything around it."[79] Appeals for anti-abolitionist unity proved effective, and abolitionists found that they could achieve their greatest successes not through creating a majority movement but rather by tirelessly challenging the status quo. As Elizabeth Margaret Chandler wrote, "there is more danger to be apprehended to any cause, from the lukewarmness of its pretended friends, than from the bitterest hostility of its professed enemies." Chandler recognized comfortable consensus as the greatest enemy of change, and post-1830 abolitionists succeeded in mounting a consistently unavoidable challenge to the problem of slavery that polarized the nation.[80]

The fight against abolitionism took on a greater level of urgency whenever fears of slave insurrection increased, as they certainly did after the Southampton Rebellion in 1831. Baxter placed considerable emphasis on the fear "that the evil should break forth at midnight, with an indiscriminate slaughter of all the whites of every description." This fear owed to two sources. One was the consistent agitation of abolitionists, but the other came from the very real history of slave resistance in the Americas.

While Channing fretted over the perceptions of Europeans, Baxter and other southerners' international attention focused on how slave rebellion shaped life in the Caribbean. The specter of Haiti had haunted the South for decades, and the more recent horror of Nat Turner's rebellion kept southerners on edge. Baxter manipulated this context into an attack on abolitionists, claiming, "As the white people have generally the advantage in numbers and incomparably the advantage in arms and military skill . . . there is reason to apprehend that an exasperated multitude would commence a promiscuous slaughter of the slaves."[81] Abolitionists' supposed concern for the slave were, for Baxter, belied by the reality that their agitation led only to rebellion and slaughter. Baxter then contrasted the destructive behavior of abolitionists with the paternalist care of enslavers and the compassionate ministry of the southern clergy, both of whom allegedly sought only peace and salvation for white and Black alike.

Baxter drew upon the history of late eighteenth-century manumissions while gesturing toward abstract arguments about the development of civilization to prove that slaves were unprepared for freedom. Only Christianity, Baxter claimed, could prepare these people for true freedom. In his words, "When society is brought to a high state of civilization, such as has been attained by only a few of the European nations, slavery disappears of course, and for this reason, free labor is better than slave labor." Baxter preferred free labor to slavery and dreamed of the day when the United States was ready to abandon slavery. But, according to Baxter, the slaveholding American republic could be transformed only through the advancement of Christianity, not through the political troublemaking of abolitionists. The "high state of civilization," Baxter maintained, "is never attained without the aid of Christianity."[82]

Baxter sought to encourage the philanthropic spirit behind abolitionism, while redirecting its radicalism toward the effective means of social transformation—in other words, toward Christian conversions. Baxter clarified that his protestations were against radical abolitionism, not against the antislavery movement writ large, assuring readers that "these observations are not intended to check the benevolence which would relieve the miseries of the slave, but to turn it into the proper channel." According to Baxter, "the sufferings of mankind proceed from one uniform source; and that is, the depravity or moral corruption of our nature." The solution to this depravity was not emancipation as abolitionists sought. The law might serve to obscure corruption, but why cover up a problem when you can solve it? The great sins of the day, Baxter proclaimed, "can be removed by the influence of revealed religion."[83]

This would all sound familiar to anyone engaged in eighteenth- and early nineteenth-century antislavery. The early pages of Baxter's *Essay on the Abolition of Slavery* relied on the rhetoric of traditional, consensus, conversionist antislavery. But this was 1836, and the older consensus no longer held. Conversionists, reacting to the radicalism of northern abolitionists, receded further into the arms of proslavery apologists. The remainder of Baxter's essay departed from the traditional conversionist narrative, reframing slavery from a temporary illustration of human sin to a benevolent institution of Christian love. Baxter and many other southern conversionists went so far as to claim that "slave and civil government, taken in the abstract, must go together."

After enumerating the many scripture passages that authorize slavery, Baxter made clear his belief that slavery would eventually vanish from the United States only through the "the benign principles of Christianity, brought fully to bear in a scriptural manner on both master and servant." Baxter even pointed to the British West Indies as an example of how the expansion of Christianity made it clear that the gospel "will banish slavery from the face of the whole earth." Abolitionism was not the answer, however. "This glorious effect will, I believe, be produced by the gospel in its own way; not by moving the question of abolition, and filling our domestic relations with strife."[84] Once again, the logic of conversionism allowed moderate and proslavery religious leaders to paint abolitionism as not only a dangerous distraction but also as an inhibitor of God's plan for liberation.

Baxter went even further, subverting the antislavery hermeneutics of the great Baptist theologian and abolitionist theologian Francis Wayland. Wayland's antislavery argument elevated the principles of the gospel above the precise language of scripture. The result was a historical argument for what Wayland understood to be the cautious antislavery of the gospel writers, claiming that "if [the gospel] had proclaimed the unlawfulness of slavery, and taught slaves to resist the oppression of their masters, it would instantly have arrayed the two parties in deadly hostility . . . and the very nature of Christian religion would have been forgotten amidst the agitations of universal bloodshed."[85]

Baxter joyously seized this argument as a weapon *against* abolition, promising that Christianity would eventually provide freedom for slaves whereas abolitionist agitation would only lead to bloodshed and upheaval. Baxter asked his readers, "Why do not the abolitionists follow what one of their ablest writers supposes to have been the plan of inspired teachers . . . lest they should array masters and servants in deadly hostility and prevent all the good effects of the gospel?" He declared to "all religious teachers in a slaveholding country" that they "must avoid proclaiming 'the unlawfulness of slavery' or they will defeat all the benefits of religious instruction."[86] The great danger of abolitionism, then, was not only the danger of violence but also the subversion of the gospel's emancipatory power. For Baxter and most American Christians, abolitionists were heretics to the joint gospel of salvation and white supremacy and their misguided idealism doomed souls and tightened shackles.

On a more practical level, conversionist proslavery advocates argued that abolitionists created fears among slaveholders that ultimately led to decreased opportunities for slaves' salvation. When abolitionists used Christianity as a weapon against slavery, slaveholders might decide that religion was too dangerous and accordingly prevent slaves from receiving religious instruction. "It is on this account," Baxter lamented, "that I deplore the circulation of abolition doctrines more than any other; they present the strongest barrier against the diffusion of that Christian influence, which is the only remedy for the evils of a slave-holding country." The ideology of conversionism led even a man who recognized the evils of slavery to attack abolitionists as opponents of human freedom. Because of this fear, Baxter hurriedly offered assurances to enslavers that gospel religion was of no immediate threat to their control and in fact sanctioned their authority as enslavers.[87]

Baxter's defense of slavery served also as a call to action. "I earnestly wish the southern churches to awake to their duty," Baxter pleaded, "and especially to the duty of giving religious instruction to the colored people. We know not what revolutions may be at the door, but there is one anchor of hope." The rise in sectionalist conflict had sounded an alarm throughout the South. Baxter and other conversionists sought to manipulate southerners' fear into a call to evangelize. Baxter warned that "if the southern churches should neglect the important duty of Christianizing the slave population, it is easy to see how that despised people may be made the instruments of our chastisement." Conversely, Baxter also warned abolitionists that if "the process [of slave conversion] be retarded by abolition sentiments, the authors of those sentiments will participate largely in the guilt."[88] This rhetoric shifted the fate of the slaves' souls from enslavers to abolitionists. Any misguided attempts at philanthropy would only produce ruin for the union, damnation for the enslaved, and hindrance of the national providential destiny that promised to bring the United States to new heights of glory.

The Death of Conversionist Antislavery

Other conversionists similarly attacked the new militant tone of Garrisonians and other abolitionists, including John Leland, the influential Baptist leader who in 1789 penned the Virginia Baptist antislavery petition. After his moving back to Massachusetts and as abolitionism intensified, Leland's opposition to slavery continued to soften. Little of his Revolutionary optimism or antislavery zeal remained at his death in 1841, and he used his experience in Virginia to attack abolitionists. In 1839, Leland asked any who would agitate on behalf of emancipation "to serve an apprenticeship of seven years in a slave holding state to qualify their minds to view the question in all its bearings."[89]

According to Leland, northerners without firsthand knowledge of the South could not understand the reality of slavery nor offer meaningful solutions. Three years earlier, Baxter similarly claimed that abolitionists knew nothing of life in the South, claiming that slavery "is a subject which people at a distance cannot understand, and with which they cannot interfere without injury to society, and to the slaves themselves."[90] As northern abolitionists stepped up their uncompromising rhetoric, Leland and other northern members of the conversionist antislavery consensus increasingly replaced their attacks on slavery with attacks against abolitionism.

Abolitionists continued to try to appeal to salvation as evidence of slavery's evil. As Maria Weston Chapman's 1839 history of abolitionism noted, "the great hope of the [abolitionists] was that the church might be roused by its instrumentality to put forth her moral power against slavery."[91] Lydia Maria Child's 1833 work *An Appeal in Favor of That Class of Americans Called Africans,* for example, included a lengthy argument that slavery prevented enslaved men, women, and children from hearing the gospel and developing their religious life. She claimed that "there are inconveniences attending a general diffusion of Christianity in a slave holding state—light must follow its path, and that light would reveal the surrounding darkness." According to Child, slavery could never flourish in a Christian community, and so to protect their property, enslavers ensured that Christianity remained a weak, ineffectual force in southern life.[92] She was wrong. In fact, Christianity became an essential component of the proslavery defense against abolitionism.

Southerners wielded the salvation of enslaved persons as a powerful weapon against abolitionists. The Methodist mission to the slaves, previously discussed, became essential evidence of how enslavers encouraged salvation and therefore how slavery was a component of God's plan for the nation. Much of this rhetoric came from William Capers himself, the clergyman who organized the mission. As editor of the *Southern Christian Advocate,* Capers engaged in a long-distance dispute with abolitionist Methodists publishing in the North.[93] *Zion's Herald,* published in Boston, was the most important interlocutor. Tracking this debate reveals how enslavers successfully seized the moral high ground of conversionism.

The editors of *Zion's Herald* had frequently mentioned Capers for years and published much of his correspondence concerning the coordination of missionary affairs. One notable piece mentioned Capers's defense against attempts to ban Black Methodists from sitting on the first floor of churches. While systems of racial segregation had been in existence for decades, exceptions had been made for the "accommodation of the old and infirm black members." A group of white churchgoers in Charleston, South Carolina, found this accommodation unacceptable and decreed that they "could not consent that their wives and daughters should sit on the same floor as colored people!" Dr. Capers battled back, assuring the white churchgoers these Black Methodists were "respectable men and though they were of another color, they were their brethren." The conflict eventually led to a schism, with the aggrieved white parishioners forming their own church that upheld uncompromising segregation.[94]

But the contributors and editor of *Zion's Herald* were growing restless of simply reprinting missionary reports, even those that highlighted the conversionist prowess of southern evangelicalism. In the mid-1830s, these Boston-based Methodists wrote less about the coordination of missionary activity and instead increasingly turned to discussions of slavery, temperance, and other social reform issues. In 1837 Capers's relationship to *Zion's Herald* faltered when he founded the *Southern Christian Advocate*. This Charleston-based periodical would serve as a sort of rival to *Zion's Herald*, and little time elapsed before the two publications grew antagonistic toward one another, presaging the 1844 division of the national Methodist Church.

Debates over slavery directly motivated the creation of the new southern publication. In a July 1837 notice by *Zion's Herald*, Capers justified the new paper by referencing "the peculiar political aspect of the times" owing to "the feeling, which is known to pervade all classes of men on the subject of our domestic institutions."[95] Just three months later, the abolitionist convictions of *Zion's Herald* proved inescapable. The September 20, 1837, edition included an abolitionist poem by Thomas Campbell. The Scotsman's poem mocked the United States, "where boasted freedom waves her Fustian flag in mockery over slaves!"[96] A few pages after reports of conversions at camp meetings in northern states, as well as the prospects of conversion in Chile and France, the same issue called for immediate emancipation.

Mocking southern claims that "they must be prepared for freedom," *Zion's Herald* asserted that "the surest way to prepare a man for slavery is to make him a slave, so the surest and best way to prepare a man for freedom is to make him free." The most important and substantial part of the article, however, attacked the logic of conversionist antislavery, claiming that converting slaves increases the power of masters by "mak[ing] them more obedient and content to be slaves."[97] No longer was conversion understood as a tool for liberation for these northern Methodists.

Conversion, while of course necessary, was presented as an insufficient response to the problem of slavery. The tone grew stronger throughout the volume as an anonymous article titled "Methodist Abolitionism" attacked southerners as deserving of "censure and reproach," asserting that "I never did believe, and never shall, that the love of God can be in the heart of that man who claims, holds, and treats his fellow-men as property; nor would I give to that man any mark or token of Christian fellowship whatever."[98] Shared commitments to Christian salvation were no longer sufficient. Abolitionists demanded purity.

Many Methodist leaders worked to restrain these heated pronouncements. Bishop Elijah Hedding issued a pronouncement in 1837 responding to Methodist abolitionism. Heddings echoed an antislavery position but provided room for proslavery apologists. A committee working with Heddings at the Genesee Conference on Slavery, held in Rochester, New York, resolved that the issue of slavery was "subordinate and not paramount, to the high and awful ends of that ministry to which we are voluntarily and solemnly devoted."[99] The imperatives of conversion, even for those who opposed slavery, were now a weapon used to oppose the expansion of abolitionism.

Despite the efforts of some church administrators to quell these hostilities, the end of 1837 left northern and southern Methodist periodicals at war with one another. In the November 1 issue, the *Zion's Herald* reprinted an attack from the *Southern Christian Advocate* that accused the northern periodical of hypocrisy for simultaneously attacking the southern church and rejoicing in the region's revivals. For William Capers, the South's ability to generate conversions both protected the region from abolitionists' attacks and proved the righteousness of its institutions, including slavery.

The trump card in the debate proved to be the high ground of millennial conversionism. As Capers wrote to the editors of *Zion's Herald*, "We adopt the language of the Herald, and say, (or rather he adopts our sentiments and puts them into words when *he* says,) 'O for the coming days when the salvation of the soul, and the advancement of the glory of god shall be the absorbing topic of thought, conversation and action among men!'" For Capers, the abolitionist meddling of the northern Methodist organ was nothing but a distraction from the church's true mission. For their part, the northern editors included personal attacks on their former partner, questioning their former belief "that Dr. Capers was not only a Christian but a gentleman—a man no less distinguished for his urbanity than for his piety."[100] In February of the next year, another abolitionist writer attacked Capers and all southerners, claiming that "the complicated sin of slavery fixes their character beyond dispute."[101]

As abolitionism gained traction within northern Methodist circles, conversionism transformed from a passive antislavery expectation into an active proslavery weapon. Southern Methodists drew on the conversionist consensus to defend their peculiar institution. Many proslavery apologists produced detailed explications of scripture, demonstrating biblical sanction for slavery, but scriptural arguments never held the power of appeals to the old conversionist consensus.

Anti-abolitionism was, of course, not confined to the South. Abolitionists remained a loathed minority throughout the antebellum era, and abolitionists were targeted everywhere they went. Northern ministers, like their southern brethren, wielded conversionism as a weapon against abolitionism. In an 1833 sermon in Vermont, Rev. Joseph Tracy proclaimed that distorted understandings of human equality had been the cause of terrible suffering. He began by attacking the radicals of the French Revolution before moving on to the advocates of wealth redistribution in the United States and the abolition of marriage. These terrifying bogeymen served as a prelude to what he understood as the most pressing danger in New England: abolitionists.

Tracy built on the discussion of family dynamics to create a metaphor comparing slaves to children: both were entitled to their liberty only when they reached an age they could use it appropriately. According to Tracy, slaves needed an education before they could earn their freedom. An education for Tracy, however, did not involve academic development but rather Christian nurture. Tracy spent most his document laying out a lengthy list of Christian lessons that must be passed along to slaves, highlighting "the Christian duty of governing the passions."[102] Emancipation without salvation merely portended ruin and race war. If Christians sought the end of slavery, they had to commit to encouraging conversions.

Tracy rejoiced that the conversion of the slaves was already well underway, citing an account of a slaveholding missionary who devoted his life to converting slaves in Georgia. The history of the early church proved to Tracy that the expansion of conversion would eliminate slavery in the United States. American conversionist efforts would "have the same effect, which it had when Paul preached it and men embraced it at Athens and at Rome." According to Tracy, if Americans would harness the same gospel as the apostle Paul, simply put, "it will abolish slavery."[103]

One year later, Simon Clough of Fall River, Massachusetts, echoed Tracy's logic but heightened the stakes, proclaiming in his very subtitle that "clergymen engaged in the dissemination of [abolitionist] principles should be dismissed from their congregations."[104] Clough made this address in response to the formation of the American Antislavery Society (AAS) and opened his document by reprinting the AAS Declaration of Sentiments. Based on the demands for immediate abolition included therein, "no minister of the Gospel," he affirmed, "can consistently become a member of that Society or advocate its measures."[105]

He began his attack with an anthropological division of humanity into five stages of development, attempting to demonstrate that slavery under a civilized people is preferable to a life of unbridled barbarism. After a long analysis of scripture, Clough concluded with a description of how Christian slaves and Christian enslavers should come together through the power of the gospel, promising that "if these relative duties between the slave and his master were duly observed, the horrors of slavery would for ever cease." Clough contrasted this dream with the inevitable result of abolitionism, namely "the horrors of civil war—our wives and children will be massacred—our fields will be covered with the slain—and the fairest portions of our country will be drenched in the blood of our fellow citizens."[106]

Few antislavery moderates went as far as Clough did. A more common response is epitomized in the creation of the American Union for the Relief and Improvement of the Colored Race (AURICR). In 1835, a number of prominent religious leaders in and around Boston joined together to create a middle ground between proslavery apologists and uncompromising abolitionists.

The first paragraph of the AURICR's *Exposition of the Object and Plans* includes a dramatic conversionist plea, identifying their purpose as "that great design in which all truly Christian enterprises unite and center." That is, of course, "establishing everywhere, and in every heart, the kingdom which is righteousness and peace and joy, and in which there is neither Barbarian nor Scythian, bond nor free, but Christ the common savior and Lord, the great restorer from moral corruption, the great deliverer from the oppression of malignant powers and from the darkness and bitterness of human woe."[107] The cornerstone of offering aid to slaves included the promise of "bringing Christianity into free and effectual contact with that great portion of our population, which, now, these influences do not affect at all, or at the best, touch only inadequately and at a disadvantage."[108]

For these Christians, abolition was a shared goal; indeed, they decreed that "we seek the abolition of this slavery." However, unlike William Lloyd Garrison, the American Antislavery Society, or other abolitionist groups, the AURICR proclaimed that "we seek it, not indeed as the ends of our association, but as a means to our end, or rather as the removal of an obstacle which cannot be surmounted." To make their attack on slavery, the AURICR privileged the establishment of God's Kingdom on Earth as the ultimate end, a goal dependent upon both abolition and national conversion. Embodying an antislavery middle ground, the AURICR claimed their mandate from the reality that "there are churches, there are ministers of the gospel, there are benevolent, active and influential individuals, who, it is believed are ready and solicitous to combine their exertions for the welfare of the colored people."

The Christianization of the United States had created a critical mass prepared to complete the holy work of abolition. To abolitionists who claimed that the promotion of Christianity "ma[d]e Christianity serve as the guardian angel of slavery," the union emphasized "the elastic spirit of Christian enterprise, which seeks the conversion of every creature." The emphasis on conversion, or the "elastic spirit," promised the surest route for a national consensus. The expansion of conversion, according to these Christians, was already succeeding in its work of liberation, for "in the districts where these efforts are begun, the slave is beginning to be regarded not merely as a chattel, but as a man, and that slavery is there about to arrive [at] . . . peaceful abolition."[109]

Joseph Tracy, the moderate clergyman who delivered the cautious attack on abolitionists in Vermont, rejoiced at the formation of the AURICR. Tracy argued that the work of John Young, a Presbyterian missionary to slaves in Kentucky, demonstrated that the national conversionist antislavery movement was destined to succeed. Speaking confidently about Young, Tracy declared that "those who are with us—in Kentucky especially—are already engaged in efficient, direct labors for the termination of slavery, in the shortest possible time, and the best possible way."[110]

But these plans came to naught. The AURICR failed to gain support from southerners, and less than a year after its formation the society disbanded. In a defeated tone, Reverend Nehemiah Adams spoke at the final meeting, telling his audience that "[God] is calling to us in these times of trouble; Come my people, enter thou into thy closet, and shut the doors about thee, hide thyself for a little moment, until the indignation be overpast." This battle was clearly over, and the forces of slavery had won. Adams cautioned fellow New Englanders, "Let us not throw ourselves upon the tempest from a mistaken bravery, or from such a sense of obligation and responsibility in regard to public events as will jeopardize our own private spiritual peace."[111]

Adams and the AURICR retreated from public reform and instead clung to the safety of spiritual quietism. The world was burning with a great tempest, and godly Americans now had no recourse but to shelter themselves in their own private spiritual peace. No clearer death knell for conversionist antislavery could have sounded, and the antislavery ground in New England would be ceded to the new, confrontational, purificationist abolitionism epitomized by Garrison and his American Antislavery Society.

◇◇◇◇ 6 ◇◇◇◇

Slavery and Schism,
1837–1845

BEGINNING IN THE LATE 1830s, debates over slavery strained and then shattered the bonds of salvation. Abolitionists avowed that slavery was a sin and that sin meant that enslavers could not carry the message of salvation. A new generation of proslavery Christians disagreed violently, claiming that not only was slavery not a sin, it was a divine institution designed to preserve and extend American salvation. A third, larger group of American Christians tried to strike a middle ground, claiming that the institution was a moral wrong, but those who participated in that institution may not themselves be sinning. For these voices in the middle, it was imperative that all American Christians should remain united in the goal of expanding American salvation.

The question of the sinfulness of slavery was explosive. However, an even greater threat came after abolitionists began to assert that enslavers could not serve as missionaries. This allegation cut at the very heart of American religious nationalism. To make matters worse, abolitionists began to oppose the very union of the United States, insisting on an uncompromising purification of all national institutions as a precursor to cooperation of any kind. The nation was ripping at its seams. For decades, national denominations and their campaigns for conversion had been among the strongest points of intersectional unity. No longer unified in the mission of extending salvation, Presbyterians, Methodists, and Baptists all splintered. Tracking the new purificationism of the 1840s and the ensuing divisions within each of these churches demonstrates how conflicts over slavery and salvation set the scene for the nation's undoing.

The loss of national religious bodies cost the United States three of its most powerful intersectional institutions as well as a source of moral authority that could have served as the best hope at avoiding the violence of war. Churches North and South not only failed to prevent the war, but, in fact, pushed the nation on the path to violence. On the eve of secession, the long-unifying discourse of extending salvation no longer held the nation together, as decades earlier that very same discourse broke national denominations apart. Conversionism created American national religious cultures in the early republic and fueled their fracture in the late 1830s and mid-1840s. The bonds of salvation both created and destroyed the United States.

Historians have long observed that the nation's churches pushed the nation toward war.[1] Historian Mark Noll has rightly noted how a theological crisis over hermeneutics (how to read the Bible) preceded and fueled the secession crisis.[2] Proslavery Southerners held the high ground of literalism, as both Old and New Testaments included literal sanctions for enslaving. Abolitionist Christians in the North responded by moving away from this way of reading the Bible, giving birth to the liberal Protestantism that would blossom over the late nineteenth and early twentieth centuries.[3] The struggle to find common readings of the Bible presented a terrifying challenge to a nation that invested so much authority in scripture, and the fallout of this crisis transformed American religion.

The hermeneutical crisis, however, was not enough to sunder national ties. Only disputes over how to extend national salvation could do that. Denominations rose and fell based on campaigns for conversion. In the late eighteenth and early nineteenth centuries, denominational bodies had formed to coordinate the extension of salvation. These campaigns united denominational bodies in ways that nothing else could, and denominational leaders worked from the beginning to suppress the explosive potential of abolitionism to undercut national unity. Yet abolitionists grew increasingly unwilling to tolerate these suppressions. Following the lead of Black activists, abolitionist ministers forced their denominations to confront the realities of slaving within their religious communities and eventually began to insist that enslavers could not serve as agents of salvation. These claims struck at the very heart of American religion: the quest to convert souls and the optimistic faith that those conversations promised salvation for the nation and for the world.

By the 1830s, abolitionists drew on a long-established purificationist impulse. However, unlike earlier activists such as Samuel Hopkins and the Quakers, this new generation foregrounded the belief that enslavers could not be trusted with the sacred duty of extending American salvation. Unlike earlier generations of Quakers, these abolitionists would no longer rest contented in personal purity or in the purity of their religious communities. They sought to save the nation from the sin of slavery and its demonic defenders. According to abolitionists, Christian piety required activism. So even if enslavers could grow the church, this new generation of abolitionists asked whether union with sin would destroy the national project of American salvation. These issues directly caused the destruction of the national Methodist and Baptist churches. The Presbyterian case was more complicated, but questions over salvation and abolitionism here also animated the split.

In all three cases, conflict emerged after the 1830s abolitionist purification movements. Proslavery churchmen fought back with new claims that slavery was not only tolerable but actually preferable to the exploitations of wage laborers in the northern states. This attempt to sanctify slavery never fully succeeded, but neither did the work of moderates who appealed to the old conversionist consensus as a means of diffusing abolitionist purification campaigns. The voices on the margins grew louder.

Expectations of conversion and efforts to coordinate its pursuit formed America's national religious cultures and the denominations they supported. Divergent understandings of how to extend salvation and the role of conversions in the fight against slavery destroyed the most powerful force in American religion. Beginning in the 1830s with the Presbyterians and culminating in the 1840s with the Methodists and then the Baptists, the loss of this force destroyed the nation's three largest denominations. The result was catastrophic for national unity. Conversionism failed, and secession approached.

Presbyterians

"The religious men of the country," the *Presbyterian Herald* asserted in November 1860, "stand apart to so great an extent in this hour of trial." With the nation itself near dissolution, this Louisville publication proclaimed that "most of the Churches have split on the very rock upon which the state is foundering. In fact, their divisions have prepared the way and laid the political foundations for the political divisions which now exist."[4] The Presbyterians knew well how religious schisms could inspire political division, as they were the first major denomination to split. Historians have disagreed on the relative influence of slavery in driving the Presbyterian division.[5] Certainly both slavery and theology divided Americans throughout the nineteenth century, and when combined, particularly in relation to issues of extending salvation, they simply proved too much to bear.

Unlike later denominational divisions, it appeared on the surface that slavery played a secondary role in the Presbyterian schism. Debates over salvation officially drove the church apart. Beginning with the Great Revival in 1800 and then accelerating after the Finneyite revivals in the 1820s, the Presbyterian General Assembly struggled to reconcile the New School supporters of revival and their Old School opponents. By the mid-1830s, glowing embers of resentment burst into open flames of antipathy. Theological debates over revival methods sparked the blaze, but debates over abolitionism provided the tinder and later fueled the inferno.[6]

In 1834, members of the Old School issued an incendiary appeal to the General Assembly calling for both the dissolution of the 1801 Plan of Union between Presbyterians and Congregationalists and an end to the New School's missionary methods. According to these complainants, Presbyterians had prioritized evangelism over traditional ecclesiology and Calvinist orthodoxy, but now the Old School would no longer tolerate this compromise. Old School critics claimed that New School conversions did not lead souls into an appropriate understanding of the faith and therefore distracted from the true mission of the church.

The memorial began by asserting that the Presbyterian Church was in a state of sin. The authors claimed that while "her purity is tarnished," it was true that "the Church may yet be purified."[7] The root complaint charged the Plan of Union with preventing rigorous Presbyterian oversight and enabling missionaries to encourage unorthodox and maybe even heretical doctrines. For the Old School, conversion without rigorous Calvinist theology was no conversion at all. Still, New Schoolers retained control of the General Assembly and decided to ignore the complaint. Rebuffed, Old Schoolers shifted tactics and instead attempted to eliminate influential New School leaders.

The synod of the Western Reserve served as the flashpoint between the Old and New Schools as well as between abolitionists and their opponents. This region of northern Ohio harbored many of the most prolific revivalists and uncompromising abolitionists in the Presbyterian church. Four notable events took place in 1835 that accelerated the controversy over both revivals and abolitionism. In this year, Charles Grandison Finney took up a position at Oberlin College, the synod of the Western Reserve adopted an abolitionist resolution, and the Old School initiated two heresy trials against New School antislavery leaders. These four events sowed the seeds of distrust that would soon choke the life from Presbyterian unity.

The arrival of Finney at Oberlin entrenched the new revivalism in the

Western Reserve. This, coupled with a provocative resolution from the Western Reserve synod, proved to anti-abolitionists and antirevivalists alike that the region must be either expelled or reformed. The synod exposed its abolitionist convictions by resolving "that slavery as it exists in the United States is a sin against God, a high-handed trespass on the rights of man; a great physical, political, and social evil, which ought to be immediately and universally abandoned."[8] In truth, New Schoolers included both abolitionists and moderates, but Old Schoolers lumped together the new revival with the new antislavery and vilified both. The very existence of the synod of the Western Reserve owed its existence to the Plan of Union and so orthodox partisans wed their anti-abolitionism and antirevivalism in opposition to the partnership between Congregationalists and Presbyterians.

Two heresy trials followed in that same year. The first targeted Albert Barnes, who in 1834 had published a book that questioned the doctrine of original sin and the traditional interpretation of justification by faith.[9] Barnes had already been under fire for his theology, having been acquitted in 1830.[10] But the publication of his work inspired the Second Philadelphia Presbytery to levy new charges against the man who perhaps more than any other codified the theology of the New School.

In the second trial, Joshua Lacy Wilson, pastor of First Presbyterian of Cincinnati, charged Lyman Beecher "with the sin of hypocrisy" and "dissimulation in important religious matters."[11] Specifically, Wilson was angry at Beecher's support of the new measures of revival. Beecher had originally opposed Charles Finney's techniques, even threatening that should Finney arrive in Connecticut, Beecher would "call out all the artillerymen and fight every inch of the way to Boston."[12] By the mid-1830s, however, Beecher supported many of these same techniques, to the dismay of many Presbyterian leaders. Both Barnes and Beecher were ultimately acquitted, but their Old School opponents were nonetheless emboldened.

Nearly all abolitionist Presbyterians advocated the new methods of revivalism. In this way, debates over conversion became inextricably enmeshed with the backlash against abolitionism. The heresy trials of Albert Barnes and Lyman Beecher played out against this backlash. Barnes later penned two abolitionists tracts, one of which would later be quoted by Frederick Douglass in his famed speech asking, "What to the Slave Is the Fourth of July?" In this speech, Douglass proclaimed, "Albert Barnes but uttered what the common sense of every man at all observant of the actual state of the case will receive as truth, when he declared that 'There is no power out of the church that could sustain slavery an hour, if it were not sustained in it.'"[13] Before he penned these words, Barnes had been annoying his Presbyterian colleagues with his abolitionist agitations. Beecher was initially an antislavery moderate, and he attempted to quell the radicalism of the so-called Lane Rebels whose abolitionism threatened to tear apart the seminary during his presidency. Still, in the mind of many southerners, he remained associated with radical abolitionism.[14]

The New School had previously dominated the General Assembly, and the abolitionist evangelist Theodore Dwight Weld estimated that abolitionists comprised nearly a fourth of delegates at the 1835 meeting.[15] However, Old Schoolers took control of the opening session of that meeting and proceeded to strike down many New School initiatives, especially those that involved cooperation with Congregationalists for the purpose of evangelism. Abolitionists still managed to present several petitions, including one that called slaveholding "a heinous sin." The General Assembly created a committee to respond to these petitions and resolved that slavery was "an evil of immense magnitude" and that Presbyterians should "use all proper means" to secure abolition.[16]

This tentative step triggered a fierce counterattack. James Smylie of Mississippi authored a tract addressing the charge that slavery was "a heinous sin." Smylie disagreed, and he blamed abolitionist dissension for the church's "little success attending the means of grace." According to Smylie, abolitionists hampered "the efforts of the Church for the extension of the Redeemer's kingdom."[17] Critics like Smylie charged abolitionists with advancing faulty theology and, worse, hindering salvation, the primary purpose of the church. According to Smylie, slavery brought salvation; abolitionism brought idolatry and death. The Princeton theologian Charles Hodge also took aim at the abolitionist petitions, claiming "to declare it [slavery] to be a heinous crime, is a direct impeachment of the word of God!" Hodge still had hope for emancipation through conversionism, however, and he proclaimed that only the effort to Christianize the South would enable "a peaceable and speedy extinction of slavery."[18] According to Hodge, abolition was a distraction, a heresy, and an obstacle to emancipation.

This anti-abolitionist backlash succeeded, and a committee charged with proposing a policy on slavery concluded that doing so "would tend to distract and divide the churches."[19] James H. Dickey, a member of the committee from the abolitionist Chillicothe Presbytery, submitted a revealing dissenting report that demonstrated the inability of abolitionists to acquiesce to the old conversionist consensus. Dickey captured the old conversionist consensus by writing, "the hope has been indulged and expressed by former assemblies, that a state of things so inconsistent with the maxims of Christianity would yield to the light of Divine truth, and be destroyed by the brightness of the Gospel, without the direct exercise of discipline."[20] Presbyterians had refused to purify the church of slavery and instead relied on conversionism to solve the problem.

But conversionism would no longer pacify Dickey and other abolitionists. Conversionism had "been used, not to put away the evil, but to give it strength, fortify its position, and spread a shield around it to defend it against the shafts of divine truth."[21] Abolitionists like Dickey increasingly believed that slavery was simply a sin, and as Christians needed to purify themselves of sin, American Christians must eliminate slavery. But anti-abolitionists still held sway and they built momentum for an aggressive condemnation of abolitionism as a distraction of the holy work of the church. The majority of Presbyterians remained in the middle of the two extremes, and they grew tired of the back and forth, successfully moving "that this whole subject be indefinitely postponed."[22] The motion carried, and the stalemate endured, at least for a while. Both abolitionists and their opponents would continue to press the issue.

Southern members remained suspicious of antislavery sympathies among the northern Old School clergy, and so Old School leaders worked to cultivate unity. They did so by attacking the widely loathed abolitionists as opponents of American salvation. Samuel Miller, a Princeton theologian, wrote an open letter to Virginia's John McElhenny that editors published in both the Philadelphia-based *Presbyterian* and the *Charlotte Observer*. Miller assured McElhenny and others that he and the northern Old School clergy believed "our abolition brethren . . . are every day deeply wounding the cause of religion."[23] The Old School included both proslavery and antislavery members; however, nearly all Old Schoolers united in denouncing the activism of Presbyterian abolitionists as inhibiting the spread of salvation.

By emphasizing unity through their shared distaste for abolition and the new methods of revival, the Old Schoolers won control of the General Assembly again in 1837 and immediately ejected four New School synods.[24] These four created their own General Assembly that same year, and several other synods peeled off to join this new body. On May 17, 1838, the two general assemblies both met at Seventh Presbyterian Church in Philadelphia. The Old School held a meeting at the front of the sanctuary and the New School held their own in the back. For everyone in the church, the situation was clear.

American Presbyterianism had been severed.[25] Later that year, the Presbytery of Hopewell in South Carolina rejoiced that the schism meant "all the Acts of the General Assembly legislating on the subject of slavery [were] null and void."[26] In truth, both sides of the schism backed away from action on slavery, but Presbyterian southerners had mostly managed to isolate themselves from religious fellowship with abolitionists.

The *Cincinnati Journal and Luminary* interpreted the schism as entirely the result of proslavery agitation: "It is not the standards which were to be protected, but the system of slavery."[27] Old Schoolers denied this initially, but by 1845, a writer in the Old School publication the *New York Observer* wrote, "the subject of slavery was one of the principal and most exciting topics of discussion, which fired the breasts of the disputants, and eventually formed one of the lines of final separation."[28] Lyman Beecher agreed and blamed proslavery firebrands for the schism, claiming "'twas slavery that did it." According to Beecher, southern ministers listened to the paranoia of politicians and "they got scared about abolition."[29]

Presaging the panicked southern hysteria over the Republican Party in 1860, southern Presbyterians greatly exaggerated the influence of abolitionism among American Presbyterians. Nonetheless, the consistent purificationist campaigning of a few abolitionist clergymen managed to foster a spirit of sectional distrust. When coupled with debates over the means of extending conversion, distrust turned into outright antipathy.

Several southern presbyteries sided with the New School in the split. However, repeated abolitionist appeals strained even New School unity. By 1850, these abolitionist agitations resulted in a reaffirming of Ashbel Green's 1818 Presbyterian General Assembly declaration. This earlier resolution, now renewed in 1850, declared that "the voluntary enslaving of one part of the human race by another as utterly inconsistent with the law of God," and all Christians were obligated "as speedily as possible to efface this blot on our holy religion, and to obtain the complete abolition of slavery throughout Christendom."[30]

Yet the 1850 renewal included the heightened charge that slavery "is an offense in the proper import of that term as used in the book of discipline." Local Presbyterian leaders were called to treat slaveholding "in the same manner as other offenses" and thereby purify the church of slavery.[31] Leaving enforcement to local leaders meant that southerners generally ignored the ruling until 1857, when twenty-one southern Presbyterians severed all connection with the New School General Assembly and instead formed the United Synod of the Presbyterian Church in the United States of America, later rebranded the United Synod of the South. Old Schoolers were stronger in their anti-abolitionist convictions and held together until secession drove them apart as well.

Proslavery ministers continued to emphasize the importance of converting slaves. Theodore Clapp, in an 1838 sermon before First Congregationalist Church in New Orleans, looked to the scriptures and concluded, "The object of New Testament preaching was not the emancipation of slaves, but their conversion to the faith and hopes of the gospel. Such should be the object of preachers at the present day."[32] The loss of the Plan of Union and the schism of the Presbyterian General Assembly only increased the importance of salvation in the contest between the North and South and between slavery and freedom.

The 1837 schism in the Presbyterian church occurred primarily over conflicts surrounding the meaning and means of salvation, but the specter of slavery haunted the debates and helped to build animosity between theological camps. Despite the schism, tensions over slavery would only grow in the coming years. Southern Presbyterian ministers increasingly encouraged the uncompromising sectionalism that led to secession. W. T. Hamilton, an Old School Presbyterian minister in Mobile, complained over un-Christian treatment from northern Presbyterians, claiming that they sinned when they denied communion to enslavers. However, in 1844, rather than turning the other cheek, he unequivocally claimed that every abolitionist "ought to be cut off from the communion of the church."[33]

The eventual sectional splits in both the New School and Old School stemmed more directly over debates on slavery and secession. In the two larger Protestant denominations, schism resulted even more directly over slavery. Yet here too, the bonds of salvation snapped only when the Americans disagreed as to whether enslavers could serve as agents of conversion. In the same year that Hamilton advocated the expulsion of all abolitionist Presbyterians, the collision of slavery and salvation destroyed the Methodist Episcopal Church, the nation's largest Protestant denomination.

But between the 1837 schism of the Presbyterian General Assembly and the 1844 dissolution of the Methodist Episcopal Church, a new purificationist movement arose that accelerated the antipathy between abolitionists and their enemies. Beginning in the early 1840s, abolitionists looked to purification with renewed zeal, convinced that American salvation must begin by purifying the nation of the sin of slavery. According to these abolitionists, any opponent of that purity was an opponent of the true gospel. Salvation required a pure nation.

Disunionism

The 1840s brought a shift in the abolitionist movement. The earlier emphasis on moral suasion, with its conversionist confidence that Americans would come to see the sinfulness of slavery, weakened, and a new uncompromising push for purification grew among abolitionists. If the United States would fail to turn toward the gospel of liberty and instead continue to bow to the demon of human bondage, then the nation must be damned. Abolitionists took aim not only against slavery, but also against all that protected it. And that included the American union.

Abolitionists increasingly believed that either enslavers had to be purged from the nation or Christians must purge themselves from a slaving United States. In pursuing this mission, abolitionists replaced an earlier emphasis on moral suasion with a new purificationist push toward disunionism. Abolitionist disunionists decried the Constitution as a compact with the devil. Southerners responded by calling for the complete elimination of abolitionism from American public life in order to protect their Christian work of expanding salvation among both the enslaved and free. The two sides grew unwilling to tolerate the existence of one another, and the conversionist middle failed to quell the incendiary attacks that set the nation ablaze. Southern religious leaders came to see slavery as an essential ally to salvation, and in order to protect both, they would eventually celebrate the dissolution of the Union through secession. But it was abolitionists, not their southern opponents, that issued the loudest calls for disunion in the 1840s.

Disunionism in the North began with an attack on the clergy. By 1842, many abolitionists began to see the clergy as enemies of liberty and distorters of the gospel. Abolitionists targeted the northern clergy's tepid conversionist antislavery as a moral abomination. Abolitionists would not prioritize the salvation of souls over the liberation of bodies, and they justified this emphasis by emphasizing the importance of purity. What conversionists saw as prioritizing spiritual matters, abolitionists attacked as an embrace of sin. The debate over whether to prioritize conversion or purification in reckoning with slavery now threatened every national institution. Its first casualties would be the nation's churches.

Anti-abolitionist religious leaders had worked for decades to protect their conversionist missions from the untiring abolitionist activists who refused to be cowed by calls for unity or the prioritization of conversion. By 1842, abolitionists in Massachusetts maintained that all but a few ministers in New England "have proved themselves, by their own professions, a great brotherhood of thieves."[34] As a result, these abolitionists claimed that conversionists had forfeited their roles as ministers of the gospel. One could not, they claimed, serve as an agent of salvation without taking an uncompromising stand against both slavery and enslavers. Clerical resistance to this attack was predictable. Ministers refused to embrace immediatism by claiming "infidelity will gain ground and hinder the conversion of the heathen."[35] The pursuit of conversions remained an essential religious justification for resisting abolitionism, but abolitionists would not relent, and soon they would add a new political rhetoric that both drew on and fueled the quest for religious purity.

At the same Massachusetts meeting that attacked the anti-abolitionist clergy, William Lloyd Garrison justified his support of disunionism by prioritizing religious purity. Notably, Garrison did not mention the salvation of souls but rather claimed that "the primary duties of every people" is "to reverence justice, to cherish liberty, and to promote righteousness."[36] Garrison could not imagine a Christian nation without first achieving abolition. In his view, salvation was impossible without purity. In the April 29, 1842, edition of the *Liberator*, Garrison decreed that there was no point in appealing to religious unity "until the professed Christian churches in our land are reclaimed from their apostacy." With the nationally unifying force of religious authority nullified, Garrison then took aim at the nation itself.

The purificationism of Garrison would find an even more compelling carrier in the Christianity of Frederick Douglass. Douglass refused to accept the Christianity of enslavers as actual Christianity. In this, he followed many abolitionists before him, including, perhaps most notably, David Walker. Douglass ended his 1845 *Narrative of the Life of Frederick Douglass, an American Slave*, by directly distilling the purificationist message. He wrote, "Between the Christianity of this land, and the Christianity of Christ, I recognize the widest possible difference."[37] For Douglass, and for many other abolitionists, there was a true gospel of love, liberty, and equality, and there was a false god of greed, cowardice, and slavery. The abolitionist message was clear: there could be no national salvation without national emancipation.

Disunionism inspired a vocal backlash. Not even all abolitionists agreed with the disunionists. In fact, Douglass himself came to reject disunionism in 1851, seeing it as surrendering the high ground of the United States Constitution. Douglass recognized the national commitment to white supremacy, yet he still believed that the founding documents of the United States served the cause of emancipation. Many other abolitionists agreed and threw their support behind the Liberty Party and its attempt to build an electoral movement around abolitionism. But the specific debate as to whether abolitionists should work within or without the system became less important than broader questions about whether God was with or against the United States of America.

The overwhelming majority of Americans were uninterested in overthrowing white supremacy, but most Americans continued to see their nation as the embodiment of God's will for humanity and the vehicle for saving the world. An article in the abolitionist *New York Evangelist* articulated the dominant view that the United States was a divine body, established by God for the salvation of the world. The author proclaimed "THE AMERICAN UNION MUST AND WILL BE PRESERVED, nay more—that it must and will be more thoroughly cemented and more widely extended." The United States would continue its practice of conquest and domination, fulfilling its manifest destiny as an agent of global salvation. But what about slavery? The author lambasted slavery but confidently predicted, "it will be abolished—we are sure of it—we know it." God hated slavery, and therefore it could not long endure. American salvation was already at work, and God would soon complete the work of abolition.[38] William Ellery Channing similarly asserted, "The Union is an inestimable good" and then attacked the purificationist impulses of disunionists.[39]

These moderate appeals did little to mollify disunionists. The tenth annual meeting of the American Antislavery Society voted "nearly three to one" to change the header of the *Liberator* to include their new purificationist rallying cry, "NO UNION WITH SLAVEHOLDERS." Moreover, the AAS undercut the logic of conversionism, asserting "revolutionary ground should be occupied by all those who abhor the thought of doing evil that good may come." Allowing the continuation of American slavery was an evil and the future promise of American salvation could not be used to justify perpetuating that evil. For an increasing number of purificationist abolitionists, abolition meant salvation, and slavery meant damnation. No political compromise or conversionist gambit could supersede the need to purify. As a result, the United States needed to be destroyed. The resolution continued, "The existing national compact should be instantly dissolved," for the AAS believed "secession from the government is a religious and political duty."[40]

The same spirit of purity that propelled political disunionism also divided denominational leaders. Abolitionists never successfully seceded from the United States. However, they did successfully secede from the Methodist Episcopal Church, the largest Protestant denomination in the nation. By the mid-1840s, however, the problem of slavery and salvation could no longer simply be blamed on a few disruptive abolitionists. Even after the defection of Methodist abolitionists, the national denomination failed to maintain unity. More and more Christians came to believe that enslavers could not serve as agents of salvation. At the same time, more and more southern Christians came to see slavery as an essential component of their Christian nation. This collision between slavery and salvation would tear apart both the Methodist and the Baptist churches.

Methodists

The Methodist Episcopal Church was the largest Protestant denomination in antebellum America, but slavery had been straining its unity from the very beginning.[41] John Wesley was unequivocal in describing the slave trade as "that execrable sum of all villanies," characterizing American slavery as "the vilest that ever saw the sun."[42] Yet the pursuit of salvation overcame the purificationist tendencies of early American Methodists, and the denomination only maintained unity by continuing to prioritize conversion over purification, isolating abolitionism as an enemy of salvation.

By the 1830s, abolitionist Methodists adopted a new militant purificationism. Their activism prompted swift and powerful resistance as most Methodists continued to hope that expanding salvation would solve the problem of American slaving. Anti-abolitionists, who made up a sizeable majority, included both proslavery members and tacitly antislavery Methodists who clung to conversionist expectations that salvation would eventually solve the problem of slavery. Tensions increased over the 1830s and early 1840s until the bonds of salvation snapped in 1844.[43] Throughout these debates, the banner of conversionism remained a coveted high ground sought after by both sides.

Anti-abolitionist Methodist polemicists repeatedly invoked the success southern missionaries achieved in spreading salvation. William Capers's widely celebrated mission to the slaves gave anti-abolitionists a powerful appeal in a nation obsessed with extending salvation. Capers weaponized his missionary work in dogged defense of slaving. Wielding the authority of the Missionary Society of the South Carolina Conference, he declared, "We denounce the principles and opinions of the Abolitionists in *toto*." Southern Methodist ministers increasingly believed that slavery was a godly institution, and they sought to prove it by spreading salvation among the enslaved. From this perspective, Black Americans belonged in slavery but their souls nonetheless deserved eternal salvation. According to Capers, the missionary society "would employ no one in the work, who might hesitate to teach thus."[44] In this manner, men like Capers portrayed the slavery debate as one between missionaries who believed that slavery was part of God's redemptive plan and divisive radicals who distorted scripture and led sinful souls to an eternity of torment. Enslavers sought salvation; abolitionists only damnation.

Yet abolitionist Methodists persisted, and 1835 provided a turning point. It was in this year that the unrelenting abolitionist minister Orange Scott began recruiting his fellow Methodists to the cause of abolition.[45] Scott gave one hundred of his fellow ministers a three-month subscription to Garrison's newspaper, the *Liberator*.[46] Through this and other means, Scott made serious inroads among antislavery New Englanders who had been growing restless with the conversionist consensus. Many Methodists surrendered conversionist antislavery in favor of a new purificationist abolitionism. They then turned their eyes toward the power of the church, yearning to wield it as a weapon in the war for national emancipation.

Abolitionists recognized the power of the nationally expansive Methodist church, and in 1835, New England abolitionists directed an appeal to Methodists in Massachusetts and New Hampshire, declaring that slavery was "a sin in the sight of Heaven, and ought to cease at once."[47] A counter-appeal invoked the old logic of conversionist antislavery by arguing two points. The first was that slavery was not necessarily a sin, but more importantly, in the second point, these anti-abolitionists assured New England Methodists that "the spirit of the gospel" led to "an irresistible tendency" toward the "destruction of slavery as a system."[48] These anti-abolitionists promised that if Methodists would simply wait for salvation to spread, slavery would be destroyed. If, however, Methodists privileged abolitionism over salvation, nothing but political and spiritual ruin would befall the nation.

Two Methodist bishops agreed with the anti-abolitionists and elevated the attack on the antislavery radicals within and without the denomination. Elijah Hedding and John Emory rebuked New England Methodists in an 1835 circular. Emory ministered to enslavers in Maryland, and he drew on his experience in his attack. The crux of their critique was the assertion that abolitionists were managing "to embarrass all our efforts, as well as by the regular ministry as by missionary means, to gain access to and promote the salvation of both the slaveholders and the slaves."[49] Again, critics of abolitionism accused the movement of slowing the spread of salvation. Most Methodists believed that they had to purify their church of the idolatry of abolitionism or the Methodist church would lose ground in their godly mission of extending salvation.

Bishops had many responsibilities but none as important as ensuring that the Methodist Church fulfilled its role in extending American salvation by generating new conversions. Disruptions caused by debates over abolition ran counter to the conversionist impulses of the church and threatened this most holy of mandates. Accordingly, Hedding and Emory advocated that all faithful Methodists condemn troublesome abolitionists.[50] Hedding and Emory knew that they could not stop Orange Scott, George Storrs, Samuel Norris, La Roy Sunderland, or several other committed Methodist abolitionists, yet they hoped to contain or exclude them. And they had considerable support in that effort from other Methodists, North and South, who had grown tired of abolitionist agitation.

At the 1836 General Conference, held in Cincinnati, a concurrent abolitionist rally attracted several Methodist delegates.[51] Anti-abolitionists at the conference used this as an opportunity to exercise denominational authority to punish these abolitionists and confirm, once and for all, that abolitionism was heresy for orthodox Methodists. After two days of railing against abolitionism, the General Conference passed two resolutions. The first condemned the speakers at the abolitionist rally, and the second stated that the General Conference was "decidedly opposed to modern abolitionism and wholly disclaim any right, wish, or intention to interfere in the civil and political relation between master and slave as it exists in the slave-holding states of this union."[52] A host of Methodist magazines published the resolution, and the Ohio Antislavery Society gave it additional life by reprinting it with a rebuttal.[53]

That same year, British Methodists sent a letter to the General Conference praising emancipation in the Caribbean and encouraging American Methodists to press for the same in the United States. The American national body of Methodists responded with an address that foregrounded the spread of conversion among enslaved people.[54] In the ongoing battle for moral capital between Britain and the United States, white American Christians cherished nothing more than claiming that God was extending salvation through their ministries, their churches, and their nation. For Methodists—a community with British origins and deep transatlantic ties—the nationalist competition to be the vanguard of salvation took on a more intimate tenor. British Methodists would not cede conversionist ground, and they almost immediately sent another message that highlighted "the conversion of great numbers of the negroes" that resulted after Caribbean emancipation.[55]

This appeal to abolitionism as an agent of salvation, rather than its opponent, emboldened abolitionist Methodists and alarmed both moderates and proslavery advocates. The latter coalition still maintained control of the conference and refused to print the letter.[56] The Methodist crusade against abolitionism hinged on portraying the movement as a threat to salvation. Testimonies of post-emancipation Caribbean conversions would undercut the most powerful proslavery argument, making it was too incendiary to print. The Ohio Antislavery Society, however, eagerly printed it along with their account of the debate at the 1836 General Conference.[57]

Bishop Hedding continued his anti-abolitionist offensive by removing Orange Scott from his position of elder in 1836. Hedding then refused to give George Storrs, another abolitionist, that same position. Methodist ecclesiology placed real power in the hands of elders, and the anti-abolitionist bishop demanded that the church hierarchy speak in one voice condemning abolitionism as an opponent of the church's conversionist mission. Scott fired back with a coercive call for purity, announcing "a new era in the history of the M. E. Church" in a published essay called *An Appeal to the Methodist Episcopal Church*.[58] Scott asserted, "The early American Methodists were warmly opposed to slavery, however mistaken they might have been in Church policy on this subject."[59] Scott believed that Methodists had long held antislavery principles, but church leaders, including the bishops who opposed him, undercut this conviction cherished by the church they purported to lead. In truth, the church had mostly made peace with slavery by the early nineteenth century, electing to emphasize church unity and the expansion of salvation and cease its calls for abolitionist purification.

Hedding had been spoiling for a fight, and Scott's polemic only fueled the fire. In 1838, Hedding took another radical action and brought charges against both Scott and another abolitionist, named La Roy Sunderland.[60] The bishop claimed that the abolitionist actions of these two ministers violated their responsibilities to their communities and to the wider Methodist denomination. According to Hedding, Methodists had to prioritize conversion and church unity. By privileging abolitionist purity over these needs, the two abolitionist ministers ran afoul of the denominational power structure. The New England Conference acquitted both, but conflict only continued to mount. In Philadelphia, ministerial candidate Lucius C. Matlack was twice rejected due to his abolitionist convictions.[61]

In the same year that Hedding took aim at abolitionists in New England, a public spat between prominent Methodists indicated the rising danger of sectionalism for the church. Gerrit Smith, an influential northern philanthropist, and William Winans, a respected Methodist minister in Mississippi, squared off, indicating the inability of conversionism to hold together abolitionists and proslavery ministers. In 1837, Winans had written to a number of respected ministers and social reformers to help raise funds for a new church to be planted in New Orleans. Gerrit Smith's response indicates how dramatically abolitionists resisted the conversionist consensus and instead prioritized the purity of the abolitionist cause.

Smith dismissed the professing Christianity of enslavers, writing, "Suppose I were invited to contribute to the cost of erecting a heathen temple, could I innocently comply with the request?" Smith, like many other abolitionists, no longer considered enslavers to be Christians. Therefore, a church created by and for enslavers could not possibly be a Christian church. Smith continued by distinguishing between "the true God—the God of the whole Bible—the God of the poor and oppressed" and "the religion of the South—the religion which justifies the oppression and murder of the Savior's poor."[62]

Winans began his reply by dismissing Smith as a sectionalist that shouted into an echo chamber while real Christians took on the important work of extending American salvation. Winans claimed that he did not see Smith's reply because it was published in abolitionist papers, sources that might be influential in the North but were in the South "inoperative." Winans claimed that "the thousands of dollars which are expended to array a moral power against slavery, are doing nothing." He did, however, grant that one possible effect of abolitionism was "to dismember the South from the Union."[63] Winans had asked Smith to contribute to the salvation of the nation through the creation of a church in a major American city. Rather than enthusiastically accept, Smith instead devoted his money to what Winans painted as a divisive, distracting, and ultimately useless abolitionist purification campaign.

Winans, of course, took greatest offense at the suggestion that southern religion was not Christian, and he fought back by foregrounding the function of the church in generating conversions. He asked Smith, "Would you, sir, have met a requisition of St. Paul to aid in propagating the religion by which he taught in Rome, at Ephesus, or at Colosse?" He then claimed that the church in New Orleans "is intended to preach . . . the same Gospel which that apostle published to those cities." Wrapped in the moral authority of the early disciples, Winans claimed that abolitionists would have to choose between the authority of the scriptures or the idolatry of abolitionism. Smith had apparently made his choice and now Winans was left to wonder what Smith would do next, imagining violence as the likely extension of what he saw as abolitionist fanaticism. He imagined that abolitionists would send "fire and sword" along with their gospel of abolition.[64]

By 1840, it was undeniable that antiabolitionists owed much of their success to their effective manipulations of conversionism. By emphasizing missionary success and the need to continue that important work, conversionists worked to marginalize the purificationist appeals of abolitionists. As a result, abolitionists attempted to organize an antislavery missionary society at the same time that Orange Scott organized an American Wesleyan Antislavery Society. The missionary organization floundered. Scott realized the power of proslavery missionary success but failed to organize an effective abolitionist counter measure.[65] By 1843, stalwart Methodist abolitionists had enough. If they could not claim the high ground of missionary conversionism, they would nonetheless pursue purity for themselves and for their church, even if it meant sundering Methodist unity.

Orange Scott, Jonathan Horton, and La Roy Sunderland announced their departure from the Methodist Episcopal Church with a published address that began by framing their decision as one that prioritized extending salvation. They wrote, "We take this step after years of consideration, and with a solemn sense of our responsibility to God; we take it with a view to his glory and the salvation of souls."[66] They formed the Wesleyan Methodist Connection, an explicitly abolitionist denomination, and justified this action as necessary for the salvation of souls.[67]

Anti-abolitionist Methodists continued to hammer on the theme of converting enslaved people. An 1843 editorial in the *Southern Christian Advocate* assured readers that "the conversion and salvation of the negro population is our great work." This great work must be protected, and increasing abolitionist agitation meant that "the south must either give up its missionary operations, or protest against ecclesiastical interference on the part of its northern brethren and presses, or else sunder its connection with the north."[68] Southern Methodists would protect their conversionist commitments even if it meant disunion or violence. Soon it would. Violence came first. In 1844, Rev. Daniel Curry professed antislavery views from his Columbus, Georgia, pulpit and he was forced to flee the state or face physical violence.[69] Southern Methodists would not tolerate antislavery in their pulpits, and soon northern Methodists would not tolerate enslavers among their ministerial colleagues.

With the question of annexing Texas dividing the nation and Methodists still reeling from the defection of the abolitionists now in the Wesleyan Connection, the specter of schism loomed over the 1844 conference held in New York City.[70] Two trials of ministers, who were also enslavers, dominated the proceedings. The first involved Francis A. Harding. Harding had been suspended from his pulpit in Baltimore after his wife inherited an enslaved man that he did not emancipate. Harding appealed his case to the General Conference, but the decision was upheld by a decisive 117 to 56 vote.[71] Southerners balked. A committee formed to soothe the resulting wounds, but after four days of work, they surrendered to the impossibility of the task.

The conflict only mounted with the second trial, which resulted from the committee on episcopacy's investigations of Bishop James O. Andrew of Georgia. Andrew had served as a bishop for twelve years. At the time of his appointment, he did not own any enslaved laborers. However, when his wife died, he inherited an enslaved woman named Kitty and an unnamed boy. Kitty refused to migrate, and the boy was too young to send away. When his second wife inherited several enslaved laborers, he quickly drew up a deed that explicitly ensured his wife's human chattel were not their common property but rather solely hers. Andrew reported the situation and offered to resign. Church discipline had allowed ministers to own enslaved people in states where manumission was illegal, as was the case in Georgia. However, this leniency was less prevalent for bishops, and the General Conference voted that Andrew should resign his office until he was able to manumit his enslaved laborers.[72]

George Foster Pierce of Georgia defended Andrew and fretted over the consequences this action would have on the spread of salvation. Pierce lamented, "No question has ever done so much harm to saving godliness as the intermeddling of the Methodist Church with the question of slavery."[73] If Methodists would continue to prioritize conversion, they must drop this disruptive insistence on antislavery purity. William A. Smith of Virginia claimed that if southern Methodist leaders allowed the national denomination to dismiss Andrews, they would "put in jeopardy all our missions among the slaves." Dr. Capers echoed this claim, and northerners were put on the defensive, forced to claim a position in opposition to that of evangelizing the enslaved.[74] Bishop

Andrew himself emphasized his conversionist labor, claiming before the General Conference that "when I was but a boy, I taught a Sunday school for slaves, in which I taught a number of them to read; and from that period till this day I have devoted my energies to the promotion of their happiness and salvation."[75]

Capers praised the bishop and explicitly invoked conversionism by claiming that Andrew deserved his episcopacy because he labored not for "the emancipation of the negro race, but what is better—what is more constitutional and more Christian—the salvation of the souls of the negroes on our great southern plantations."[76] Capers then reverted to history, reminding Methodists of the partnership of his former schoolmaster William Hammett and the revered Methodist founder John Wesley. According to Capers, Hammett (with Wesley's sanction) adopted no rules on slavery in his fledgling southern mission despite Wesley's avowed antislavery. Hammett adopted this policy for the same reasons "which prevented Mr. Wesley and after him the Wesleyan English Conference, from ever enjoining any rule respecting slavery for the missions in the West Indies."[77] Salvation was the primary goal, and if attacking slavery hindered the expansion of salvation, then those attacks would be sinful.

Southern Methodists were unanimous in interpreting the decision as a direct attack on their attempts to convert the enslaved. William Smith explicitly stated that any action that jeopardized the mission to slaves would mean that "a division of our ecclesiastical confederation would become a high and solemn duty."[78] That duty was quickly put into action. North Carolina Methodists wrote, "We regard the officious, and unwarranted interference of the Northern portion of the Church with the subject of slavery alone, a sufficient cause for a division of our Church."[79] Southerners called a meeting on May 1, 1845, in Louisville to plan their new denomination, a denomination that would privilege conversion over antislavery purity. On that day, half a million Methodists became members of the Methodist Episcopal Church, South. Slavery had torn white American Methodism in two.

Methodists in the South had been aggressive in securing conversions among both enslaved and free, Black and white. And they had been wildly successful. These conversionist ambitions stemmed from both pious desires to expand the salvation of souls and defensive tactics to tighten the shackles of slavery. For several decades, this tactic worked, but increasing abolitionist insistence on slavery's sin convinced enough Methodists that enslavers could not serve as acceptable agents of salvation. Methodists were not alone in this conviction and the crisis that it caused. The experience of American Baptists was nearly identical.

Baptists

Southern Baptists, like Methodists, experienced a brief burst of confrontational purificationist antislavery in the earliest years of the new nation.[80] However, as we saw with the career of John Leland, this was but a moment. By the nineteenth century, Baptists mostly went one of three ways: They either left the national denomination like David Barrow, rested in the emancipatory expectations of conversionist causation, or came to believe that slavery was not a sin at all but rather a divinely ordained institution to spread Christian salvation. Everything changed in the 1830s when a new generation of northern Baptists heeded the abolitionist call to purify their church. These Baptist abolitionists took two often-overlapping courses of action. First, they attacked the pro-slavery ideology of influential national Baptist leaders like Richard Furman. Second, they questioned the conversionist expectation that the expansion of salvation would work to purify their church of slaving. They sought purity now and they would achieve it through coercion.

Baptist abolitionists were most active in Maine. In 1837, one association even voted "we, as the professed followers of Jesus Christ, have no fellowship or communion with those who, under the character of Christians, continue to hold their fellow men in bondage."[81] Abolitionism soon spread to New Hampshire and Vermont. The Shaftsbury Association of Vermont sent its own antislavery materials directly to southern Baptists, informing slaveholders that they could not be given communion or allowed to preach in Vermont.[82] In Massachusetts, Cyrus Pitt Grosvenor, pastor of First Baptist Church in Boston and then Second Baptist in Salem, served as the first president of the Anti-Slavery Society of Salem and Vicinity.

In a speech before the antislavery society, Grosvenor began by claiming that killing tyrants would not incur God's wrath. Coming just three years after Nat Turner's rebellion, these were weighty words. Grosvenor also engaged in a bit of regional pride, claiming that this society was more committed to the cause of liberty than any other "even in New England, where the principles of liberty are better understood and the blessings of liberty are more highly valued by the citizens at large than in any other portion of the world." After discussing the promise of abolition embedded in the Declaration of Independence, Grosvenor spent the bulk of the text explaining the society's insistence on "immediate, simultaneous emancipation." Throughout, Grosvenor asserted that slavery hindered the spread of the gospel, claiming that "a Christian slaveholder in

Georgia told me in his own house, ten years ago, that he wished to instruct his slaves, but was prevented by law."[83] Grosvenor sanctioned slave rebellion and denied the conversionist power of slavery, the two most important hot button issues in religious discussions about slavery and abolition.

Abolitionism grew slowly among white Baptists. The legacy of prioritizing religious liberty made many Baptists wary of looking to legal coercion, but by 1840, enough antislavery Baptists came to see human bondage as a sufficient violation of soul liberty to warrant formal action. The conflict began in earnest. In April of that year, the American Baptist Antislavery Convention met in New York. They issued an address to southern Baptists calling for abolition and proclaiming that they "cannot, at the lord's table cordially take as a brother's hand, which plies the scourge on a woman's naked flesh ... and which shuts up the Bible from human eyes."[84] The convention also created a Foreign Provisional Missionary Committee that wanted to separate from slavery and enslavers completely. For these Baptist abolitionists, working to extend salvation alongside enslavers would not bring true salvation. It would merely taint the church with sin.[85] Unlike the Methodists, with their highly publicized and highly successful mission to the slaves, Baptists scrambled for the conversionist trump card.

Southerners erupted at the formation of the American Baptist Antislavery Convention, and the national denomination was forced to respond. In November of 1840, the Board of Managers of the Baptist General Convention announced, "with painful interest, indications of a tendency on the part of some of their beloved brethren and co-adjutors, to withdraw from the missionary connection." The convention neither denounced nor supported this secessionist movement but rather rested in hope that the "unseasonable diversion of our thoughts to irrelevant subjects" would not disturb their more important work "to send the glad tidings of salvation to the heathen."[86] The denomination had formed under the imperative of extending salvation, and it prayed that it would endure for the same reason.

But pursuing salvation was no longer enough. Both sides were spoiling for a fight. The Maine Baptist Anti-Slavery Convention met two months later in January 1841 and claimed that of 214 Baptist ministers in Maine, 180 supported immediate emancipation.[87] In late February, Elon Galusha organized an ecumenical meeting "of every denomination in western New York," encouraging Christians to "withdraw all ecclesiastical connection with those slaveholders and slave-holding churches."[88] Baptists in Camden, South Carolina, called for

Galusha's removal, while the influential Charleston Association supported the idea of separation and called for southerners to form their own missionary board.[89] At the Georgia Baptist State Convention, B. M. Sanders claimed that neutrality was insufficient. He thundered, "Between us and the abolitionists we know no neutrals. Those who are not for us are against us."[90] Both enslavers and abolitionists increasingly saw missionary cooperation impossible across the divide. Salvation required either a commitment to slavery or to abolition.

At the 1841 Triennial Convention in Baltimore, proslavery southerners went on the offensive, gathering a week early to strategize. At the same time, several moderates met with the goals of heading off the southern firebrands and maintaining unity through prioritizing conversions. This group of moderates assured southerners that no new measures "should be suffered to interfere with the harmonious operations of our beloved associations." More importantly, the document charged that abolitionists "invade the prerogative of Jesus Christ" by hindering "the holy enterprise of disseminating the truth of God."[91] These moderates clung to the conversionist consensus that had held Baptists together since the late eighteenth century. But even their grip began to loosen.

The convention itself began with a victory for southerners as the South Carolina proslavery stalwart Richard Fuller replaced the abolitionist Elon Galusha. The Bostonian Baron Stow saved his position as recording secretary only by assuring southerners that he opposed and refused to share the 1840 address from the American Baptist Antislavery Convention. Stow promised that he thought "it not only impolitic and inexpedient, but uncourteous and unchristian."[92] Perhaps most important, William Bullein Johnson of South Carolina became the convention's president.[93] No one had done more for proslavery Baptists than Johnson and Fuller, and the two now sat in the highest positions at the convention.

Incensed, abolitionists abandoned the convention and began again to imagine a national ministry free from enslavers. By 1843, they had planted the seeds of what would become the Free Mission Society, a Baptist abolitionist missionary organization. The *Christian Reflector*, a Baptist abolitionist paper published by Cyrus Grosvenor in Worcester, Massachusetts, called for support from "the Friends of Missions in the Baptist Denomination of the United States who believe that missions ought not to be supported by the gain of, or any connivance with oppression."[94] The official Baptist Board of Foreign Missions responded quickly, asserting that funds could not go to missionaries except through their authority. But the point was made; Baptist abolitionists had begun envisioning an exclusively abolitionist missionary society.[95] National conversionism was crumbling.

Southerners were again put on their heels when the Triennial Convention opened in 1844. Richard Fuller tried to head off controversy by moving that "cooperation in this [missionary organization] does not involve nor imply any concert or sympathy as to any matters foreign from the subject designated." Dr. Cone of New York seconded, but after debate, a more direct assertion by G. B. Ide of Philadelphia replaced the preamble, proclaiming that "in co-operating together as members of the convention in the work of foreign missions, we disclaim all sanction either expressed or implied whether of slavery or anti-slavery, but as individuals we are perfectly free to both express and promote our own views on these subjects in a Christian manner and spirit."[96] The tenuous unity would not last long.

Abolitionists working in the Home Missionary Society decided to force the issue. Samuel Adlam, a Maine abolitionist, tricked conservatives into debating whether enslaving should disqualify missionaries. Adlam proposed a resolution he intended to vote against that claimed, "a minister being a slaveholder should present no barrier to his being employed as a missionary."[97] Adlam knew that southerners would eagerly agree with this resolution but that enough northern Baptists would dissent, ending the uneasily silence and force Baptists to decide once and for all whether enslavers could serve as agents of salvation. The gambit worked.

The resolution caused such a stir that the chair immediately adjourned the session, leaving the topic to be broached two days later when Fuller again headed off schism by proposing a countermeasure that "the Home mission Society clearly defines its object to be the promotion of the Gospel in North America . . . to introduce the subjects of slavery or antislavery into this body, is in direct contravention of the whole letter and purpose of the said Constitution . . . our cooperation in this body does not imply any sympathy either with slavery or antislavery."[98] Fuller's motion carried, and the meeting resumed its business without another flareup. As Fuller well knew, silence supported slavery, and so enslavers simply had to decry discussion as divisive distraction.

But abolitionists would not relent. The Baptist Association of Wisconsin met in 1844, from June 26 to June 27, and blamed "the union of religious societies in the free and slave states" for allowing "slave holding ministers and churches the right to make heathen and perpetuate heathenism at home." What others would call Christian unity, the Wisconsin Baptists called "the sum of all villainies." What southerners had called missionary work, they attacked as fostering heathenism. The Wisconsinites concluded by turning the Psalms against all Baptists who were unwilling to expel enslavers; they claimed "when thou sawest a thief then thou consentedst with him and hast made thyself partaker with adulterers."[99] Three months later, the Baptist Antislavery Convention declared "the Baptist Triennial Convention and its Board have, in our opinion, manifested an incurable proslavery spirit." Since the board was willing to appoint enslavers as missionaries, "the time has come, for a distinct and permanent missionary organization."[100]

It looked increasingly likely that abolitionists would splinter off and a union of southern and moderate northerners would take hold of the existing denominational positions of authority. This is perhaps exactly what would have happened had proslavery Baptists not pushed the moderates as they did in October 1844. In that month, the Georgia Baptist Convention recommended James E. Reeve as a missionary to the Cherokee. In the very proposal, Georgians noted that Reeve was an enslaver, and the board decided 7 to 5 against appointing Mr. Reeve. However, the exact language claimed they rejected Reeve not because he owned enslaved laborers but because his very application identified him as an enslaver. According to this logic, the southerners who advanced his candidacy nullified his qualifications by introducing slavery into the discussion when it did not belong. Neither northern abolitionists nor southern fire-eaters would muffle their attacks. The only question remained was which side would retain the authority of the denomination when the other finally removed themselves from the national fellowship.

Southerners rose to the challenge. Alabama Baptists pushed the issue of Reeve's candidacy further and demanded clarification from the Foreign Missions Board in Boston, asking in November 1844 if an enslaver would be accepted as a missionary. The board shifted from its earlier policy of silence and responded clearly that if anyone "should offer himself as a missionary, having slaves, and should insist on retaining them as his property, we could not appoint him. One thing is certain, we can never be a party to any arrangement which would imply approbation of slavery."[101]

Francis Wayland, president of the General Board, then reaffirmed this decision, writing that while all qualified northerners and southerners are eligible for missionary service, this principle might make some "responsible for institutions which they could not, with a good conscience, sanction." In such a case, the board would not expect anyone to act against their conscience but rather "refer the case to the Convention for its decision."[102]

Many southerners interpreted these resolutions as a violation of the message of neutrality offered at the 1844 convention. Virginians took action first, proposing the creation of a new missionary board for all of those disappointed with the recent activity of the Boston-based national board. A new convention met in Augusta, Georgia, on May 8, 1845. All the attendees came from slaveholding states. The Southern Baptist Convention was born, and the national Baptist General Convention had been sundered.

BY THE 1840S, THE old tactics of preserving unity by foregrounding salvation had pretty much failed. As national denominations splintered, so too did national missionary organizations. The 1845 meeting of the American Board of Commissioners for Foreign Missions doubled down on its belief that conversion would solve the problem of slavery. These missionary leaders condemned abolitionist purificationism and instead unanimously accepted a report resolving that spreading the gospel would "lead to the correction of all the social wrongs and disorders." In their view, attacking slavery would eliminate a symptom not a cause. Real emancipation could only arrive through the triumph of the gospel. The latter had to come first because in their view "the souls among the heathen are, in fact, regenerated by the Holy Spirit, before they are freed from all participation in these social and moral evils.[103] Salvation must precede emancipation.

Abolitionists disagreed, believing that national salvation would be impossible without first achieving purity through emancipation. This spirit of purification did not mean that abolitionists were willing to surrender the pursuit of conversions, however. They responded to the ABCFM's moderation by forming their own missionary society, the American Missionary Association (AMA), in 1846. The abolitionist AMA maintained a biracial leadership and refused to accept funds from enslavers.[104] For these abolitionists, salvation could only result from intuitions untainted by the sin of slavery. The number of abolitionists and anti-abolitionist Christians willing to put their differences aside in pursuit of fostering conversions dwindled further.

Presbyterians, Methodists, and Baptists all splintered over debates rooted in the intersections of conversion and slavery. How do we save souls? Who is equipped to do this work? Will slavery disappear as salvation expands? In the earliest years of the republic all of these denominations largely agreed on these three questions, and they built national denominations on those shared commitments to salvation. The national denominations in turn created powerful nationalisms and networks that launched a benevolent empire of social reform. The rise of social reform alongside missionary coordination enabled a new abolitionism to form, and these new abolitionists no longer suspended the pursuit of emancipation in the name of coordinating campaigns for salvation. As soon as abolitionists privileged purity over extending conversions, denominational unity was doomed.

Many Presbyterians, Baptists, and Methodists, both North and South, described the schism as a great tragedy. However, these lamentations only accelerated sectional animosities as nearly all parties placed the blame for dissolution on the other side. As historian Edward R. Crowther has recognized, sectional epithets increased in the aftermath of these schisms.[105] These epithets took on a specific nature when the logistics of separation proved contentious and then litigious. Implementing the Methodist Plan of Separation, for example, proved so heated that the distribution of some property had to be settled by the courts. Debates over pensions, land, and the publishing house turned into a flurry of lawsuits that reached the Supreme Court.[106] Battles over salvation and slavery descended into scrambles over property.

John G. Jones, a respected Methodist minister in Mississippi, bemoaned the schism, calling it an "unprecedented disaster," claiming, "To this writer it was the darkest day he had ever seen." More importantly for Jones, he believed the schism slowed the growth of Methodism in Mississippi. He reflected, "Instead of our usual increase we had a decrease of sixty white members, with an increase of only seven hundred and twelve colored and twelve Indian members." Despite this he nonetheless claimed that schism was necessary. In his view, Mississippi Methodists either had the choice "to rend the body of Christ" or "lose the fruits of self-sacrifice among the slaves of the South or their owners."[107] For Jones, it was worth slowing the pace of growth in order to protect slavery and the opportunities for additional conversions that it provided.

Other Southern Methodists celebrated their schism as another example of a Providentially directed division, much like that which inspired early Methodists "to establish an independent Church in America." Despite the difficulty of the schism, Southern Methodists claimed that "the star of Divine Providence [was] leading the way, and the salvation of the Southern Church and the African race" would ensue. And they claimed that the early evidence indicated that they were correct. This collection of Southern Methodist writers rejoiced that "the seal of heaven's approbation has been set upon their course—the gracious work of the Lord has been gloriously revived—thousands have been brought to the knowledge of salvation, and Ethiopia with glad heart is stretching out her hands unto God."[108] The famed Psalm used by colonizationists now adorned proslavery celebrations of human bondage.

Celebrations of the denominational schisms meshed easily with rising secessionist sentiments. In 1850, Methodists in Charleston claimed that northerners would continue encroaching upon the rights of the South. They reinterpreted the 1844 Methodist schism as the first step in a wider process of southern resistance. The dissolution of the national denomination, according to the *Charleston Southern Christian Advocate*, was a sacrifice "laid on the altar of constitutional right." No longer simply a religious matter, the Methodist schism had been reinterpreted as a political act designed to save the Constitution.[109]

The loss of these three denominations did not immediately spell the death of the republic, yet it greatly damaged one of the most powerful sources of American nationalism: denominational identity. Moreover, denominational schisms weakened the moral authority of ministers that could have been used to prevent secession and war. The loss of these national churches put greater strain on other national institutions, most notably political parties.

By the mid-1840s, denominations were by no means the only national institutions capable of maintaining unity in the republic. With the fracture of denominations, the importance of political parties only increased. The eventual dissolution of the Democratic Party was the last national fissure prior to secession, yet both statesmen and ministers connected the actions of politicians to the churches. They believed that the loss of the nation's largest Protestant denominations portended damnation for the union.

In 1850 John C. Calhoun wrote a speech claiming that of all of the things tying together the United States "the strongest of those of spiritual and ecclesiastical nature, consisted in the unity of the great religious denominations, all of which originally embraced the whole union." With the loss of the national Baptist and Methodist denominations, he predicted that divisiveness over slavery "will finally snap every cord."[110] Calhoun was not alone in recognizing that national denominations offered an essential source of American nationalism, and that without these religious nationalisms, the sectional divide would only grow.

Few Americans better understood the fragility of national unity than Henry Clay. Having spent his career brokering sectional compromises over the status of slavery in the West, Clay knew the divisive power of slavery and the potentially unifying power of American religious nationalism. Yet at the end of his life, he gave preeminence to ecclesiastical division as the greatest threat to the nation, claiming that "this sundering of the religious ties which have hitherto bound our people together, I consider the greatest source of danger to our country. If our religious men cannot live together in peace, what can be expected of us politicians?"[111] Even those who blamed "sagacious and gifted politicians," like the Yankee-turned-southerner Robert Livingston Stanton, acknowledged that fire-eaters "could effect nothing until the religious union of the North and South was dissolved."[112]

The words of Calhoun, Clay, and Stanton proved prophetic. Religious union between North and South did indeed dissolve, and the nation crumbled. By the end of the 1840s American Christians concluded that conversionism no longer provided a valid solution to the problem of slavery. A new radical purificationism grew in strength after the dissolution of national denominations. Untethered to one another, American Christians pulled their churches and their nation toward secession and war.

Conclusion

Secession and Salvation

NEITHER THE QUEST FOR conversions nor the confrontational agitation of abolitionists ended slavery in the United States. American emancipation came only as a consequence of the horrors of civil war and the deaths of over 750,000 Americans. But those deaths and the war that caused them partly resulted from the collision of salvation and slavery. From the beginnings of the nation, Christian Americans believed their nation could serve the kingdom of God. A minority privileged purity, believing that God's kingdom would become manifest only when the church and the nation had proven themselves worthy. The majority of Americans sought to fulfill this holy work by extending Christian conversion, confident that God would save both their souls and their world.

The bonds of salvation formed powerful American nationalisms and took on institutional reality through national denominations. But the problem of slavery remained. The colonizationist movement sprung from denominational networks, pairing visions of salvation with the amelioration of slavery. Yet the quixotic scheme, so impractical that it could only endure when connected to millennial promises of divine aid, drew opposition from Black Christians who eventually rallied white allies to their side. Emboldened by experience in organizing ever-larger conversionist endeavors, white Christian reformers returned to the problem of slavery, heeding the calls of Black activists to insist that the nation purify itself from slavery. But slavery swelled in size and strength, and American commitments to human bondage permeated the social, economic, and political fabric of the nation. Tensions between abolitionists and their opponents unraveled America's churches and then destroyed the nation.

American nationalism had thrived through coordinated efforts to expand salvation. When abolitionists began to prioritize purity instead of extending conversion, the United States lost one of its most powerful forces for national unity. Any hope of bridging that divide vanished after abolitionists and their opponents redefined one another as not Christians at all. When Americans could no longer recognize themselves as participants in a shared project for establishing the kingdom of God, the nation lost itself.

To be clear, religious discord or denominational fracture did not cause the Civil War. Slavery did. Southerners seceded to protect slavery, and northerners went to war to preserve the United States, convinced that God had ordained the union to save the world. But the spirit of secession thrived only after debates over slavery and salvation had destroyed national denominations and convinced many Americans that their former coreligionists were no longer Christians. The English writer Harriet Martineau recognized in 1837, the same year of the first of these denominational schisms, that "the democracy of America is planted down deep into the Christian religion."[1] When the largest Protestant national denominations fell, American democracy did not hold for long.

Even after the loss of national denominations, many Americans continued to understand the United States as a heaven-sent redeemer for the world. As the nation marched toward secession and war, conversionists continued organizing the expansion of salvation, as confident and committed in their work as the generations that came before. New, powerful purificationist movements emerged, however, first from abolitionists and then from southern secessionist fire-eaters. Both camps were convinced that the other represented an existential threat to American salvation. The purificationist currents from the poles drowned out the conversionist majority and swept the nation toward secession.

While radicals pushed northerners toward a disunionist purification, southern Christians sought to save their vision of American salvation from what they saw as the irreligion of abolitionism. In their mind, abolitionists represented an anti-Christian idolatry that threatened the religious destiny of the nation. In describing this destiny, southern Christians grew more explicit in connecting slavery and white supremacy with the kingdom of God. Political debates over slavery morphed into competing visions for a godly social order. Over the course of the 1850s, attacks against abolitionism became generalized assaults on the North and eventually the United States.[2] The South was not a monolith, but it was nearly so in its hatred of abolitionism. In reality, abolitionists remained a loathed minority among northerners as well. The reality of a shared commitment of salvation had been obscured by partisan claims of purity over slavery and abolition.

Southern ministers enabled the march toward secession. But before they could fulfill their eventual secessionist function, the southern clergy first had to conquer their own theology of political non-interference called "the spirituality of the church." This ideology claimed that in order to maintain its spiritual function, the church must maintain a distance from the sinful world of politics. From the very beginning, however, this ideology had notable cracks.

As southern ministers repeatedly defended slavery from abolitionist attacks, the spirituality of the church seemed to apply only to critiques of slavery, not to critiques of abolitionism. Nonetheless, this discourse had real consequences in how southerners envisioned their relationship to the state. Divorcing Christianity from politics either undercut arguments for the nation's redemptive role in God's divine plan or shifted agency for that project away from ministers and toward statesmen. Clergy deployed either strategy depending on the needs of the moment. However, this all began to change after the dissolution of the national denominational bodies.

Denominational schisms required the southern clergy to build new denominational structures. This process led ministers to exert greater influence over public life.[3] We can see this transformation through the ministry of William A. Smith of the Methodist Randolph-Mason College, just outside of Richmond. In 1856 he published his reflections on the moral philosophy of slavery, unsurprisingly declaring it to be consistent with American ideals of liberty, Christian holiness, and universal moral law. Smith's preface begins by noting, "Since the year 1844, I have been frequently called on to discuss this subject on various popular occasions in Virginia and North Carolina."[4] The year 1844 marked a turning point for southern Methodists. The schism offered an opportunity for clergymen to gain new social power by defending slavery. They eagerly rose to the challenge and by so doing, transformed the relationship between religion and southern society.

Proslavery Christianity, however, remained rooted in conversionism. By the time the schisms had rent American Christianity, the majority of southerners had become convinced that slavery was an agent of salvation and abolitionism was a demonic challenge to both social stability and gospel truth. The Christian status of slavery, however, hinged on whether enslavers would encourage the conversion of their enslaved laborers. By making this move, southern religious leaders drew on the old emphasis on conversion to shift the burden of defending slavery against abolitionism onto enslavers while simultaneously elevating their own status as ministers.

According to the southern clergy, enslavers had a choice, if they could submit themselves and their enslaved laborers to the salvation of Christ and the guidance of the church, they would reap the blessings of God. If they failed to join the mission of expanding salvation, they damned both themselves and the institution of slavery. Clergymen claimed that failing to expand salvation would expose the South to the violence of abolitionists. William A. Smith's defense of slavery closed with a discussion of "the duty of master's to slaves" that asserted that "religion holds the scales of justice between masters and slaves." If enslavers did not cultivate their own Christian faith as well as the Christian faith of their enslaved laborers, they were failing as southern citizens.[5] These appeals largely succeeded and the clergy rose to greater prominence in southern society, intensifying the role of religion and religious leaders in the mounting sectional crisis.

The Compromise of 1850, and the Fugitive Slave Act in particular, increased the rancor among religious communities. In the North, the prolific revivalist Charles Grandison Finney aligned with disunionists. After accepting that revivals would not end slavery in the South, he called for "the dismemberment of our hypocritical union."[6] If the United States would be a Christian nation, it had to purify itself from the irredeemable sinful South. After years of coordinated conversion campaigns, enslavers had successfully demonstrated that slavery could serve as an agent of salvation among the enslaved. As a result, antislavery agitators increasingly divorced discussions of slavery from discussions of salvation. Finney's transformation personified wider trends how American Christians reckoned with slavery. Conversionism withered, and new disunionist purificationisms blossomed.

In the South, James Osgood Andrew, the bishop whose censure catalyzed the dissolution of the national Methodist church, encouraged southerners to prepare for all manners of secession as early as 1850. He called for immediate southern independence in education and economics. Andrew was not yet ready to condemn the union, but he did feel the time had come for southerners to organize should it be necessary for Christians to support the dissolution of the nation.[7] For Andrew and others, nothing could threaten slavery's function in extending salvation, not even the American union.

The most important secessionist Christian voice emerged in 1850 when South Carolina Presbyterian minister James Henley Thornwell reinvigorated proslavery theology by merging a conversionist appeal for salvation with a purificationist call to destroy the idolatry of abolitionism.[8] In his view, "the world

is the battle ground—Christianity and Atheism the combatants; and the progress of humanity the stake."[9] These attacks only gained strength in the 1850s,
as higher criticism slowly began to spread among a small selection of northern
intellectuals. For southern Christians already inclined to view their northern
coreligionists as idolators before a throne of abolitionism, higher criticism and
its rejection of literalist biblical hermeneutics provided further evidence that
northern Christians had abandoned their obligation to spread salvation.[10]

For many northerners, the Fugitive Slave Act proved that the Constitution
had failed and the South had seized the federal government. Harriet Beecher
Stowe's incendiary novel *Uncle Tom's Cabin* captured the debate. In one passage, Senator John Bird of Ohio and his wife Mary discuss the passage of the
law. Mary is indignant, calling it "downright cruel and unchristian." For Mary,
there could be no political compromise with sin, and in her estimation, the
law is a grave sin. Many northerners agreed and worked to subvert the law. In
Boston, the application of the law through the highly publicized capture and
re-enslavement of Anthony Burns inspired Amos Adams Lawrence to reflect,
"We went to bed one night old-fashioned, conservative, compromise Union
Whigs & woke up stark mad Abolitionists."[11]

But Lawrence and Mary Bird were outliers. Stowe's Senator John Bird better represented the reaction of most Americans by defending the law. White
supremacy and nationalism combined to buttress the Fugitive Slave Law.
Americans believed they owed a sacred duty to their countrymen, but the intersectional commitment to white supremacy prevented the vast majority from
recognizing Black Americans as Americans at all. As a result, the biblical in-
junction to treat your neighbor as yourself became interpreted as an obligation
to protect the property of your enslaving white neighbor over the life and liberty of your Black neighbor.[12] The vast majority of Americans still clung to the
union as a cherished agent for global redemption, and this faith inspired most
Christians to shrug off the appeals of abolitionists.

Colonization continued to offer a third way, rooted in both white supremacy
and the prioritization of salvation for both the United States and Africa. John
Henry Hopkins, an anti-abolitionist Episcopal bishop from Vermont, called
colonization "a call of Providence" that promised "safety to the South, peace
to the Union, freedom to the slave, and regeneration to Africa.[13] For Americans who were both antislavery and anti-abolitionist, the movement maintained its appeal, but the opposition of Black Americans and loss of support
from abolitionist ministers denied the movement the authority it once had.

Even visions of African salvation and calls for unity in pursuit of that noble aim could not stem the tide of sectionalist purificationism. Henry C. Wright wrote of a Michigan abolitionist meeting that attacked the United States as a protector of sin and called for "a Northern Republic, on the basis of 'No Union with Slaveholders.'" These midwesterners declared that the Christianity of the United States was not Christianity at all.[14] Southern proslavery polemicists similarly appealed to the discourse of purity. According to the *Liberator*, the *Louisiana Courier* proclaimed that abolitionist ideas had infected the South and called upon all southerners to "cast away every one at all infected with the leprosy of New England politics, and fall back upon our own native sons for leaders."[15] Abolitionists and proslavery prophets both yearned to live in a nation free of one another.

Political events continued to inspire calls for disunion. The Supreme Court decision that Black Americans could never be true Americans inflamed many abolitionists. Disunionist abolitionists framed the Dred Scott case as proof that enslavers had seized control of all three branches of government. As a result, disunionists called for representatives throughout the free states to gather in Cleveland in order to begin planning for northern secession.[16] The Panic of 1857, however, convinced organizers to delay the event.

Many abolitionists ignored the organizers' decision to delay. The cause was too important, and so despite the formal abandonment of the convention many still traveled from Pennsylvania, Indiana, Michigan, and all over Ohio in order to purify themselves and their states from the slaving United States. Those assembled correctly noted that many Americans believed that their nation would save the world regardless of its unsavory methods of maintaining unity. The convention dismissed this as a "Jesuitical doctrine" that "the eternal law of right repudiated." What mattered was "the regions of conscience and the Higher Law," and there the Union was deemed "a crime and a curse." For these abolitionists, purity was the standard for holiness, and any compromise with sin was itself sinful.[17] A nation could serve God only if it first made itself holy.

These uncompromising calls for purity had more and more Americans looking to either disunionism or secession. In an 1859 graduation address at the University of South Carolina, Judge Longstreet, a Methodist minister, warned the graduates that "we are on the eve of a lamentable revolution." In fact, he believed that "the revolution is actually begun" and these students had to decide on which side to stand. On one side was the idolatry and murder ascribed to John Brown, who had recently failed to instigate slave rebellion in Virginia, and on the other was the Christian piety of the South. The Union, in his view, was already lost, and the North was to blame. He was certain that when the South arose to its duty to secede, there would be no war, but if there was, it would be an easy victory for the South, largely because he expected the aid of "all Europe." Moreover, he predicted a quick dissolution of the North, as, "the only bond of union with her people is hatred of slavery." Longstreet had grown so convinced that the North was united in its abolitionism that he believed it to be the sole issue that anyone in the North valued.[18]

Delusions of abolitionist hegemony in the North convinced more and more southern Christians that protecting, much less expanding, salvation required complete separation from abolitionist idolaters. By 1860, southern Methodists were seeking to build an ecumenical but sectional publishing house in order to protect itself from northern writers whom they called "cadets enlisted for a war against the South." According to Robert Abbey, the financial secretary of the Southern Methodist Publishing House, "all [of the North's] books are engendered to this purpose" of destroying the southern way of life.[19]

Joseph Otis, editor of the Baptist *Western Recorder,* predicted an armed conflict and blamed abolitionists for the coming violence, invoking the imperative of salvation and reminding readers that slavery enabled the "regeneration of many of Africa's sons, who are now heralds of the cross in their benighted fatherland."[20] For Otis, the war would be between salvation and damnation. He was not alone. Benjamin Morgan Palmer preached in his New Orleans Presbyterian Church on the eve of Louisiana's secession that God had anointed southerners "to conserve and to perpetuate the institution of domestic slavery as now existing." He accused northerners of abandoning Christianity in favor of atheism and other European heresies.[21]

Secession sprouted in soil that had been watered by proslavery Christianity. In 1860, Thornton Stringfellow boldly asserted in the subtitle of a well-circulated tract that slavery benefited "human happiness and divine glory [when] considered in the light of Bible teachings, moral justice, and political wisdom."[22] Denominational schism and rising sectionalism both politicized the clergy and prepared the wider populace to turn to their ministers for commentary on politics. In return, southern ministers framed secession as essential to preserve their physical safety and their Christian way of life—both rooted in slavery. Salvation for these southerners could not be divorced from the protection of slavery. And so they went to war.

When secession finally did arrive, abolitionists were put in the awkward position of distinguishing their long-standing calls for disunion from this new movement for southern secession. Disunionists claimed that there was not a Constitutional right to secession, only the moral right of disunion in pursuit of righteousness. According to them, since southern secession was made to protect slavery, the South's movement was both illegal and immoral. Simply put, the editorial concluded that disunionism "is based upon the eternal fitness of things, and animated by a noble, disinterested, and philanthropic spirit. The latter is the concentration of all diabolism."[23]

About a week before the firing on Fort Sumter, the Northampton, Massachusetts, Congregationalist Zachary Eddy embraced disunionism, tying the prospects of future American conversions to the need to purify the North from the South, believing that severing ties with southern enslavers would enable the United States to "develop all those forces of a high, Christian civilization." However, by the end of the month, he called for war to support the Union.[24] These reversals were common among disunionist abolitionists. Southern secession enabled abolitionists to reclaim the popular moral high ground that the United States was God's agent for global salvation. Their task now was to connect the destruction of secession with the destruction of slavery.

The arrival of war enabled abolitionists to pair conversionism with purificationism. Emancipation activists claimed that the war could not be won, and therefore the nation could not fulfill its destiny of saving the world, unless the republic first embraced righteousness by destroying slavery. After the election of Abraham Lincoln, with rumors of secession swirling about, Henry Ward Beecher took the pulpit in Brooklyn for a Thanksgiving Day sermon. Beecher began with a message of salvation. He declared, "Christ came to save the world." But first, the United States needed to be purified. Beecher recognized the importance of conversionism to proslavery rhetoric, explaining that southerners asserted that "slaves are missionaries. Slave-ships bring heathen to plantation Christianity." But he did not even address this claim. For Beecher and for his congregants, the call to purity was more important than a reckoning over the meaning, nature, or prospects for extending salvation.[25]

Many northern ministers sacralized the war for union as a pursuit of godly purity that would restore the nation's potential as an agent for global salvation. Henry W. Bellows, minister of All Souls Church in New York City, proclaimed in January 1861, "We will go to war to save order and civilization." Bellows connected the United States with God's divine plan for the world, "If our country be Christ's true heritage, in assailing it, He is assailed, and in that case we have nothing to fear."[26]

The paradigm of purity continually shaped how abolitionist ministers understood the violence and death of the war. Many blamed battlefield losses on the continued presence of slavery in the laws of the nation but looked to the Emancipation Proclamation as ensuring future divine aid on the battlefield.[27] Others flipped the agency and claimed that the war itself functioned as a purifying agent designed to improve the American people.[28] Many northern Christians believed that the violence of the war was purifying the United States of its lethargic, decadent sins. In order to endure this horrific, bloody process of purification, American ministers looked toward a postwar future of greater glory.

Abraham Lincoln encouraged this belief, claiming in his second inaugural address that the war occurred not because of the wishes of secessionists or the desire to preserve the Union. Rather, he asserted, "the Almighty has His own purposes." According to Lincoln, God himself ordained the war to purify the nation. Lincoln described a scale with the wealth of slavery on the one side and the blood of Americans on the other. He imagined that God would not allow the war to cease until enough blood had been spilled that the scale might balance. Centuries of injustice necessitated the great cataclysm of the war, and God demanded a sacrifice in blood. Emancipation, however, promised "a new birth of freedom," enabling the nation to fulfill its divinely ordained destiny. Tragically, from the very beginning, white Christian imaginations of national glory foretold the eventual failings of America's new birth of freedom.

For Nathaniel West, a Presbyterian minister in Brooklyn, the struggles of the war "foretoken a future of national exaltation in righteousness." The war was purifying the nation for a future work of good. West prophesied, "God is preparing the world, by the overthrow of all organized systems of error and iniquity, for millennial glory." He promised that the United States would be at the center of that millennium. But his vision, and the vision of most Americans, had no room for Black people. He envisioned "one bold energetic Anglo-Saxon race, predominating vastly over all the rest; one common Christianity, teaching in its various evangelic forms the open Bible in its purity."[29] The Christian nationalism fostered by the war was sufficient to destroy the institution of chattel slavery but woefully insufficient in addressing the enduring sin of white supremacy.

Conversionism, then, did not die with the war or with emancipation. Both the Confederacy and the Union sought to save the world through their own brand of conversionist ideology: the former through a belief that Christianity was dependent upon slavery and white supremacy, the latter through a belief that the world could be redeemed only if "government of the people, by the people, for the people, shall not perish from the earth." American messianic nationalism amplified after the Civil War partly by ignoring or even sacralizing American white supremacy. The bonds of salvation returned with even greater strength. Ensuing generations continued to connect the extension of American power with Christian glory. The war and the transformation of the United States into an industrial capitalist, imperialist superpower created unprecedented new weapons for Americans to deploy in pursuing their divine mission. Long after emancipation, Americans continued to believe that their nation was divinely destined to expand salvation and in so doing, save the world. Americans and the rest of the world continue to reckon with the consequences of this faith.

NOTES

Introduction

Note to chapter epigraph: Joshua Marsden, *Grace Displayed: An Interesting Narrative of the Life, Conversion, Christian Experience, Ministry, and Missionary Labors of Joshua Marsden* (New York, 1814), 190.

1. Marsden, *Grace Displayed*, 190.

2. Disestablishment was one cause that did animate usually politically resistant white Christians in both the North and the South, but this animation was short-lived. Once they secured disestablishment, these Christian activist networks fell dormant. By the late eighteenth century, slavery, on the other hand, was no longer seen by most Christians as an obstacle for conversion. See Katharine Gerbner, *Christian Slavery: Conversion and Race in the Protestant Atlantic World* (Philadelphia: University of Pennsylvania Press, 2018).

3. I refer to my actors as conversionists and their ideology as conversionism largely because all other terms are too narrow. These beliefs transcended the theological boundaries implied by labels like evangelicalism or even missionary Christianity. Even the nascent anti-missions movement shared a belief that conversion would remake the world, and while evangelicals were more zealous in extending salvation, nearly all Christians believed that conversion would solve the world's problems more effectively than political action.

4. Paul E. Johnson's *A Shopkeeper's Millennium: Society and Revivals in Rochester, New York, 1815–1837* (New York: Hill & Wang, 1978) argues that market changes and status anxieties fueled reform. Histories that emphasize biracial cooperation include Manisha Sinha, *The Slave's Cause A History of Abolition* (New Haven, CT: Yale University Press, 2017); Richard Newman, *Transformation of American Abolitionism: Fighting Slavery in the Early Republic* (Chapel Hill: University of North Carolina Press, 2002); and John Stauffer, *Black Hearts of Men: Radical Abolitionists and the Transformation of Race* (Cambridge, MA: Harvard University Press, 2002). The best political history of antislavery in the early republic is Matthew Mason, *Slavery and Politics in the Early Republic* (Chapel Hill: University of North Carolina Press, 2006). See also Paul J. Polgar, *Standard-Bearers of Equality: America's First Abolition Movement* (Chapel Hill: University of North Carolina Press, 2019); and Nicholas Wood, "Considerations of Humanity and Expediency: The Slave Trades and African Colonization in the Early National Antislavery Movement" (PhD diss., University of Virginia, 2013). Historians of the later abolitionist movement have foregrounded

ideology, including W. Caleb McDaniel, *The Problem of Democracy in the Age of Slavery: Garrisonian Abolitionists and Transatlantic Reform* (Baton Rouge: Louisiana State University Press, 2013), and Luke E. Harlow, *Religion, Race, and the Making of Confederate Kentucky, 1830–1880* (New York: Cambridge University Press, 2014). Works focusing on the earlier era, however, have largely focused on political action rather than ideological formation.

5. Newman, *Transformation of American Abolitionism*, 2.

6. Sinha, *The Slave's Cause*.

7. Robert H. Abzug, *Cosmos Crumbling: American Reform and the Religious Imagination* (New York: Oxford University Press, 1994), viii.

8. David Brion Davis, "The Emergence of Immediatism in British and American Antislavery Thought," *Mississippi Valley Historical Review* 49, no. 2 (1962): 205–24.

9. Manisha Sinha, for example, explicitly decries the divide separating studies of gradualism and immediatism. Sinha, *The Slave's Cause*.

10. Tracy Fessenden, *Culture and Redemption: Religion, the Secular, and American Literature* (Princeton, NJ: Princeton University Press, 2007), 61; and John Lardas Modern, *Secularism in America* (Chicago: University of Chicago Press, 2011), 21.

11. The historiography on religion and the English Civil War is robust, and the role of millennial religion is documented even in synthetic works. See Michael Braddick, *God's Fury, England's Fire: A New History of the English Civil Wars* (London: Penguin, 2009), and Carla Gardina Pestana, *The English Atlantic in an Age of Revolution, 1640–1641* (Cambridge, MA: Harvard University Press, 2007).

12. Nathan O. Hatch, "The Origins of Civil Millennialism in America: New England Clergymen, War with France, and the Revolution," *William and Mary Quarterly* 31, no. 3 (July 1974): 407–30.

13. Robert H. Abzug, *Cosmos Crumbling: American Reform and the Religious Imagination* (New York: Oxford University Press, 1994).

14. Nicholas Guyatt, *Providence and the Invention of the United States, 1607–1876* (New York: Cambridge University Press, 2007).

15. Nathan O. Hatch, *The Democratization of American Christianity* (New Haven, CT: Yale University Press, 1989).

16. For an example of scholarship that foregrounds denominational authority, see Jon Butler, *Awash in a Sea of Faith: Christianizing the American People* (Cambridge, MA: Harvard University Press, 1992), esp. 98–128 and 257–88.

17. Sam Haselby and Benjamin Park have offered exciting correctives to this trend, but more attention is required to understand how national denominations came into existence and how their creation shaped life in the early republic. Sam Haselby, *The Origins of American Religious Nationalism* (New York: Oxford University Press, 2015); Benjamin E. Park, *American Nationalisms: Imagining Union in the Age of Revolutions, 1783–1833* (New York: Cambridge University Press, 2017).

18. Marsden, *Grace Displayed*, 210.

19. Intellectual historians are understandably drawn to the task of unfolding logically consistent intellectual systems. The legacy of Perry Miller's spectacular dissection of Ramist logic in the *New England Mind* has led to equally impressive cartographies of American Calvinism in the eighteenth and early nineteenth centuries. For a synthesis of this work, see E. Brooks Holifield, *Theology in America: Christian Thought from the Age of the Puritans to the Civil War* (New Haven,

CT: Yale University Press, 2003). For Miller, see *The New England Mind: The Seventeenth Century* (Cambridge, MA: Harvard University Press, 1939).

20. For more on the Quaker propensity to make antislavery alliances with non-Quakers, see Kirsten Sword, "Remembering Dinah Nevil: Strategic Deceptions in Eighteenth-Century Antislavery," *Journal of American History* 92, no. 2 (Sept. 2010): 314–43.

21. The best study on the War of 1812 and American Christianity remains William Gribbin, *The Churches Militant: The War of 1812 and American Religion* (New Haven, CT: Yale University Press, 1973). This study builds on Gribbin's insights to track how the war inspired denominational leaders to expand their efforts from salvation to reform.

22. See, for example, McDaniel, *The Problem of Democracy in the Age of Slavery;* Christopher L. Brown, *Moral Capital: Foundations of British Abolitionism* (Chapel Hill: University of North Carolina Press, 2006); and R. J. M. Blackett, *Building an Antislavery Wall: Black Americans in the Atlantic Abolitionist Movement, 1830–1860* (Baton Rouge: Louisiana State University Press, 1983).

23. Marsden, *Grace Displayed,* 204–5.

24. Daniel Walker Howe, *What Hath God Wrought: The Transformation of America, 1815–1848* (New York: Oxford University Press, 2007).

25. Eric Burin, *Slavery and the Peculiar Solution: A* History *of the* American Colonization Society (Gainesville: University Press of Florida, 2005); Beverly C. Tomek, *Colonization and Its Discontents: Emancipation, Emigration, and Antislavery in Antebellum Pennsylvania* (New York: New York University Press, 2011); and, for the opposite perspective, Douglas R. Egerton, "'Its Origin Is Not a Little Curious': A New Look at the American Colonization Society," *Journal of the Early Republic* 5, no. 4 (Winter 1985): 463–89.

26. James T. Campbell, *Middle Passages: African American Journeys to Africa, 1787–2005* (New York: Penguin Books, 2006); Amos Beyan, *African American Settlements in West Africa: John Brown Russwurm and the American Civilizing Efforts* (New York: Palgrave Macmillan, 2005); and James Sidbury, *Becoming African in America: Race and Nation in the Early Black Atlantic* (New York: Oxford University Press, 2007).

27. Marsden, *Grace Displayed,* 214.

Chapter One

1. John Leland, *The Writings of the Late Elder John Leland,* edited by L. F. Greene (New York: G. W. Wood, 1845), 171, 173.

2. Leland, *Writings,* 94.

3. Leland, *Writings,* 51.

4. Leland, *Writings,* 174.

5. David Brion Davis, *The Problem of Slavery in the Age of Revolution, 1770–1823* (Ithaca, NY: Cornell University Press, 1975).

6. Even in the antebellum North, scholarship on the disappearance of slavery highlights the role of contentious political action. For a wide-ranging survey of global abolition, see Seymour Drescher, *Abolition: A History of Slavery and Antislavery* (New York: Cambridge University Press, 2009). See also Joanne Pope Melish, *Disowning Slavery: Gradual Emancipation and "Race" in New England, 1780–1860* (Ithaca, NY: Cornell University Press, 2000); Margot Minardi, *Making*

Slavery History: Abolitionism and the Politics of Memory in Massachusetts (New York: Oxford University Press, 2010); Leslie M. Harris, *In the Shadow of Slavery: African Americans in New York City, 1626–1863* (Chicago: University of Chicago Press, 2002); Gary B. Nash, *Freedom by Degrees: Emancipation in Pennsylvania and Its Aftermath* (New York: Oxford University Press, 1991); Leslie Alexander, *African or American? Black Identity and Political Activism in New York City, 1784–1861* (Urbana: University of Illinois Press, 2010); and Richard S. Newman, *Transformation of American Abolitionism: Fighting Slavery in the Early Republic* (Chapel Hill: University of North Carolina Press, 2002).

7. Historian Benjamin Quarles first called the American Revolution the nation's longest, most sustained slave revolt. During the tumult of the war, over eighty thousand Black men and women liberated themselves. Benjamin Quarles, *The Negro in the American Revolution* (Chapel Hill: University of North Carolina Press, 1961/1996).

8. Eva Sheppard Wolf, *Race and Liberty in the New Nation: Emancipation in Virginia from the Revolution to Nat Turner's Rebellion* (Baton Rouge: Louisiana State University Press, 2006).

9. For more on declining tobacco productivity and its influence on slavery, see Alan Kulikoff, *Tobacco and Slaves: The Development of Southern Cultures in the Chesapeake, 1680–1800* (Chapel Hill: University of North Carolina Press, 1986); Barbara Hahn, *Making Tobacco Bright: Creating an American Commodity, 1617–1937* (Baltimore: Johns Hopkins University Press, 2011); and Steven Stoll, *Larding the Lean Earth: Soil and Society in Nineteenth-Century America* (New York: Hill & Wang, 2002).

10. The 1777 constitution of Vermont partially banned slavery. In 1780 Pennsylvania passed a gradual emancipation act. Similar laws followed from New Hampshire, Connecticut, Rhode Island, New York, and finally New Jersey in 1804. Massachusetts achieved abolition through a 1783 legal decision. The Northwest Ordinance in 1787 banned the introduction of new enslaved persons in the Northwest Territories.

11. For more on Scottish moral philosophy and its influence on American Christianity, see Mark A. Noll, *America's God: From Jonathan Edwards to Abraham Lincoln* (New York: Oxford University Press, 2002).

12. For more on how theological and denominational rivalries created anxieties in the early republic, see Samuel Hasselby, *The Origins of American Religious Nationalism* (New York: Oxford University Press, 2015).

13. For a discussion of early American conversion narratives, see Lincoln Mullen, *The Chance of Salvation: A History of Conversion in America* (Cambridge, MA: Harvard University Press, 2017).

14. For more on Scottish moral philosophy and its influence on the United States, see Franklin Court, *The Scottish Connection: The Rise of English Literary Study in Early America* (Syracuse, NY: Syracuse University Press, 2001); and Roger L. Emerson, "The Scottish Literati and America, 1680–1800," in Ned C. Landsman, ed., *Nation and Province in the First British Empire: Scotland [and] the Americas, 1600–1800* (Lewisburg, PA: Bucknell University Press, 2001), 183–220.

15. Thomas Reid, *The Works of Thomas Reid*, ed. William Hamilton Bart (Edinburgh: Maclachlan Stewart & Co., 1846), 95.

16. Gideon Mailer, *John Witherspoon's American Revolution* (Chapel Hill: University of North Carolina Press, 2017); Jeffry H. Morrison, *John Witherspoon and the Founding of the American Republic* (Notre Dame, IN: University of Notre Dame Press, 2005).

17. Sarah Knott, *Sensibility and the American Revolution* (Chapel Hill: University of North Carolina Press, 2009). For Knott on class, see p. 18; on gender, see p. 52

18. In 1822, Methodists trumpeted Scottish moral philosophy, issuing Reid's complete works through the church's publishing house. E. Brooks Holifield, *The Gentlemen Theologians: American Theology in Southern Culture, 1795–1860* (Durham, NC: Duke University Press, 1978), 118–19.

19. Timothy Dwight, *A Sermon Preached at Northhampton, on the Twenty-Eighth of November, 1781* (Hartford, CT, 1781), 28–29.

20. *Minutes of the Warren Association, at Their Meeting, in Middleboro, Sept 7 and 8, 1784* (1784), cited in Ruth Bloch, *Visionary Republic: Millennial Themes in American Thought, 1756–1800* (New York: Cambridge University Press, 1985), 256 n44.

21. For examples of how evangelical hegemony stymied religious liberty, see David Sehat, *The Myth of American Religious Freedom* (New York: Oxford University Press, 2010).

22. Thomas Paine, *The Rights of Man: Being an Answer to Mr. Burke's Attack on the French Revolution* (London, 1817), 114.

23. Richard Price, *Observations on the Importance of the American Revolution, and the Means of Making It a Benefit to the World* (London, 1785), 3.

24. Timothy Dwight, *A Sermon Preached at Northhampton, on the Twenty-Eighth of November, 1781* (Hartford, CT, 1781), 31.

25. Thomas Reese, *An Essay on the Influence of Religion, in Civil Society* (Charleston, SC: 1788), 18.

26. Ezra Stiles, *The United States Elevated to Glory and Honour* (Worcester, MA: Isaiah Thomas, 1785), 70, 20.

27. Joseph Benson, *Four Sermons, on the Second Coming of Christ, and the Future Misery of the Wicked* (Philadelphia, 1797), 64, 83.

28. John Blair Smith, *The Enlargement of Christ's Kingdom, the object of a Christian's prayers and exertions. A discourse, delivered in the Dutch Church, in Albany; before the Northern Missionary Society in the State of New-York, at their organization, Feb. 14, 1797* (Schenectady, NY: C. P. Wyckoff, 1797), 8.

29. Smith, *The Enlargement of Christ's Kingdom*, iii.

30. The literature on free Black communities in the early republic is vast but important. Starting points include Gary B. Nash, *Forging Freedom: The Formation of Philadelphia's Black Community, 1720–1840* (Cambridge, MA: Harvard University Press, 1991); Christopher Cameron, *To Plead Our Own Cause: African Americans in Massachusetts and the Making of the Antislavery Movement* (Kent, OH: Kent State University Press, 2014); Julie Winch, *Between Slavery and Freedom: Free People of Color in America From Settlement to the Civil War* (Lanham, MD: Rowman & Littlefield, 2014); and Nicholas P. Wood, "A 'class of Citizens': The Earliest Black Petitioners to Congress and Their Quaker Allies," *William and Mary Quarterly* 74, no. 1 (Jan. 2017), 109–44.

31. *Annals of the Congress of the United States*, 4th Congress, 2nd Session [March 1795-March 1797] VI (Washington, DC: 1849), cols. 2015–2024.

32. *Acts and Proceedings of the Synod of New York and Philadelphia, 1787 and 1788* (Philadelphia: Jane Aitken, 1803), 3.

33. Acts and Proceedings, 3–4.

34. Acts and Proceedings, 3–4.

35. It is possible, however, to exaggerate the commitment to abolitionism among Quakers. While many abolitionists were Quakers, it would be wrong to claim that most Quakers were ab-

olitionists. See, for example, Jean R. Soderlund, *Quakers and Slavery: A Divided Spirit* (Princeton, NJ: Princeton University Press, 2016).

36. Jack D. Marietta, *The Reformation of American Quakerism, 1748–1783* (Philadelphia: University of Pennsylvania Press, 1984). See also Sydney V. James, *A People among Peoples: Quaker Benevolence in Eighteenth-Century America* (Cambridge, MA: Harvard University Press, 1963); and James Walvin, *The Quakers: Money and Morals* (London: John Murray, 1997).

37. This process was not always smooth. For a case study in a particularly fraught story of Quaker antislavery, see A. Glenn Crothers, *Quakers Living in the Lion's Mouth: The Society of Friends in Northern Virginia, 1730–1865* (Tallahassee: University Press of Florida, 2012).

38. Thomas Chalkley, "Some Considerations on the Call, Work, and Wages of the Ministers of Christ, 1720," in *A Collection of the Works of Thomas Chalkley* (Philadelphia, 1790), 548–49.

39. John Woolman, *Journal of John Woolman* (Boston, 1871), 160–68.

40. For other examples of British Quakers encouraging reform, see the work of John Stephenson and Samuel Spavold. For Stephenson, see the diary of George Churchman and for Spavold, see the diary of John Parrish, both in the Quaker Collection at Haverford College.

41. January 5, 1762, Elizabeth Wilkinson Journal, Quaker Collection, Haverford College.

42. July 27, 1762, Elizabeth Wilkinson Journal.

43. February 7, 1763, George Churchman Diary.

44. Job Scott, *The Works of That Eminent Minister of the Gospel, Job Scott, late of Providence Rhode Island,* edited by John Comly, Vol. II (Philadelphia, 1831), 71–73.

45. Journal of Job Scott, 71–21, 215.

46. John Fothergill, *An Account of the Life and Travels in the Work of the Ministry of John Fothergill* (Philadelphia: James Chattin, 1754), 81–81.

47. Benjamin Holme, "An Epistle to Friends in America," in *The Collection of the Epistles and Works of Benjamin Holme* (London: L. Hinde, 1754), 161–62.

48. May 10, 1762, Elizabeth Wilkinson Journal.

49. John Churchman, *An account of the gospel labours: and Christian experiences of a faithful minister of Christ, John Churchman* (Philadelphia: James Phillips, 1780), 281.

50. Letter, no date, John Parrish to James Thornton, John Parrish papers, Quaker Collection, Haverford College.

51. John Parrish, *Remarks on the slavery of the black people, addressed to the citizens of the United States, particularly to those who are in legislative or executive stations in the general or state governments; and also to such individuals as hold them in bondage* (Philadelphia, 1806), 3. For a comparison of the 1805 draft and the published piece, see Richard S. Newman, "John Parrish, 'Notes On Abolition' (circa 1805)," Quakers and Slavery, available at http://web.tricolib.brynmawr.edu/speccoll/quakersandslavery/commentary/people/parrish_john.php.

52. 1798, no month and day given, Diary of John Parrish.

53. Samuel Hopkins, *The Works of Samuel Hopkins* (Boston: Doctrinal Tract and Book Society, 1852), 622.

54. Sarah Deutsch, "Those Elusive Guineamen: Newport Slavers, 1735–1774," *New England Quarterly* 55, no. 2 (1982): 230.

55. Hopkins, *Works,* 615.

56. For more detail on slavery in Newport, see Jay Coughtry, *The Notorious Triangle: Rhode Island and the African Slave Trade 1700–1807* (Philadelphia: Temple University Press, 1981); Deutsch,

"Those Elusive Guineamen," 229–53; and Elaine F. Crane, "'The First Wheel of Commerce': New-port, Rhode Island and the Slave Trade, 1760–1776," *Slavery and Abolition* 1, no. 2 (1980): 178–98.

57. The Providence abolitionists largely depended on the organizing and publishing activity of Moses Brown. For more about the activism of Moses Brown, particularly his combative rela-tionship with his brother John, who became the most vocal defender of slavery in Rhode Island, see Charles Rappleye, *Sons of Providence: The Brown Brothers, the Slave Trade, and the American Revolution* (New York: Simon & Schuster, 2017).

58. Samuel Hopkins, *Sin, thro' divine interposition, an advantage to the universe; and yet this no excuse for sin, or encouragement to it* (Boston: J. Kneeland, 1773).

59. Hopkins, *Works*, 624.

60. Hopkins, *A Dialogue Concerning the Slavery of the Africans, in Works*, 575.

61. For a detailed discussion of how Hopkinsian disinterested benevolence modified Ed-wardsean pure virtue, see Joseph A. Conforti, *Samuel Hopkins and the New Divinity Movement: Calvinism, the Congregational Ministry, and Reform in New England between the Great Awakenings* (Grand Rapids, MI: Wm. B. Eerdmans, 1981). 109–24. See also Kenneth P. Minkema and Harry S. Stout, "The Edwardsean Tradition and the Antislavery Debate, 1740–1865," *Journal of American History* 92, no. 1 (June 2005):47–74; and Kenneth P. Minkema, "Jonathan Edwards on Slavery and the Slave Trade," *William and Mary Quarterly* 54, no. 4, Religion in Early America (Oct., 1997): 823–34.

62. Hopkins met several formerly enslaved men through his parishioner Sarah Osborn, who in 1774 reported to the census that she had six Black boarders. For more on Hopkins, Osborn, and the Black men and women who radicalized Hopkins, see Catherine Brekus, *Sarah Osborn's World: The Rise of Evangelical Christianity in Early America* (New Haven, CT: Yale University Press, 2013), esp. 286–88.

63. Phillis Wheatley to Samuel Hopkins, February 9, 1774, and May 6, 1774, in Phillis Wheat-ley, *Complete Writings*, edited by Vincent Caretta (New York: Penguin Books, 2001), 151–52, 157–58.

64. Caesar Sarter, "Address, To those who are Advocates for holding the Africans in Slav-ery," *The Essex Journal and Merimack Packet*, August 17, 1774. For more on Sarter and Black New England abolitionists, see Christopher Cameron, *To Plead Our Own Cause: African Americans in Massachusetts and the Making of the Antislavery Movement* (Kent, OH: Kent State University Press, 2014).

65. Hopkins, "Dialogue Concerning the Slavery of the Africans," in *Works*, 585.

66. Hopkins, "Slave Trade and Slavery," in *Works*, 617–18.

67. Hopkins, "Discourse upon the Slave Trade and the Slavery of the Africans," in *Works*, 606.

68. Hopkins, "Slave Trade and Slavery," in *Works*, 614–15, 619–20.

69. Phillis Wheatley, "Letter to Reverend Samson Occum," *Connecticut Gazette*, March 11, 1774.

70. First Congregational Church Records, March 5, 1784, cited in Joseph E. Conforti, *Samuel Hopkins and the New Divinity Movement*, 134–35.

71. Hopkins, "Slave Trade and Slavery," in *Works*, 615. The three scriptures are Jeremiah 22:13, Habakkuk 2:12, and Ezekiel 24:13.

72. For more on Lemuel Haynes, see John Saillant, *Black Puritan, Black Republican: The Life and Thought of Lemuel Haynes, 1753–1833* (New York: Oxford University Press, 2002).

73. Isaac first published this argument in "Evangelical Revolt: The Nature of the Baptists' Challenge to the Traditional Order in Virginia, 1765 to 1775," *William and Mary Quarterly* 31,

no. 3 (July 1974): 345–68. See also Rhys Isaac, *The Transformation of Virginia, 1740–1790* (Chapel Hill: University Press of North Carolina, 1982); Donald G. Matthews, *Religion in the Old South* (Chicago: University of Chicago Press, 1977); Christine Heyrman, *Southern Cross: The Beginnings of the Bible Belt* (Chapel Hill.: University of North Carolina Press, 1997).

74. Charles F. Irons, *The Origins of Proslavery Christianity: White and Black Evangelicals in Colonial and Antebellum Virginia* (Chapel Hill: University of North Carolina Press, 2008). See also Janet Moore Lindman, *Bodies of Belief: Baptist Community in Early America* (Philadelphia: University of Pennsylvania Press, 2008); Randolph Ferguson Scully, *Religion and the Making of Nat Turner's Virginia: Baptist Community and Conflict, 1740–1840* (Charlottesville: University of Virginia Press, 2008); Jewel Spangler, *Anglican Monopoly, Evangelical Dissent, and the Rise of the Baptists in the Late Eighteenth Century* (Charlottesville: University of Virginia Press, 2008); Monica Najar, *Evangelizing the South: A Social History of Church and State in Early America* (New York: Oxford University Press, 2008).

75. John Leland, *The Writings of the Late Elder John Leland*, edited by L. F. Greene (New York: G. W. Wood, 1845), 171 and 173.

76. Mark S. Scarberry, "John Leland and James Madison: Religious Influence on the Ratification of the Constitution and on the Proposal of the Bill of Rights" (Sept. 2, 2008). Available at SSRN: http://ssrn.com/abstract=1262520.

77. Leland, *Writings*, 174.

78. Leland, *Writings*, 96.

79. January 30, 1816, Daniel Chapman Banks Diary, Filson Library.

80. Leland, *Writings*, 171–75.

81. Leland, *Writings*, 51.

82. Leland, *Writings*, 171–74.

83. Leland, *Writings*, 672. Leland's shift from abolitionist to anti-abolitionist is treated in Bruce Gourley, "John Leland: Evolving Views of Slavery, 1789–1839," *Baptist History and Heritage* (Winter 2005): 104–16. As the title indicates, Gourley sees rupture in Leland's views. If, however, we foreground Leland's conversionism, we can track notable continuities that tie together his early antislavery activism with his later anti-abolitionism.

84. The best biographical treatment of Asbury is John Wigger, *American Saint: Francis Asbury and the Methodists* (New York: Oxford University Press, 2012). See also John Wigger, *Taking Heaven by Storm: Methodism and the Rise of Popular Christianity in America* (Urbana: University of Illinois Press, 2001); Cynthia Lynn Lyerly, *Methodism and the Southern Mind, 1770–1810* (New York: Oxford University Press, 2006); Dee Andrews, *The Methodists and Revolutionary America, 1760–1800: The Shaping of an Evangelical Culture* (Princeton, NJ: Princeton University Press, 2000); and Russell E. Richey, *Early American Methodism* (Bloomington: Indiana University Press, 1991).

85. Francis Asbury, *The Journal and Letters of Francis Asbury*, edited by Elmer T. Clark et al. (London: Epworth Press, 1958), 1:488.

86. Thomas Coke, *The Journals of Dr. Thomas Coke*, edited by John A. Vickers (Nashville, Tennessee: Kingswood Books, 2005), 87. For more on the pivotal role of Thomas Coke in the Methodist response to slavery, see Christopher Cannon Jones, "Methodism, Slavery, and Freedom in the Revolutionary Atlantic, 1770–1820" (PhD diss., College of William and Mary, 2016), esp. 127–35.

87. Thomas Coke to Ezekiel Cooper, April 23, 1795, in Thomas Coke, *The Letters of Dr. Thomas Coke*, edited by John A. Vickers (Nashville, TN: Kingswood Books, 2013), 200.

88. Asbury, *Journal,* Vol. II: 151.

89. Asbury, *Journal II,* 156.

90. Asbury, *Journal II,* 580.

91. Asbury, *Journal II,* 281.

92. Asbury, *Journal II,* 591.

93. James Sidbury, *Ploughshares into Swords: Race, Rebellion, and Identity in Gabriel's Virginia, 1730–1810* (New York: Cambridge University Press, 1997), 76–77. See also Douglas R. Egerton, *Gabriel's Rebellion: The Virginia Slave Conspiracies of 1800 and 1802* (Chapel Hill: University of North Carolina Press, 1993).

Chapter Two

1. François Furstenberg's study of civil texts demonstrates how American nationalism included the belief that enslaved men and women tacitly consented to their enslavement, for if they were as desirous and capable of freedom as white Americans, they would have it. François Furstenberg, *In the Name of the Father: Washington's Legacy, Slavery, and the Making of a Nation* (New York: Penguin, 2006). For more on how the rise of the American democracy influenced American attitudes toward slavery and white supremacy, North and South, see Padraig Riley, *Slavery and the Democratic Conscience: Political Life in Jeffersonian America* (Philadelphia: University of Pennsylvania Press, 2015).

2. Christian organizing drew on powerful fears of a backsliding republic. Amanda Porterfield, *Conceived in Doubt: Religion and Politics in the New American Nation* (Chicago: University of Chicago Press, 2012).

3. For Baptist denominational formation, see Robert Baylor Semple, *History of the Rise and Progress of Baptists in Virginia* (Richmond, 1810); Reuben Edward Alley, *A History of Baptists in Virginia* (Richmond, 1974); Thomas S. Kidd and Barry G Hankins, *Baptists in America: A History* (New York: Oxford University Press, 2015). For Presbyterian denominational formation see Leonard J. Trinterud, *The Forming of an American Tradition: A Reexamination of Colonial Presbyterianism* (Philadelphia: Westminster Press, 1949); and William Harrison Taylor, *Unity in Christ and Country: American Presbyterians in the Revolutionary Era, 1758–1801* (Tuscaloosa: University of Alabama Press, 2017).

4. Samuel Haselby, *The Origins of American Religious Nationalism* (New York: Oxford University Press, 2015).

5. For more on how religious leaders imagined the space of the West, see Amy Derogatis, *Moral Geography: Maps, Missionaries, and the American Frontier* (New York: Columbia University Press, 2003). As Derogatis notes, the process of converting the nation had as much, if not more, to do with subduing space and asserting institutional authority as it did with encouraging personal religious changes.

6. Judge Edmund Pendleton wrote to James Madison in 1787 that "parties or factions are tumors that will arise in the political body" and require "dangerous amputations." Madison agreed and outlined the many dangers of factionalism that same year in Federalist 10. "To James Madison from Edmund Pendleton, 7 April 1787," *The Papers of James Madison,* vol. 17, edited by David B. Mattern et al. (Charlottesville: University Press of Virginia, 1991), 515–18. See also "The Federalist

Number 10," *The Papers of James Madison,* vol. 10, edited by Robert A. Rutland et al. (Chicago: University of Chicago Press, 1977), 263–70.

7. According to historian Johann Neem, American nationalism stemmed not from state action, but through grassroots organizing and cultural fusion. Johann Neem, "Civil Society and American Nationalism, 1776–1865," in Elisabeth S. Clemens and Doug Guthrie, eds. *Politics and Partnerships: The Role of Voluntary Associations in America's Political Past and Present* (Chicago: University of Chicago Press, 2010), 29–53. See also Neem, "Taking Modernity's Wager: Tocqueville, Social Capital, and the American Civil War," *Journal of Interdisciplinary History* 41, no. 4 (Spring 2011): 591–618.

8. "Extracts from a letter received from the Rev. Robert Finley, at Basking Ridge, New Jersey, Dec. 23, 1804," *The General Assembly's missionary magazine; or evangelical intelligencer,* edited by William P. Farrand (Philadelphia: William P. Farrand, 1806), 353–56.

9. Isaac V. Brown, *Memoirs of the Rev. Robert Finley, D. D., late pastor of the Presbyterian congregation at Basking Ridge, New-Jersey, and president of Franklin college, located at Athens, in the state of Georgia. With brief sketches of some of his cotemporaries, and numerous notes* (New Brunswick, NJ: Terhune & Letson, 1819), 51.

10. American Protestants of nearly all theological stripes relied on transatlantic connections wedded to the British Empire. For more on the power of these connections, see Katherine Carté Engel, "Connecting Protestants in Britain's Eighteenth-Century Atlantic Empire," *William and Mary Quarterly* 75, no. 1 (Jan. 2018): 37–70.

11. *Acts and Proceedings of the Synod of New York and Philadelphia, 1787 and 1788* (Philadelphia: Jane Aitken, 1803), 3–4.

12. Thomas Coke, *The substance of a sermon, preached at Baltimore, in the state of Maryland, before the general conference of the Methodist Episcopal Church, on the 27th of December, 1784, at the ordination of the Rev. Francis Asbury, to the Office of a Superintendent* (London: J. Paramore for T. Scollick, 1785), 6.

13. Coke, *The substance of a sermon . . .,* 22.

14. *The Society for Propagating the Gospel among the Indians and Others in North America, 1787–1887* (Cambridge, MA: Printed for the Society, 1887), 27.

15. *The Records of the General Association of Ye Colony of Connecticut, Begun June 20, 1738, Ending June 19, 1799* (Hartford, CT: Case, Lockwood, & Brainard, 1888), 120–25.

16. For more on the Connecticut Society for the Promotion of Freedom and for the Relief of Persons Unlawfully Holden in Bondage, see James D. Essig, "Connecticut Ministers and Slavery, 1790–1795," *Journal of American Studies* 15, no. 1 (April, 1981), 27–44.

17. Marilyn Westerkamp, "Division, Dissension, and Compromise: The Presbyterian Church during the Great Awakening," *Journal of Presbyterian History* 78, no. 1, Special Issue: Presbyterians in Times of Controversy (Spring 2000): 3–18.

18. *Acts and Proceedings of the General Assembly of the Presbyterian Church in the United States of America, 1789* (Philadelphia: Jane Aitken, 1803), 7. Presbyterian Historical Society.

19. *Acts and Proceedings,* 7. For more on the spiritual importance of Washington, see Furstenberg, *In the Name of the Father.*

20. *Acts and Proceedings,* 7.

21. This letter was signed by Isaac Backus, Nathan Plimpton, and Asaph Flether. See Alvah Hovey, *A Memoir of the Life and Times of the Rev. Isaac Backus* (Boston: Gould & Lincoln, 1858), 229–30.

22. *Minutes of the Philadelphia Baptist Association, from A.D. 1707, to A.D. 1807: being the first one hundred years of its existence,* edited by A. D. Gillette (Philadelphia: American Baptist Society, 1851), 343, 350.

23. Savannah Baptist Society for Foreign Missions, "To the Inhabitants of Georgia and the Adjacent Parts of South Carolina," in Samuel Boykin, ed., *History of the Baptist Denomination in Georgia, Volume I* (Atlanta: Jas. P. Harrison, 1881), 79–80.

24. Richard S. Newman, *Freedom's Prophet: Bishop Richard Allen, the AME Church, and the Black Founding Fathers* (New York: New York University Press, 2008).

25. For more on the work of the Free African Society, see Newman, *Freedom's Prophet;* Carol V. R. George, *Segregated Sabbaths; Richard Allen and the Emergence of Independent Black Churches 1760–1840* (New York: Oxford University Press, 1973); and Julie Winch, *Philadelphia's Black Elite: Activism, Accommodation, and the Struggle for Autonomy, 1787–1848* (Philadelphia: Temple University Press, 1988).

26. There is some disagreement regarding when the walk-out occurred. Allen's memoirs and AME tradition date the event to 1787; Richard Allen, *The Life, Experience, and Gospel Labours of the Rt. Rev. Richard Allen* (Philadelphia: Martin & Boden, 1833), 13–15. Historians, however, have convincingly argued that the more likely date is 1793; see J. Gordon Melton, *A Will to Choose: The Origins of African American Methodism* (Lanham: Rowman & Littlefield, 2007), and Dennis C. Dickerson, *The African Methodist Episcopal Church: A History* (New York: Cambridge University Press, 2019).

27. Christopher Cameron, *To Plead Our Own Cause: African Americans in Massachusetts and the Making of the Antislavery Movement* (Kent, OH: Kent State University Press, 2014), 90.

28. *Petition for freedom to the Massachusetts Council and the House of Representatives, January 1777.* Massachusetts Historical Society.

29. John Marrant, *A Sermon Preached on the 24th Day of June 1789, Being the Festival of St. John the Baptist* (Boston: Thomas and John Fleet, 1789).

30. Craig Steven Wilder, *In the Company Of Black Men: The African Influence on African Americans in New York City* (New York: New York University Press, 2001), 52. See also Craig Steven Wilder, "The Rise and Influence of the New York African Society for Mutual Relief, 1808–1865," *Afro-Americans in New York Life and History* 22 (July 1998).

31. Jefferson clung to this belief even after the Missouri Crisis illustrated how debates over slavery threatened to tear apart the nation. See "From Thomas Jefferson to John Holmes, 22 April 1820," Founders Online, National Archives, version of Jan. 18, 2019.

32. Richard Lovett, *The History of the London Missionary Society, 1795–1895* (London: Oxford University Press, 1899), I:49–50.

33. *New York Missionary Magazine and Repository of Religious Intelligence* I (Jan. 1800): 9.

34. Alexander McWhorter, *The Blessedness of the Liberal: A Sermon, Preached in the Dutch Middle Church, before the New York Missionary Society, at their First Institution, November 1, 1796* (New York: T. and J. Swords, 1796), 5.

35. John Rodgers, the influential Presbyterian, served as president while John H. Livingston, a leader in the Dutch Reformed Church, was vice president. Secretary John M. Mason was from the Associate Reformed Church. Of the nine other officers, four were Dutch Reformed, three Presbyterian, one Associate Reformed, and another Baptist. This diverse roster set the NYMS apart as a singular example of the possibilities of American ecumenism, but the society struggled in its efforts to turn ecumenical enthusiasm into results.

36. For more on the NYMS mission to the Chickasaw, see R. Pierce Beaver, *Pioneers in Missions: A Sourcebook on the Rise of American Missions* (Grand Rapids, MI: William Eerdman's, 1966), 235–48.

37. For information on both missions, see *New York Missionary Magazine and Religious Intelligencer, Volume II* (New York, 1801), 401–6.

38. Nathaniel Emmons, *To All Who Are Desirous of the Spread of the Gospel of Our Lord Jesus Christ* (Boston, 1799), 6.

39. Emmons, *To All Who Are Desirous,* 6.

40. *Massachusetts Baptist Missionary Magazine (MBMM)* I (Sept. 1803): 6.

41. *MBMM* I: 5–8, 11–12, 93, 159, 191, 220.

42. Charles L. Chaney, *The Birth of Missions in America* (South Pasadena, CA: William Carey Library, 1976), 163.

43. Massachusetts Society for Promoting Christian Knowledge, *An Account of the Massachusetts Society for Promoting Christian Knowledge* (Andover, MA: Flagg & Gould, 1815), 3.

44. Chaney, *The Birth of Missions in America.*

45. Gillette, *Minutes of the Baptist General Association,* 350, 370, 381.

46. Diary of Nancy Cranch, July 4, 1819, Cranch Family Papers, Library of Congress, cited in Linda Kerber, *Women of the Republic: Intellect and Ideology in Revolutionary America* (Chapel Hill: University of North Carolina Press, 1980), 111. For more on the complex ways in which women navigated patriarchy in their activism, see Nancy F. Cott, *The Bonds of Womanhood: "Woman's Sphere" in New England, 1780–1830* (New Haven, CT: Yale University Press, 1977). See also Elizabeth R. Varon, *We Mean to Be Counted: White Women and Politics in Antebellum Virginia* (Chapel Hill: University of North Carolina Press, 1998).

47. Cent Society Address, 1802, Broadside, Massachusetts, Historical Society.

48. After two years, the BFSMP began distributing their donations equally among the MMS and the Massachusetts Baptist Missionary Society. *A Brief Account of the Origin and Progress of the Boston Female Society for Missionary Purposes, with Extracts from the Reports of that Society, in May, 1817 and 1818* (Boston: Lincoln & Edmands, 1818), 3. See also *Massachusetts Missionary Magazine* 2, no. 5 (1804): 279–381.

49. R. Pierce Beaver, *American Protestant Women in World Missions: A History of the First Feminist Movement in North America* (Grand Rapids, MI: William B. Eerdman's, 1980), 18. See also Dana L. Robert, *American Women in Mission: A Social History of Their Thought and Practice* (Macon, GA: Mercer University Press, 1997).

50. In 1803 three women joined the MMS, and a fourth joined the following year. Beaver, *American Protestant Women in World Missions,* 24.

51. In 1829, the membership of the BFSMP had grown entirely Baptist, prompting the founders to rename the society the Boston Baptist Female Society for Missionary Purposes. There is no indication that this change resulted from tensions but rather simply from natural turnover as orthodox Congregationalists defected to Baptist churches as a result of the triumph of liberal Congregationalism. See *Constitution of the Boston Baptist Female Society for Missionary Purposes* (Boston: True & Greene, 1830).

52. Absalom Jones and Richard Allen, *Narrative of the Proceedings of the Black People during the Late Awful Calamity in Philadelphia in the Year 1793; and a Refutation of Some Censures Thrown*

upon Them in Some Late Publications (Philadelphia: Printed for the authors, by William W. Woodward, 1794).

53. "The Petition of the People of Colour, Freemen within the City and Suburbs of Philadelphia," December 30, 1799, Slave Trade Committee Records (STCR), HR 6A-F4.2, National Archives (NA), Washington, DC. See also Nicholas P. Wood, "A 'Class of Citizens': The Earliest Black Petitioners to Congress and Their Quaker Allies," *William and Mary Quarterly* 74, no. 1 (Jan. 2017): 109–44.

54. Newman, *Freedom's Prophet*, 153–54. See also William Douglass, *Annals of the First African Church in the United States of America, now styled The African Episcopal Church of St. Thomas, Philadelphia* (Philadelphia: King & Baird, 1862), 118.

55. Absalom Jones, Probate Inventory, 1818, microfilm, Winterthur Library, Winterthur, DE. See also Julie Winch, *Philadelphia's Black Elite: Activism, Accommodation, and the Struggle for Autonomy, 1787–1848* (Philadelphia: Temple University Press. 1988); and Gary Nash, *Forging Freedom: The Formation of Philadelphia's Black Community, 1720–1840* (Cambridge, MA: Harvard University Press, 1988).

56. Cameron, *To Plead Our Own Cause.* See also Corey D. B. Walker, *A Noble Fight: African American Freemasonry and the Struggle for Democracy in America* (Urbana: University of Illinois Press, 2008); and Stephen Bullock, *Revolutionary Brotherhood: Freemasonry and the Transformation of the American Social Order, 1730–1840* (Chapel Hill: University of North Carolina Press, 1996).

57. Kyle T. Bulthuis, *Four Steeples over the City Streets: Religion and Society in New York's Early Republic Congregations* (New York: New York University Press, 2014). See also Leslie M. Harris, *In the Shadow of Slavery: African Americans in New York City, 1626–1863* (Chicago: University of Chicago Press, 2003); and Leslie M. Alexander, *African or American? Black Identity and Political Activism in New York City, 1784–1861* (Champaign: University of Illinois Press, 2008).

58. For more on how national political parties struggled with the issue of slavery, see Matthew Mason, *Slavery and Politics in the Early American Republic* (Chapel Hill: University of North Carolina Press, 2016); as well as John Craig Hammond and Matthew Mason, *Contesting Slavery: The Politics of Bondage and Freedom in the New American Nation* (Charlottesville: University of Virginia Press, 2011).

59. For more on Barrow's antislavery ideology, see Keith Harper, "'A Strange Kind of Christian': David Barrow and Involuntary, Unmerited, Perpetual, Absolute, Hereditary Slavery, Examined; on the Principles of Nature, Reason, Justice, Policy, and Scripture," *Ohio Valley History* 15, no. 3 (Fall 2015): 68–77; Vivien Sandlund, "'A Devilish and Unnatural Usurpation': Baptist Evangelical Ministers and Antislavery in the Early Nineteenth Century—A Study of the Ideas and Activism of David Barrow," *American Baptist Quarterly* 13 (1994): 262–77; and Randolph Scully, "'Somewhat Liberated': Baptist Discourses of Race and Slavery in Nat Turner's Virginia, 1770–1840," *Explorations in Early American Culture* 5 (2001): 328–71.

60. Carter Tarrant, *History of the Baptist Ministers and Churches in Kentucky &c., Friends to Humanity* (Frankfurt, KY, 1808), 21.

61. Minutes of the Elkhorn Association of Baptists, met at Bryan's, August 10, 1805, 3–4.

62. Minutes of the North-District Association of Baptists held at Bethel Meeting House, in the county of Montgomery, state of Kentucky, fifth, sixth, seventh, and eighth days of October, 1805.

63. Minutes of the North-District Association of Baptists, 1806, 3–4.

64. Minutes of the North-District Association of Baptists, 1807.

65. Minutes of the North-District Association of Baptists, 1808.

66. David Barrow, *Involuntary, unmerited, perpetual, absolute, hereditary slavery, examined [microform] on the principles of nature, reason, justice, policy, and scripture* (Lexington: 1808), 7.

67. For context on this letter from Barrow as well as a full text reproduction, see Carlos R. Allen Jr., "David Barrow's Circular Letter of 1798," *William and Mary Quarterly* 20, no. 3 (July 1963): 440–51, quote at 449.

68. Sandlund, "'A Devilish and Unnatural Usurpation,'" 263. For more on this schism, see Tarrant, *History of the Baptist Ministers and Churches in Kentucky*, 6–24.

69. For more on Bourne, see Ryan McIlhenny, *To Preach Deliverance to the Captives: Freedom and Slavery in the Protestant Mind of George Bourne, 1780–1845* (Baton Rouge: Louisiana State University Press, 2020). See also Andrew E. Murray, *Presbyterians and the Negro—A History* (Philadelphia: Presbyterian Historical Society, 1966).

70. George Bourne, *Marriage Indissoluble and Divorce Unscriptural* (Harrisonburg, VA: Davidson & Bourne, 1813).

71. *Minutes of the General Assembly of the Presbyterian Church in the United States of America from Its Organization, 1789–1820* (Philadelphia: Presbyterian Board of Publications, 1847), 601.

72. Howard McKnight Wilson, *Lexington Presbytery Heritage: The Presbytery of Lexington and Its Churches in the Synod of Virginia, Presbyterian Church in the United States* (Verona, VA: McClure Press, 1971), 90–91.

73. William Henry Foote, *Sketches of Virginia: Historical and Biographical, Volume 2* (Philadelphia: J. B. Lippincott, 1855), 361.

74. Wilson, *Lexington Presbytery*, 91.

75. Foote, *Sketches of Virginia*, 362.

76. Murray, *Presbyterians and the Negro*, 23

77. John W. Christie and Dwight L. Dumond, eds., *George Bourne and* The Book and Slavery Irreconcilable (Wilmington: Historical Society of Delaware and the Presbyterian Historical Society, 1969).

78. David Brion Davis, *The Problem of Slavery in the Age of Revolutions* (Ithaca: Cornell University, 1975), 33.

79. Bourne, *Book and Slavery Irreconcilable*, 89.

80. Bourne, *Book and Slavery Irreconcilable*, 155.

81. For more on the Germantown Protest, see Katherine Gerbner, "'We are against the traffick of mens-body': The Germantown Quaker Protest of 1688 and the Origins of American Abolitionism," *Pennsylvania History: A Journal of Mid Atlantic Studies* 74, no. 2 (Spring 2007): 149–72.

82. *Minutes of the General Assembly, 1789–1820*, 627.

83. *Extracts from the Minutes of the General Assembly of the Presbyterian Church in the United States of America, 1818* (Philadelphia: Thomas and William Bradford, 1818), 20.

84. "1818 Declaration" in *Extracts from the Minutes of the General Assembly of the Presbyterian Church of America* (Philadelphia: Thomas and William Bradford, 1818), 28–29.

85. "1818 Declaration," 31–32.

86. Bertram Wyatt-Brown, "Prelude to Abolitionism: Sabbatarian Politics and the Rise of the Second Party System," *Journal of American History* 58, no. 2 (Sept. 1971): 316–41.

87. Richard S. John, "Taking Sabbatarianism Seriously: The Postal System, the Sabbath, and

the Transformation of American Political Culture," *Journal of the Early Republic* 10, no. 4 (Winter 1990): 517–67.

88. Postmaster General Gideon Granger had instructed all postmasters to sort mails on Sunday, but Wylie's decision to open his post office was his own.

89. *Records of the Synod of Pittsburg, From its First Organization, September 29, 1802 to October, 1832, inclusive* (Pittsburgh: Luke Loomis, 1852), 62.

90. *Minutes of the Presbyterian General Assembly,* I:456.

91. *Minutes of the Presbyterian General Assembly,* I:508.

92. Richard Peters, ed., *The Public Statutes at Large of the United States of America,* (17 vols., Boston, 1850), II:595.

93. *Records of the Synod of Pittsburgh,* p. 74.

94. John, "Taking Sabbatarianism Seriously," 523.

95. "11th Congress, 3rd Session, Remonstrance Against the Delivery of Letters, Papers, and Packets, at the Post Office on the Sabbath." Communicated to the House of Representatives, January 31, 1811. *American State Papers, Class CII,* 44–45.

96. *Extracts from the Minutes of the Synod of New York and New Jersey, A.D. 1811* (Elizabethtown, NJ: Shepard Kollock, 1811), 40.

97. *Minutes of the Presbyterian General Assembly,* 1:485.

98. *Minutes of the Presbyterian General Assembly,* I:513–14.

99. John, "Taking Sabbatarianism Seriously," 525.

100. See Elizabeth Twadell, "The American Tract Society, 1814–1860," *Church History* 15, no. 2 (June 1946): 117.

101. *First Annual Report of the New York Religious Tract Society* (New York: J. Seymour, 1813).

102. *A Brief History of the American Tract Society, instituted at Boston, 1814, and its relations to the American Tract Society at New York, instituted 1825* (Boston: T. R. Marvin, 1857), 6.

103. "The Cent Society," *Connecticut Evangelical Magazine and Religious Intelligencer* 2, no. 9 (Sept. 1809): 359.

104. John Fea, *The Bible Cause: A History of the American Bible Society* (New York: Oxford University Press, 2016).

105. For more on the role of Federalists in the benevolent empire, see Jonathan Den Hartog, *Patriotism and Piety: Federalist Politics and Religious Struggle in the New American Nation* (Charlottesville: University of Virginia Press, 2015); and Linda K. Kerber, *Federalists in Dissent: Imagery and Ideology in Jeffersonian America* (Ithaca, NY: Cornell University Press, 1970).

106. *An Answer to the Objections of the Managers of the Philadelphia Bible Society, Against a Meeting of Delegates from the Bible Societies in the Union to Agree on Some Plan to Disseminate the Bible in Parts without the United States* (Burlington, NJ: David Allinson, 1815), 3.

107. Clifford S. Griffin, *Their Brothers' Keepers: Moral Stewardship in the United States, 1800–1865* (New Brunswick, NJ: Rutgers University Press, 1960); Joseph F. Kett, "Temperance and Intemperance as Historical Problems," *Journal of American History* 67, no. 4 (March 1981): 878–85; Joseph R. Gusfield, *Symbolic Crusade: Status Politics and the American Temperance Movement* (Urbana: University of Illinois Press, 1986).

108. W. J. Rorabaugh, *The Alcoholic Republic: An American Tradition* (New York: Hill & Wang, 1978); Ian R. Tyrrell, *Sobering Up: From Temperance to Prohibition in the Antebellum South, 1800–1860* (Wesport, CT: Greenwood Press, 1979); Jack S. Blocker, *American Temperance Movements:*

Cycles of Reform (Boston: Twayne Publishers, 1989); Stephen Wills Murphy, "'It Is a Sacred Duty to Abstain': The Organizational, Biblical, Theological, and Practical Roots of the American Temperance Society" (PhD diss., University of Virginia, Charlottesville, 2008); James R. Rohrer, "The Origins of the Temperance Movement: A Reinterpretation," *Journal of American Studies* 24, no. 2 (Aug. 1990): 228–35.

109. *Minutes of the Presbyterian General Assembly,* I:467, 485, 498, and 511.

110. For Mercer's role in the creation of the ACS, see Douglas R. Egerton, "'Its Origin Is Not a Little Curious': A New Look at the American Colonization Society," *Journal of the Early Republic* 5, no. 4 (Winter 1985): 463–80. Egerton blames a "Princeton Theological junto" for crediting Rev. Robert Finley with the idea of colonization, when Mercer came to the idea before Finley. Egerton is correct in noting the importance of Princetonians in the formation and memory of the ACS, and while Mercer came to the idea of colonization first, it was the clergymen and their associates who directed the destiny of the society and the colonizationist movement as a whole, for the unifying discourse of conversion was essential in maintaining the fractious coalition of colonizationists.

111. Egerton, "'Its Origin Is Not a Little Curious,'"

112. Egerton, "'Its Origin Is Not a Little Curious.'"

Chapter Three

1. Daniel Coker, *Journal of Daniel Coker* (Baltimore: Edward J. Coale, 1820), 12.

2. For a history that emphasizes antislavery in colonization, see Burin, *Slavery and the Peculiar Solution.* Beverly C. Tomek unfolds the important differences between how competing antislavery movements responded to colonization in Pennsylvania in *Colonization and Its Discontents: Emancipation, Emigration, and Antislavery in Antebellum Pennsylvania* (New York: New York University Press, 2011). For a study that emphasizes how colonization related to the later abolitionist movement, see David Brion Davis, *The Problem of Slavery in the Age of Emancipation* (New York: Alfred A. Knopf, 2014), esp. 83–192.

3. Douglas R. Egerton identifies southern enslavers as the progenitors of the movement in "'Its Origin Is Not a Little Curious.'" Nicholas Guyatt compares African colonization with Indian removal and emphasizes racial anxieties in motivating both: Nicholas Guyatt, "The Outskirts of Our Happiness: Race and the Lure of Colonization in the Early Republic," *Journal of American History* 95, no. 4 (March 2009): 986–1011.

4. James T. Campbell, *Middle Passages: African American Journeys to Africa, 1787–2005* (New York: Penguin, 2006); Amos Beyan, *African American Settlements in West Africa: John Brown Russwurm and the American Civilizing Efforts* (New York: Palgrave Macmillan, 2005); and James Sidbury, *Becoming African in America: Race and Nation in the Early Black Atlantic* (New York: Oxford, 2007).

5. P. J. Staudenraus's wide-ranging 1961 study of the movement gives the most attention to religious impulses but ultimately he bends his interpretation toward political questions surrounding the endurance of slavery in the United States: P. J. Staudenraus, *The African Colonization Movement, 1816–1865* (New York: Columbia University Press, 1961).

6. For more on this process, see Cassandra Pybus, *Epic Journeys of Freedom: Runaway Slaves of*

the American Revolution and Their Global Quest for Liberty (Boston: Beacon Press, 2007); Alexander X. Byrd, *Captives and Voyagers : Black Migrants across the Eighteenth-Century British Atlantic World* (Baton Rouge: Louisiana State University Press, 2010); and Simon Schama, *Rough Crossings: Britain, the Slaves and the American Revolution* (New York: HarperCollins, 2006).

7. Rosalind Cobb Wiggins, *Captain Paul Cuffe's Logs and Letter, 1808–1817: A Black Quaker's "Voice from within the Veil"* (Washington, DC: Howard University Press, 1996); Jeffrey Fortin, "Cuffe's Black Atlantic World, 1807–1817," *Atlantic Studies* 4, no. 2 (October 2007): 245–66; Sheldon H. Harris, *Paul Cuffee: Black America and the African Return* (New York: Simon & Schuster, 1972); and Lamont D. Thomas, *Paul Cuffe: Black Entrepreneur and Pan-Africanist* (Urbana: University of Illinois Press, 1988).

8. For more on the lived experience of early Liberian colonization, see Claude Andrew Clegg, *The Price of Liberty: African Americans and the Making of Liberia* (Chapel Hill: University of North Carolina Press, 2004); and Marie Tyler-McGraw, *An African Republic: Black and White Virginians in the Making of Liberia* (Chapel Hill: University of North Carolina Press, 2009).

9. Robert Finley, *Thoughts on the Colonization of Free Blacks* (Washington, DC, 1816). While some historians question Finley's status as the father of colonization, the literature produced by the ACS consistently credited the Presbyterian educator and divine as its founder. Whatever his role in the organizational establishment, the ubiquity of his tract and his reputation at the time as the movement's founder illustrates his symbolic importance and requires scholarly attention. For accounts downplaying Finley's role, see Douglas Egerton, "'Its Origin Is Not a Little Curious'"; and also Joseph S. Moore, "Covenanters and Antislavery in the Atlantic World," *Slavery And Abolition* 34, no. 4 (2013): 539–61.

10. Finley, *Thoughts*, 8.

11. Finley, *Thoughts*, 1.

12. St. George Tucker, *Letter to a member of the General Assembly of Virginia, on the subject of the late conspiracy of the slaves: with a proposal for their colonization* (Baltimore, 1801), 12.

13. Thomas Branagan, *Serious remonstrances: addressed to the citizens of the northern states, and their representatives, being an appeal to their natural feelings and common sense, consisting of speculations and animadversions on the recent revival of the slave trade in the American republic* (Philadelphia, 1805), 92–93.

14. Finley, *Thoughts*, 1.

15. Skeptics may claim Finley's location at a New Jersey–based site made it easier for him to privilege African conversion over the prevention of slave revolts, a danger that certainly disproportionately affected southerners. But there is no indication that Finley's brief career as the president of the University of Georgia changed any of his views.

16. Finley, *Thoughts*, 5.

17. James S. Green, *Proceedings of a Meeting Held at Princeton, New Jersey, July 14, 1824 to form a Society in the State of New Jersey, to cooperate with the American Colonization Society* (Princeton, NJ, 1823), 33.

18. Anthony Benezet, *A Short Account of That Part of Africa, Inhabited by the Negroes* (Philadelphia, 1762), 22.

19. Henry Clay, *Speech of the Hon. Henry Clay before the American Colonization Society in the Hall of the House of Representatives, January 20, 1827* (Washington, DC: Columbian Office, 1827), 12.

20. Finley, *Thoughts*, 8.

21. Edward Dorr Griffin, *A Plea for Africa* (New York, 1817), 30.

22. Finley, *Thoughts*, 2.

23. Prince Saunders, *A Memoir Presented to the American Convention for Promoting the Abolition of Slavery, and Improving the Condition of the African Race* (Philadelphia, 1818).

24. Society for Promoting the Emigration of Free Persons of Color to Haiti, *Information for the free people of color, who are inclined to emigrate to Haiti* (New York, 1824).

25. Letter, Jean Pierre Boyer to Lording Daniel Dewey, April 30, 1824, in Loring Daniel Dewey, *Correspondence Relative to the Emigration to Haiti, of the Free People of Color, in the United States* (New York, 1824), 11.

26. Green, *Proceedings of a Meeting Held at Princeton*, 31.

27. Theodore Frelinghuysen, *An Oration: Delivered at Princeton, New Jersey, November 16, 1824 before the New Jersey Colonization Society* (Princeton, 1824), 12–13.

28. Benjamin Rush, *An Address to the Inhabitants of the British Settlements on the Slavery of the Negros in America, Second ed. By A Pennsylvanian* (Philadelphia, 1773), 27.

29. Abiel Holmes, *The Life of Ezra Stiles* (Boston: Thomas & Andrews, 1798).

30. Granville Sharp, *The Just Limitations of Slavery in the Laws of God* (London, 1776), 26, 29–31. Sharp included a passage of a sermon his grandfather delivered before the House of Commons in 1679.

31. For the long history of Anglo-Christian racist understandings of Africa, see Winthrop Jordan, *White over Black: American Attitudes toward the Negro, 1550–1812* (Chapel Hill: University of North Carolina Press, 1968): and the "Constructing Race" special issue of the *William and Mary Quarterly*, 3rd Series, 54 (Jan. 1997).

32. William Augustus Muhlenberg, *A sermon in memory of the Rev. Samuel Bacon, and John P. Bankson, May, 1820* (Philadelphia, 1820), 23.

33. See, for example, Emily Conroy-Krutz, *Christian Imperialism: Converting the World in the Early Republic* (Ithaca, NY: Cornell University Press, 2015)); Derek Peterson, ed. *Abolitionism in Britain, Africa, and the Atlantic* (Athens: Ohio University Press, 2010); and Gale Kenny, *Contentious Liberties: American Abolitionists in Post-Emancipation Jamaica, 1834–1866* (Athens, GA: Georgia University Press, 2010).

34. Griffin, *Plea for Africa*, p. 31.

35. Finley, *Thoughts*, 8.

36. Finley, *Thoughts*, 3–4.

37. Elias B. Caldwell, *A View of the Exertions Lately Made for the Purpose of Colonizing the Free People of Color in the United States, In Africa, or elsewhere* (Washington DC, 1817), 8.

38. Caldwell, *A View of the Exertions Lately Made.*

39. Finley, *Thoughts*, 6–8.

40. Muhlenberg, *A sermon in memory of the Rev. Samuel Bacon, and John P. Bankson*, 12.

41. Griffin, *Plea for Africa*, p. 31.

42. James Patterson, *A Sermon on the Effects of the Hebrew Slavery as Connected with the Slavery in this Country, Preached in the Seventh Presbyterian Church in the City of Philadelphia, at an United Meeting of Christians of Different Religious Persuasions to Celebrate Our National Independence, July 4, 1825* (Philadelphia: S. Probasco, 1825), 20–21.

43. James Beattie, *Personal Slavery Established by the Suffrages of Custom and Right Reason: Being a Full Answer to the Gloomy and Visionary Reveries of all the Fanatical and Enthusiastical Writers*

on the Subject (Philadelphia, 1773), 3. For a longer discussion of the irony involved in the tract, see Lester B. Scherer, "A New Look at Personal Slavery Established," *William and Mary Quarterly,* Third Series, 30, no. 4 (Oct. 1973): 646.

44. Absalom Jones, *A thanksgiving sermon, preached January 1, 1808, in St. Thomas's, or the African Episcopal, Church, Philadelphia: on account of the abolition of the African slave trade, on that day, by the Congress of the United States* (Philadelphia, 1808), 18.

45. *Poulson's American Daily Advertiser,* December 20, 1816. Julie Winch remarks how through *Poulson's,* Philadelphia's large free people of color population would have heard of the meeting only five days after it occurred. Julie Winch, *A Gentleman of Color: The Life of James Forten* (New York: Oxford, 2002), 189.

46. Green, *Proceedings of a Meeting Held at Princeton,* 32–33.

47. American Society for Colonizing the Free People of Color of the United States, *Memorial of the president and board of managers of the American Society for Colonizing the Free People of Color of the United States. January 14, 1817* (Washington, DC, 1817), 1–2, 3–4, 5.

48. Thomas Hart Benton, *Abridgment of the Debates of Congress from 1789 to 1856, Volume 5* (New York, 1857), 712.

49. Samuel Miller, *A Sermon Preached at New-Ark October 22, 1823, Before the Synod of New-Jersey, for the Benefit of the African School, under the Care of the Synod* (Trenton, NJ: George Sherman, 1823), 21. See also the 1823 report of the Baptist General Convention where the convention concluded that "the duty of sending the Gospel to Africa, certainly rests with greater weight on Christians in this country than on any other." "Report of the African Mission," *The Latter Day Luminary* 4, no. 6 (June 1, 1823): 183.

50. *Address of the Colonization Society of Loudoun, Virginia* (Annapolis, MD, 1819), 4–5.

51. Anthony Benezet, *A Short Account of That Part of Africa, Inhabited by the Negroes* (Philadelphia, 1762), 22–23.

52. Peter Kolb, *The Present State of the Cape of Good Hope,* vol. 3 (London, 1731), 359. See Maruice Jackson's biography of Benezet for more on how the reformer employed early studies of Africa for the antislavery crusade. Maurice Jackson, *Let This Voice Be Heard: Anthony Benezet, Father of Atlantic Abolitionism* (Philadelphia: University of Pennsylvania Press, 2009).

53. William Law, *An extract from a treatise on the spirit of prayer, or The soul rising out of the vanity of time into the riches of eternity. With some thoughts on war: Remarks on the nature and bad effects of the use of spirituous liquors. And considerations on slavery* (Philadelphia, 1780).

54. Guyatt, "The Outskirts of Our Happiness."

55. Rush, *An Address,* 2, 27.

56. For more on Anthony Benezet and his use of European thought, see Jackson, *Let This Voice Be Heard.*

57. Carl Bernhard Wadström, *An Essay on Colonization* (London, 1794–95), 95.

58. Phillis Wheatley, *The Collected Works of Phillis Wheatley,* ed. John Shields (New York: Oxford, 1988), 175–76.

59. Ralph Randolph Gurley, *A Discourse, Delivered on the Fourth of July, 1825* (Washington, DC, 1825), 18.

60. American Convention for Promoting the Abolition of Slavery and Improving the Condition of the African Race, *Minutes of the proceedings of a special meeting of the Fifteenth American Convention for Promoting the Abolition of Slavery, and Improving the Condition of the African Race*

assembled at Philadelphia, on the tenth day of December, 1818, and continued by adjournments until the fifteenth of the same month, inclusive (Philadelphia, 1818), 52.

61. Beilby Porteus reprinted in *Substance of the report of the court of directors of the Sierra Leone Company to the general court, held at London on Wednesday the 19th of October, 1791* (London, 1791), 29–30.

62. Finley, *Thoughts*, 3–4.

63. Elias B. Caldwell, *A View of the Exertions Lately Made for the Purpose of Colonizing the Free People of Color in the United States, In Africa, or elsewhere* (Washington DC, 1817), 3.

64. American Convention for Promoting the Abolition of Slavery and Improving the Condition of the African Race, *Minutes of the proceedings of a special meeting of the fifteenth American Convention for Promoting the Abolition of Slavery, and Improving the Condition of the African Race: assembled at Philadelphia, on the tenth day of December, 1818, and continued by adjournments until the fifteenth of the same month, inclusive* (Philadelphia, 1818), 21.

65. Finley, *Thoughts*, 3.

66. Finley, *Thoughts*, 8.

67. Wheatley, *Collected Works*, 178.

68. Muhlenberg, *A sermon in memory of the Rev. Samuel Bacon, and John P. Bankson*, 25.

69. Naimbanna also sent another son to North Africa, to study under Islamic tutors, and yet another to France, to learn under Catholics.

70. *Substance of the report of the court of directors of the Sierra Leone Company to the general court, held at London on Wednesday the 19th of October, 1791* (London, 1791), 15–20.

71. William Gilpin, *Moral Contrasts: or, The Power of Religion Exemplified under Different Characters* (London, 1798), 196–98.

72. *Substance of the report of the court of directors of the Sierra Leone Company to the general court* (London, 1791); Zachary Macaulay, *The African Prince* (London, 1796). See also Gilpin, *Moral Contrasts*, and Hannah More, *The Black Prince* (Philadelphia, 1800).

73. Robert Goodloe Harper, *A letter from Gen. Harper, of Maryland, to Elias B. Caldwell, Esq. secretary of the American Society for Colonizing the Free People of Colour, in the United States, with their own consent. Published by order of the society* (Baltimore, 1818), 29, 32.

74. Alvin Wilson Skardon, *Church Leader in the Cities: William Augustus Muhlenberg* (Philadelphia: University of Pennsylvania Press, 1971).

75. Muhlenberg, *A sermon in memory of the Rev. Samuel Bacon, and John P. Bankson*, 6.

76. G. A. Robertson, *Notes on Africa* (London, 1819), 431.

77. Green, *Proceedings of a Meeting Held at Princeton*, 33.

78. Muhlenberg, *A sermon in memory of the Rev. Samuel Bacon, and John P. Bankson*, 6.

79. Finley, *Thoughts*, 8.

80. Russell Parrott, *An Oration on the Abolition of the Slave Trade* (Philadelphia, 1812), 10.

81. Absalom Jones, *Thanksgiving sermon*, 20–21.

82. For a full treatment of Richard Allen's views on colonization, see Richard Newman, *Freedom's Prophet: Bishop Richard Allen, the AME Church, and the Black Founding Fathers* (New York: New York University Press, 2008).

83. Winch, *The Life of James Forten*, 191.

84. James Forten and Russell Parrott, "An Address To The Humane And Benevolent Inhabitants Of The City And County Of Philadelphia," published in *Minutes of the Proceedings of a Special Meeting of the Fifteenth American Convention* (Philadelphia, 1817), 69–72.

85. Letter, Phillis Wheatley to John Thornton, October 20, 1774, in *The Collected Works of Phillis Wheatley*, 184.

86. *Proceedings of the General Convention of the Baptist Denomination in the United States, 1817* (Philadelphia: Printed by order of the Convention, 1817), 180.

87. Robert Finley, "Dialogues on the African Colony," in Isaac V. Brown, *Memoirs of the Rev. Robert Finley, D.D.: Late Pastor of the Presbyterian Congregations at Basking Ridge, New-Jersey, and President of Franklin College, Located at Athens, in the State of Georgia* (New Brunswick, NJ, 1819), 251.

88. Finley, "Dialogues," 274–75.

89. Ephraim Bacon, *Abstract of a journal of Ephraim Bacon, assistant agent of the United States, to Africa : with an appendix, containing extracts from proceedings of the Church Missionary Society in England, for the years 1819–20. To which is prefixed An abstract of the journal, of the Rev. J. B. Cates* (Philadelphia, 1821), 5, 10–11.

90. Letter, Samuel Wilson, May 18, 1818. *The Second Annual Report of the American Society for the Colonization of Free People of Color* (Washington, DC, 1819), 150.

91. This letter was signed by John Kizzell, William Martin, George Davis, George Lewis, R. Robertson, Samuel Wilson, Peter Mitchell, Perry Locke, Thomas Williams, John Kizzell Jr., and Pompey Rutledge and dated May 19, 1819. *Second Annual Report*, 1819, 152.

92. Green, *Proceedings of a Meeting Held at Princeton*, 33.

93. Gurley, *A Discourse, Delivered on the Fourth of July 9, 1824*, 14–15.

94. Gurley, *A Discourse*, 14–15.

95. Gurley, *A Discourse*, 17–18.

96. Broadside, June 17, 1825, Brand Papers, Virginia Historical Society.

97. Coker, *Journal*, 14, 21.

Chapter Four

1. *The African Repository and Colonial Journal* (Washington, DC: American Colonization Society: 1826), 5.

2. Mathew Carey, *Letters on the Colonization Society and on Its Probable Results* (Philadelphia: L. Johnson, 1832), 19.

3. *The Sixth Annual Report of the American Society for Colonizing the Free People of Colour of the United States* (Washington: Davis & Force, 1823), 73.

4. Carey, *Letters on the Colonization Society*, 19.

5. *Journals of the General Conference of the Methodist Episcopal Church, Volume 1 1796–1836* (New York: Carlton & Phillips, 1855), 183.

6. *Journals of the General Conference of the Methodist Episcopal Church, Volume 1 1796–1836*, 291.

7. *Journals of the General Conference of the Methodist Episcopal Church, Volume 1 1796–1836*, 290–91.

8. *The African Repository and Colonial Journal* (Washington, DC: American Colonization Society: 1826), 222.

9. "Colonization," *Masonic Mirror and Mechanics Intelligencer* 1, no. 29 (July 9, 1825), 2.

10. *Proceedings of the Fifth Triennial Meeting of the Baptist General Convention, Held in New York, April 1816* (Boston: Lincoln & Edmands, 1826), 17.

11. Mathew Carey, *Letters on the Colonization Society and on Its Probable Results* (Philadelphia: L. Johnson, 1832), 19. For more on how Fourth of July celebrations fostered the American imperial imagination, see Caitlyn Fitz, *Our Sister Republics: The United States in an Age of American Revolutions* (New York: Norton, 2016).

12. David Kazanjian's study of colonizationist rhetoric has shown how colonizationists linked colonial American history with their understandings of early Liberia. Both colonizations were providential opportunities to save the world. David Kazanjian, *The Colonizing Trick: National Culture and Imperial Citizenship in Early America* (Minneapolis: University of Minnesota Press, 2003).

13. For one example among many, see "Colonization Society: Intelligence from the Colony," *Missionary Herald* 17, no. 10 (Oct. 1821): 322. See also Gale L. Kenney, "Race, Sympathy, and Missionary Sensibility in the New England Colonization Movement," *New Directions in the Study of African American Recolonization, edited by Beverly Tomek and Matthew J. Hetrick* (Tallahassee: University Press of Florida, 2017), 33–49.

14. *Daily National Intelligencer* (Oct. 7, 1823).

15. *African Repository and Colonial Journal,* May 1, 1825, 66.

16. *African Repository and Colonial Journal,* April 1, 1825, 35.

17. "American Board of Commissioners for Foreign Missions," *African Repository and Colonial Journal* 1, no. 8 (Oct. 1825): 248. For more on the ABCFM and its relation to Liberia, see Emily Conroy-Krutz, *Christian Imperialism: Converting the World in the Early American Republic* (Ithaca, NY: Cornell University Press, 2015), esp. 153–78.

18. "German Mission to Liberia," *African Repository and Colonial Journal* 3, no. 6 (Aug. 1827): 183.

19. Jehudi Ashmun, "Missions to Africa," *African Repository and Colonial Journal,* 3, no. 9 (Nov. 1827): 259–60.

20. Ashmun, "Missions to Africa," 262.

21. Ashmun, "Missions to Africa," 269.

22. "American Board of Commissioners for Foreign Missions," 248.

23. For more on how climate became a rationale for colonization, see Ikuko Asaka, *Tropical Freedom: Climate, Settler Colonialism, and Black Exclusion in the Age of Emancipation* (Durham, NC: Duke University Press, 2017).

24. "African School," *Genius of Universal Emancipation* 1, no. 13 (Nov. 19, 1825): 100. For more on the African School, see James J. Gigantino II, *The Ragged Road to Abolition: Slavery and Freedom in New Jersey, 1775–1865* (Philadelphia: University of Pennsylvania Press, 2015), 183–84; and Graham Russell Hodges, *Root and Branch: African Americans in New York and East Jersey, 1613–1863* (Chapel Hill: University of North Carolina Press, 1999), 219–20.

25. John Ford, "African School," *Religious Intelligencer* 8, no. 42 (March 20, 1824): 663.

26. "Education of People of Color," *Religious Intelligencer* 9, no. 34 (Jan. 22, 1825): 542.

27. See also Eric Robert Papenfuse, "The Evils of Necessity: Robert Goodloe Harper and the Moral Dilemma of Slavery," *Transactions of the American Philosophical Society* 87, no. 1 (1997).

28. "African Free Schools in the United States," *African Repository and Colonial Journal* 3, no. 9 (Nov. 1827): 271–72. For more on Black schools in antebellum America, see Hillary J. Moss, *Schooling Citizens: The Struggle for African American Education in Antebellum America* (Chicago: University of Chicago Press, 2009). For more on how Americans dreamed of converting the world

by training nonwhite missionaries, see John Demos, *The Heathen School: A Story of Hope and Betrayal in the Age of the Early Republic* (New York: Knopf, 2014).

29. "African School," *Genius of Universal Emancipation* 1, no. 13 (Nov. 19, 1825): 100.

30. "African School," *Genius of Universal Emancipation* 1, no. 13 (Nov. 19, 1825): 100.

31. "An Address to the Public, By the Managers of the Colonization Society of Connecticut, *African Repository and Colonial Journal* 4, no. 4 (June 1828): 116.

32. Cary quoted in Andrew Billingsley, *Mighty Like a River: The Black Church and Social Reform* (New York: Oxford University Press, 2003), 69.

33. See Miles Mark Fisher, "Lott Cary, the Colonizing Missionary," *Journal of Negro History* 7, no. 4 (Oct. 1922): 390.

34. Burin, *Slavery and the Peculiar Solution*, 17.

35. "Conversion of Africans," *Evangelical and Literary Magazine* 6, no. 5 (May 1823): 279.

36. "Colonization Society," *North American Review* 18, no. 1 (Jan. 1, 1824): 41.

37. For more on how colonizationists and other missionaries dismissed failure, see Conroy-Krutz, *Christian Imperialism*, 102–29.

38. Richard Furman to Sarah Yanswort, March 4, 1799, and Furman to Haynsworth, January 7, 1790. Richard Furman, letter to an unidentified person, cited in James A. Rogers, *Richard Furman: Life and Legacy* (Macon, GA: Mercer University Press, 2001), 222.

39. Richard Furman, *Rev. Dr. Richard Furman's Exposition of the Views of the Baptists, relative to the colored population of the United States* (Charleston, SC: A. E. Miller, 1823), 1.

40. Furman lived just a few blocks from Denmark Vesey's home. Rogers, *Richard Furman*, 223.

41. Furman, *Exposition of the Views of the Baptists*, 7.

42. Richard Fuller and Francis Wayland, *Domestic Slavery Considered as a Scriptural Institution* (New York: Lewis Colby, 1845).

43. Furman, *Exposition of the Views of the Baptists*, 16–17.

44. Frederick Dalcho, *Practical considerations founded on the scriptures: relative to the slave population of South-Carolina* (Charleston: A. E. Miller, 1823), 6. For more on Furman and Dalcho, see Robert Pierce Forbes, *The Missouri Compromise and Its Aftermath: Slavery and the Meaning of America* (Chapel Hill: University of North Carolina Press, 2009), 149–52.

45. Dalcho, *Practical considerations*, 3.

46. Dalcho, *Practical considerations*, 33.

47. John Holt Rice and William Maxwell, *A Memoir of the Rev. John H. Rice, D.D., First Professor of Christian Theology in Union Theological Seminary, Virginia: First Professor of Christian Theology in Union Theological Seminary, Virginia* (Philadelphia: J. Whetham, 1835), 311–13.

48. George A. Baxter, *Sermon Preached before the Presbytery of Lexington at the Installation of the Rev. Thomas Caldwell: Pastor of the Churches of Lebanon and Windy Cove, April 30, 1825* (Lexington, VA: Valentine M. Mason, 1825).

49. See Donald G. Mathews, "The Methodist Mission to the Slaves," *Journal of American History* 51, no. 4 (March 1965): 615–31, and *Slavery and Methodism: A Chapter in American Morality, 1780–1845* (Princeton, NJ: Princeton University Press, 1965). See also Erskine Clark, *Dwelling Place: A Plantation Epic* (New Haven, CT: Yale University Press, 2007).

50. Charles Cotesworth Pinckney, *An Address delivered in Charleston before the Agricultural Society of South Carolina* (Charleston: A. E. Miller, 1829), cited in Jeffrey Robert Young, *Proslavery*

and Sectional Thought in the Early South, 1740–1829: An Anthology (Columbia: University of South Carolina Press, 2006), 246, 248.

51. *Minutes of the Annual Conference of the Methodist Episcopal Church*, vol. 1 (1829–39), vol. 2 (1839–45), and *Minutes of the Annual Conferences of Methodist Episcopal Church, South* (1858–65), cited in Janet Duitsman Cornelius, *Slave Missions and the Black Church in the Antebellum Southern United States* (Columbia: University of South Carolina Press, 1999), 47–48n6. See also Donald Blake Touchstone, "Planters and Slave Religion in the Deep South (PhD diss., Tulane University, 1973).

52. "A Carolinian," *Genius of Universal Emancipation* 1, no. 7 (Jan. 1822): 110–11. For more on how anticolonizationists deployed the West, see Brandon Mills, "Situating the African Colonization Movement in the History of U.S. Expansion," Beverly Tomek and Matthew Hetrick, eds., *New Directions in the Study of African American Recolonization* (Tallahassee: University Press of Florida, 2017), 166–83.

53. "From the Georgia Journal to the American People," *Daily National Intelligencer,* July 9, 1819, 2.

54. *Georgia Journal,* Jan. 18, 1820. Quoted in Matthew Mason, *Slavery and Politics in the Early American Republic* (Chapel Hill: University of North Carolina Press, 2006), 124.

55. "From a South Carolina Correspondent," *Daily National Intelligencer,* August 4, 1819, 2.

56. Matthew Mason, *Slavery and Politics in the Early American Republic* (Chapel Hill: University of North Carolina Press, 2006), 164–66.

57. Charles Irons has demonstrated how a focus on religious conversion fueled the development of proslavery Christianity. See Charles Irons, *The Origins of Proslavery Christianity: White and Black Evangelicals in Colonial and Antebellum Virginia* (Chapel Hill: University of North Carolina Press, 2008).

58. Douglass Egerton, "Averting a Crisis: The Proslavery Critique of the American Colonization Society," *Civil War History* 43, no. 2 (June 1997): 144.

59. *Register of Debates, a Century of Lawmaking for a New Nation; U.S. Congressional Documents and Debates, 1774–1875.* Feb. 18, 1825.

60. Whitemarsh Seabrook, *A Concise View of the Critical Situation, and Future Prospects of the Slave-Holding States* (Charleston, SC: A. E. Miller, 1825), 16.

61. Herman Vandenburg Ames, *State Documents on Federal Relations: The States and the United States, Vol. V* (Philadelphia: Published by the Department of History at the University of Pennsylvania, 1906), 208–9, 211–13.

62. Elizabeth Varon, for example, shows how southern anticolonization proslavery dissolved the gradualist antislavery of evangelical women in Virginia. Varon, "Evangelical Womanhood and the Politics of the African Colonization Movement in Virginia," in John R. McKivigan and Mictchel Snay, eds., *Religion and the Antebellum Debate over Slavery* (Athens: University of Georgia Press), 169–95.

63. *Controversy between Caius Gracchus and Opimius* (Georgetown,DC: James C. Dunn, 1827). See Lacy Ford, *Deliver Us from Evil: The Slavery Question in the Old South* (New York: Oxford University Press, 2009), 308–310.

64. *Controversy,* 31.

65. *Controversy*, 41.

66. *Controversy*, 44.

67. *Controversy*, 45.

68. *Controversy*, 79–80.

69. *Controversy*, 92–93, 114.

70. "Review," *African Repository and Colonial Journal* 3, no. 1 (March 1827): 3–6.

71. "An Essay for the Fourth of July, on the American Colonization Society," *African Repository and Colonial Journal* 3, no. 12 (Feb. 1826): 372.

72. Lundy was one of the last abolitionists to retain hope for colonization, attempting to create a freedmen's coloniy in Texas in the 1830s. Merton L. Dillon, *Benjamin Lundy and the Struggle for Negro Freedom* (Urbana: University of Illinois Press, 1966).

73. "African Colonization," *Philanthropist* 7, no. 13 (Feb. 2, 1822): 200–201.

74. "African Colonization," 200–201.

75. For more on John Russwurm, see Winston James, *The Struggles of John Brown Russwurm: The Life and Writings of a Pan-Africanist Pioneer, 1799–1851* (New York: New York University Press, 2010).

76. "Colonization Society," *Freedom's Journal* 1, no. 13 (June 8, 1827): 50–51.

77. "African Discoveries," *Colored American*, March 25, 1827.

78. Letter from Bishop Allen," *Freedom's Journal* 1, no. 34 (Nov. 2, 1827): 143.

79. See Richard S. Newman, *Freedom's Prophet: Bishop Richard Allen, the AME Church, and the Black Founding Fathers* (New York: New York University Press, 2008).

80. "Letter from Bishop Allen," 143.

81. "Letter from Bishop Allen," 143.

82. David Walker, *Walker's Appeal, in Four Articles; Together with a Preamble, to the Coloured Citizens of the World, but in Particular, and Very Expressly, to Those of the United States of America, Written in Boston, State of Massachusetts, September 28, 1829* (Boston: David Walker, 1830), 30, 5–6. Stephen Marini, "Hymnody and Development of American Evangelicalism," Edith Blumhofer and Mark A. Noll, eds., *Singing the Lord's Song in a Strange Land: Hymnody in the History of North American Protestantism* (Tuscaloosa: University of Alabama Press, 2004), 33.

83. Walker, *Appeal*, 50.

84. For more on the differences among the three editions and the increased importance of religious themes, see Peter P. Hinks's editor's note in Hinks, ed., *David Walker's Appeal to the Colored Citizens of the World* (University Park: Pennsylvania State University Press, 2000), xlv–li.

85. Peter Hinks, *To Awaken My Afflicted Brethren: David Walker and the Problem of Antebellum Slave Resistance* (University Park: Pennsylvania State University Press, 1997), 78–79.

86. *Freedom's Journal*, December 19, 1828.

87. Walker, *Appeal*, 2.

88. Walker, *Appeal*, 2.

89. Walker, *Appeal*, 2.

90. William Lloyd Garrison, *Thoughts on African Colonization: or an Impartial Exhibition of the Doctrines, Principles, and Purposes of the American Colonization Society, together with the Resolutions, Addresses, and Remonstrances of the People of Color* (Boston, 1832), 29.

Chapter Five

1. For more on the revival in Enfield and the sermon known as "Sinners in the Hands of an Angry God," see George M. Marsden, *Jonathan Edwards: A Life* (New Haven, CT: Yale University Press, 2003), esp. 214–26.

2. For more on Finney's revival in Rochester, see Paul E. Johnson, *A Shopkeeper's Millennium: Society and Revivals in Rochester, New York, 1815–1837* (New York: Hill & Wang, 1978); and Keith J. Hardman, *Charles Grandison Finney, 1792–1875: Revivalist and Reformer* (Syracuse, NY: Syracuse University Press, 1987).

3. Jonathan Edwards, "Sinners in the Hands of an Angry God," in *Sermons and Discourses, 1739–1742 (WJE Online Vol. 22)*, edited by Harry S. Stout, accessed Nov. 12, 2008, at http://edwards.yale.edu.

4. Charles Grandison Finney, *Lectures on the Revivals of Religion: The Life and Works of Charles G. Finney,* edited by Richard M. Friedrich (Fenwich, MI: Alethea in Heart, 1868/2005), 252.

5. Robert Abzug has described this process as "sacralizing the world," as reformers sought to transform their world into the Kingdom of God: *Cosmos Crumbling: American Reform and the Religious Imagination* (New York: Oxford University Press, 1994).

6. Charles G. Finney, "Sinners Bound to Change Their Own Hearts," in *Sermons on Important Subjects* (New York: John S. Taylor, 1845), 3–28.

7. Charles G. Finney, *Lectures on Revivals of Religion* (Cambridge, MA: Harvard University Press, 1960), 33.

8. These sales estimates come from Marion L. Ball, *Crusade in the City: Revivalism in Nineteenth-Century Philadelphia* (Cranberry, NJ: Associated University Press, 1977), 97.

9. For more on Finney's relationship to reform, see James H. Moorehead, "Social Reform and the Divided Conscience of Antebellum Protestantism," *Church History* 48, no. 4 (Dec. 1979): 416–30.

10. Charles G. Finney, *Lectures on Revivals,* 242–43.

11. Charles G. Finney, *Lectures on Systematic Theology* (Oberlin, OH: James M. Fitch, 1846), 421.

12. For more on Oberlin and abolitionism, see Carol Lasser and Gary Kornblith, *Elusive Utopia: The Struggle for Racial Equality in Oberlin, Ohio* (Baton Rouge: Louisiana State University Press, 2018).

13. James H. Moorehead, "Charles Finney and the Modernization of America," *Journal of Presbyterian History* 62, no. 2 (1984): 99.

14. Finney, *Lectures on Revivals of Religion,* 281.

15. Finney, *Lectures on Systematic Theology.*

16. Charles G. Finney, "Letters on Revival—No. 23," *Oberlin Evangelist,* Jan. 21, 1846.

17. The best treatment of Garrison's faith is James Brewer Stewart, *William Lloyd Garrison and the Challenge of Emancipation* (Arlington Heights, IL: Harlan Davidson, 1992).

18. "To the Public," *Liberator,* Jan. 1, 1831.

19. For more on the use of moral suasion by Black Americans, see Tunde Adeleke, "Afro-Americans and Moral Suasion: The Debate in the 1830's," *Journal of Negro History* 83, no. 2 (Spring 1998): 127–42.

20. Constitution of the New England Antislavery Society, with an address to the public (Boston: Garrison & Knapp, 1832), 7.

21. Angelina E. Grimké, *Appeal to the Christian Women of the South* (New York: American Antislavery Society, 1836), 26. The literature on Angelina Grimké is voluminous. See Katharine Du Pre Lumpkin, *The Emancipation of Angelina Grimké* (Chapel Hill: University of North Carolina Press, 1974). See also Gerda Lerner, *The Grimké Sisters from South Carolina: Pioneers for Women's Rights and Abolition* (New York: Oxford University Press, 1998).

22. Minutes and Proceedings of the First Annual Meeting of the American Moral Reform Society (Philadelphia: Merrihew & Gunn, 1837), 5.

23. Maria Weston Chapman, *Right and Wrong in Massachusetts* (Boston: Dow & Jackson's Antislavery Press, 1839), 3–4. Despite Chapman's historicizing of abolitionism, few women engaged in either the colonizationist movement or in its opposition. As Bruce Dorsey has acknowledged, "colonization reformers constituted the solution to slavery as political, national, and masculine." This masculinization of colonization contributed to the participation of women in the abolitionist movement. Bruce Dorsey, *Reforming Men and Women: Gender in the Antebellum City* (Ithaca, NY: Cornell University Press, 2002), 140.

24. *Hints and Sketches by an American Mother* (New York: John S. Taylor, 1839), 139–40.

25. William Lloyd Garrison, *Thoughts on African Colonization; or an Impartial Exhibition of the Doctrines, Principles, and Purposes of the American Colonization Society, together with the Resolutions, Addresses, and Remonstrances of the People of Color* (Boston: 1832), 10. Repeated from a passage from the April 23, 1831, edition of the *Liberator.*

26. Garrison, "Part Two," *Thoughts on Colonization.*

27. James G. Birney, *Letter on Colonization, addressed to the Rev. Thornton J. Mills* (New York, 1834).

28. Letter, July 8, 1834, Theodore Dwight Weld to James Birney. James G. Birney Papers, Box 1, Folder 35. Clements Library. University of Michigan.

29. *Hints and Sketches,* 139.

30. Maria Stewart's "Address Delivered at the African Masonic Hall, Boston" (Feb. 27, 1833), in *Pamphlets of Protest: An Anthology of Early African-American Protest Literature, 1790–1860,* edited by Richard Newman, Patrick Rael, and Philip Lapansky (New York: Routledge, 2013), 126.

31. Peter Williams quoted in Garrison, *Impartial Thoughts,* 64–64.

32. Garrison, *Thoughts on African Colonization,* 31.

33. Garrison, *Thoughts on* African *Colonization,* 26.

34. *Resolutions of the People of Color at a meeting held on the 25th January, 1831, with an address to the citizens of New York in answer to those of the New York Colonization Society* (New York, 1831). See especially the handwritten manuscript at the end of the Google Books copy: https://books .google.com/books?id=UW5kmgEACAAJ&printsec=frontcover&source=gbs_ge_summary_r& cad=0#v=onepage&q&f=false.

35. Erastus Hopkins, *The Objections to African Colonization Stated and Answered* (Philadelphia, 1833), 1.

36. Hopkins, *Objections Stated and Answered,* 4.

37. Hopkins, *Objections Stated and Answered,* 18.

38. Hopkins, *Stated and Answered,* 21, 24.

39. Garrison, *Thoughts on African Colonization,* 26.

40. Garrison, *Thoughts on African Colonization,* 32.

41. Garrison, *Thoughts on African Colonization,* 25. *Controversy between Caius Gracchus and Opimius* (Georgetown, DC: James C. Dunn, 1827).

42. Garrison, *Thoughts on African Colonization*, 36.

43. Cyril Pearl, *Remarks on African Colonization and the Abolition of Slavery: In Two Parts, by a Citizen of New England* (Windsor, VT, 1833), 37.

44. Pearl, *Remarks*, 17.

45. Birney, *Letter on* Colonization, 39.

46. Garrison, *Thoughts on African Colonization*, 70–71.

47. Garrison, *Thoughts on African Colonization*, 28.

48. Birney, *Letter on Colonization*, 36.

49. Birney, *Letter on Colonization*, 36.

50. Birney, *Letter on Colonization*, 41.

51. *Examination of Mr. Thomas C. Brown, a free colored citizen of S. Carolina, as to the actual state of things in Liberia in the years 1833 and 1834: at the Chatham Street Chapel, May 9th & 10th, 1834* (New York, 1834), 5–8.

52. *Examination of Mr. Thomas C. Brown*, 12–13.

53. *Examination of Mr. Thomas C. Brown*, 15.

54. *Examination of Mr. Thomas C. Brown*, 22–23.

55. *Examination of Mr. Thomas C. Brown*, 28–30.

56. *Examination of Mr. Thomas C. Brown*, 31.

57. "Journal of Dr. Crocker," *Baptist Missionary Magazine* 20, no. 3 (March 1840): 50.

58. George S. Brown, *Brown's Abridged Journal, containing a brief account, of the life, trials, and travels of Geo. S. Brown, six years a missionary in Liberia, West Africa* (Troy, NY, 1849), 110.

59. Archibald Alexander, *A History of Colonization on the Western Coast of Africa* (Philadelphia, 1846), 525–26.

60. "Liberia," *Colored American*, Dec. 15, 1838.

61. "Original Communication to the Rev. John Seys, Missionary to Africa," *Colored American*, Dec. 22, 1838.

62. "Highly Important," *Colored American*, December 15, 1838.

63. For more on Turner's revolt, see Patrick H. Breen, *The Land Shall Be Deluged in Blood: A New History of the Nat Turner Revolt* (New York: Oxford University Press, 2016); and David F. Allmendinger Jr., *Nat Turner and the Rising in Southampton County* (Baltimore: Johns Hopkins University Press, 2014). For more on the wider context in Southhampton, especially the role of women and children in the rebellion, see Vanessa Holden, *Surviving Southampton: Gender, Community, Resistance, and Survival during the Southampton Rebellion of 1831* (Urbana: University of Illinois Press, forthcoming).

64. William Ellery Channing, *Slavery* (Boston: J. Munroe & Company, 1835), 3.

65. Channing, *Slavery*, 3–4.

66. Channing, *Slavery*, 5–6.

67. Channing, *Slavery*, 152.

68. Conrad E. Wright, "The Channing We Don't Know," *The Unitarian Controversy: Essays on American Unitarian History* (Boston, 1994), 155–66, esp. 157.

69. John Lardas Modern, *Secularism in America* (Chicago: University of Chicago Press, 2011).

70. William Ellery Channing, "Unitarian Christianity: Discourse at the Ordination of the Rev. Jared Sparks," in *The Works of William Ellery Channing, Volume 3* (Boston, 1903), 59–103.

71. Letter from William Ellery Channing, Feb. 22, 1819, Reel One, WEC Papers, MHS.

72. Letter from William Ellery Channing to Catharine Maria Sedgwick, May 20, 1821. WEC Papers, MHS.

73. Letter from William Ellery Channing to the committee of the American Unitarian Association concerning the Ministry-at-Large of the Benevolent Fraternity of Churches, July, 11833. Reel Two, WEC Papers, MHS.

74. Letter from William Ellery Channing to Ezra Stiles Gannett, August 6, 1833. Reel Two, WEC Papers, MHS.

75. Earlier discussions of slavery are found in Channing's extended review of the character of John Milton, originally published by the *Christian Examiner* in 1826 and briefly in published sermons at the commencement of the War of 1812. Both can be found in William Ellery Channing, *Discourses, Reviews, and Miscellanies* (Boston, 1830), 51–52, 586.

76. Channing, *Slavery*, 5.

77. Channing, *Slavery*, 150.

78. Channing, *Slavery*, 140.

79. George A. Baxter, *An Essay on the Abolition of Slavery* (Richmond, 1836), 3.

80. Elizabeth Margaret Chandler, *Essays, Philanthropic and Moral, principally relating to the abolition of slavery in America,* edited by Benjamin Lundy (Philadelphia: T. E. Chapman, 1845), 12.

81. Chandler, *Essay on Abolitionism*, 3.

82. Chandler, *Essay on Abolitionism*, 8.

83. Chandler, *Essay on Abolitionism*, 8.

84. Chandler, *Essay on Abolitionism*, 10, 17.

85. Francis Wayland, *The Elements of Moral Science* (Boston: Gould & Lincoln, 1835/1854), 225, cited in Baxter, *Essay on Abolition,*18.

86. Baxter, *Essay on Abolition*, 18.

87. Baxter, *Essay on Abolition*, 19.

88. Baxter, *Essay on Abolition*, 23.

89. Leland, *Writings*, 698.

90. Baxter, *Essay on Abolition*, 5.

91. Maria Weston Chapman, *Right and Wrong in Massachusetts* (Boston: Dow & Jackson's Anti-Slavery Press, 1839), 15.

92. Lydia Maria Child, *An Appeal in Favor of That Class of Americans Called Africans* (Boston: Allen & Ticknor, 1833), 56.

93. See the 1837 and 1838 editions of *Zion's Herald.*

94. "From our Southern Correspondent," *Zion's Herald* 6, no. 10 (March 11, 1835), 38.

95. William Capers, "Southern Christian Advocate," *Zion's Herald* 8, no. 28 (July 12, 1837), 110.

96. Thomas Campbell, "Slavery," *Zion's Herald* 8, no. 38 (Sept. 20, 1837), 1.

97. "They Must Be Prepared for Freedom," *Zion's Herald* 8, no. 38 (Sept. 20, 1837), 150.

98. "Methodist Abolitionism," *Zion's Herald* 8, no. 38 (Sept. 20, 1837), 152.

99. "Report on Slavery," *Zion's Herald* 8, no. 43 (Oct. 25, 1837), 172.

100. "Wonderful Instance of Sudden Conversion," *Zion's Herald* 8, no. 44 (Nov. 1, 1837), 174.

101. "Southern Religion—Dr. Capers," *Zion's Herald* 9, no. 7 (Feb. 14, 1838), 1.

102. Joseph Tracy, *A Sermon before the Vermont Colonization Society, at Montpelier, October 17, 1833* (Windsor, VT: Chronicle Press, 1833), 16.

103. Tracy, *Sermon*, 17.

104. Simon Clough, *A Candid Appeal to the Citizens of the United States, Proving That the Doctrines Advanced and the Measures Pursued by the Abolitionists, Relative to the Subject of Emancipation, are inconsistent with the teachings and directions of the Bible, and that those clergymen engaged in the dissemination of these principles, should be immediately dismissed by their respective congregations as false teachers* (New York: A. K. Bertron, 1834).

105. Clough, *Candid Appeal,* 5.

106. Clough, *Candid Appeal,* 36–38.

107. *Exposition of the Object and Plans of the American Union for the Relief and Improvement of the Colored Race* (Boston, 1835), 1. See James R. Stirn, "Urgent Gradualism: The Case of the American Union for the Relief and Improvement of the Colored Race, *Civil War History* 25, no. 4 (Dec. 1979): 309–28.

108. *Exposition of the Object and Plans,* 2–3.

109. *Exposition of the Object and Plans,* 8–10.

110. Joseph Tracy, *Boston Recorder* (Dec. 26, 1834).

111. Nehemiah Adams, "Address" in *Report of the Executive Committee of the American Union, at the Annual Meeting of the Society, May 25, 1836* (Boston: Perkins & Marvin, 1836), 36. Nehemiah Adams is an interesting case study in the role of conversionism in fueling proslavery Christianity. Twenty years after losing faith in the antislavery movement, Adams published a widely read firsthand account of slavery that proved to be powerful propaganda for proslavery apologists. See Nehemiah Adams, *A Southside View of Slavery* (Boston: Ticknor & Fields, 1854).

Chapter Six

1. The best study of denominational schisms remains C. C. Goen, *Broken Churches, Broken Nation: Denominational Schisms and the Coming of the Civil War* (Macon, GA: Mercer University Press, 1985). See also Mitchell Snay, *Gospel of Disunion: Religion and the Rise of Southern Separatism, 1830–1861* (Chapel Hill: University of North Carolina Press, 1984); Richard J. Carwadine, *Evangelicals and Politics in Antebellum America* (New Haven, CT: Yale University Press, 1993); John Patrick Daly, *When Slavery Was Called Freedom: Evangelicalism, Proslavery, and the Causes of the Civil War* (Lexington: University Press of Kentucky, 2004); Douglas M. Strong, *Perfectionist Politics: Abolitionism and the Religious Tensions of American Democracy* (Syracuse, NY: Syracuse University Press, 1999); and Eugene D. Genovese, "Religion in the Collapse of the American Union," *Religion and the American Civil War,* edited by Randall M. Miller and Harry S. Stout (New York: Oxford University Press, 1998), 43–73. Other historians of the sectional crisis have missed the important role of denominational schism in fueling secession. David Potter, for example, begins his study of sectionalism in 1846, already after the denominations had split: Potter, *The Impending Crisis, 1848–1861,* completed and edited by Don E. Fehrenbacher (New York: Harper & Row, 1976). For more on how churches pushed the nation toward violence, see Harry S. Stout, *Upon the Altar of the Nation: A Moral History of the Civil War* (New York: Viking Penguin, 2006).

2. Mark A. Noll, *The Civil War as a Theological Crisis* (Chapel Hill: University of North Carolina Press, 2006).

3. The best study of the changes in northern theology as a result of slavery debates is Molly

Oshatz, *Slavery and Sin: The Fight against Slavery and the Rise of Liberal Protestantism* (New York: Oxford University Press, 2012).

4. *Louisville Presbyterian Herald* 30, no. 21 (Nov. 1860): 2.

5. For a useful overview of how historians have evaluated the role of slavery in the schism of 1837, see Goen, *Broken Churches, Broken Nation,* 72–73.

6. The best overview of the 1837 schism is George M. Marsden, *The Evangelical Mind and the New School Presbyterian Experience* (New Haven, CT: Yale University Press, 1970), 59–87. See also James H. Moorhead, "The 'Restless Spirit of Radicalism': Old School Fears and the Schism of 1837," *Journal of Presbyterian History* 78, no. 1 (Spring 2000): 19–33; Robert W. Doherty, "Social Bases for the Presbyterian Schism of 1837–1838, the Philadelphia Case," *Journal of Social History* 2, no. 1 (Fall 1968): 69–79; C. Bruce Staiger, "Abolitionism and the Presbyterian Schism of 1837–1838," *Journal of American History* 36, no. 3 (Dec. 1949): 391–414; Earl R. MacCormac, "Missions and the Presbyterian Schism of 1837," *Church History* 32, no. 1 (March 1963): 32–45; Elwyn A. Smith, "The Role of the South in the Presbyterian Schism of 1837–38," *Church History* 29, no. 1 (March 1960): 44–63; and Catherine Glennan Borchert, "Excinded!: The Schism of 1837 in the Presbyterian Church in the United States of America and the Role of Slavery" (PhD diss., Case Western Reserve University, Cleveland, OH, 2009).

7. *Christian Advocate,* vol. 12 (Philadelphia: A. Finley, 1834), 273.

8. Zebulon Crocker, *The Catastrophe of the Presbyterian Church, in 1837* (New Haven, CT: B & W Noyes, 1838), 66. See also Chris Padgett, "Evangelicals Divided: Abolition and the Plan of Union's Demise in Ohio's Western Reserve," in *Religion and the Problem of Slavery in Antebellum America,* edited by John R. McKivigan and Mitchell Snay (Athens: University of Georgia Press, 1998), 66.

9. Albert Barnes, *Notes, Explanatory and Practical on the Epistle to the Romans, Designed for Bible-classes and Sunday-Schools* (New York: Leavitt, Lord, & Co., 1834). For more on Barnes, see Kenneth G. Cleaver, "An Examination of Albert Barnes' Handling of the Bible in the Debate on Slavery in Mid-Nineteenth-Century America," (PhD diss., Trinity Evangelical Divinity School, Deerfield, IL, 2002).

10. Barnes had earlier gotten himself in trouble by challenging orthodox understandings of salvation in a sermon titled "The Way of Salvation," which was later published along with its criticism and defense. See Barnes, *The Way of Salvation; A Sermon, Delivered at Morristown, New Jersey, February 8th, 1829, By Albert Barnes. Together with Mr. Barnes' Defense of the Sermon, Read Before the Synod of Philadelphia, at Lancaster, October 29th, 1830, and His 'Defense' Before the Second Presbytery of Philadelphia, in Reply to the Charges of the Rev. Dr. George Junkin* (New York: Leavitt & Lord, 1836). For more context, see Bryant M. Kirkland, "Albert Barnes and Doctrinal Freedom," *Journal of the Presbyterian Historical Society* 29, no. 2 (June 1951): 97–106.

11. Joshua Lacy Wilson, *Wilson's Plea in the Case of Lyman Beecher, D.D.* (Cincinnati: R. P. Brooks, 1837), 35.

12. Lyman Beecher, *Autobiography, Correspondence etc., of Lyman Beecher, D.D,* edited by Charles Beecher, Vol. II (New York: Harper & Brothers, 1865), 101. See also Lyman Beecher, *The Autobiography of Lyman Beecher* (Cambridge: Belknap Press of Harvard University Press, 1961); Stuart C. Henry, *Unvanquished Puritan: A Portrait of Lyman Beecher* (Grand Rapids, MI: William B. Eerdmans, 1973); and James W. Fraser, *Pedagogue for God's Kingdom: Lyman Beecher and the Second Great Awakening* (New York: University Press of America, 1985).

13. See Albert Barnes, *An inquiry into the Scriptural views of slavery* (Philadelphia: Parry & McMillan, 1846), 383; and Frederick Douglass, *Oration, Delivered in Corinthian Hall, Rochester, by Frederick Douglass, July 5th, 1852* (Rochester, NY: Lee, Mann & Co., 1852), 30.

14. For more on Lyman Beecher and slavery, see J. Earl Thompson, Jr., "Lyman Beecher's Long Road to Conservative Abolitionism," *Church History* 42, no. 1 (March 1973): 89–109.

15. Theodore Dwight Weld to Elizur Wright, Jr., June 6, 1835, in Gilbert H. Barnes and Dwight L. Dumond, eds., *Letters of Theodore Dwight Weld, Angelina Grimke Weld, and Sarah Grimke, 1822–1844,* 2 vols. (Gloucester, MA: Peter Smith, 1964), I,

16. For both the petitions and the response from the General Assembly, see Charles Hodge, "The General Assembly of 1835, Biblical Repertory, VII, 451. See also H. Shelton Smith, *In His Image, but... Racism in Southern Religion, 1780–1910* (Durham, NC: Duke University Press, 1972), 77–78.

17. James H. Smylie, *A review of a letter, from the Presbytery of Chillicothe, to the Presbytery of Mississippi, on the subject of slavery* (Woodville, MS: Wm. A. Norris, 1836), 7.

18. Hodge's remarks were initially published in an April 1836 edition of the *Biblical Repertory,* but were widely reprinted: Charles Hodge, "Slavery," *Biblical Repertory and Princeton Review* 8 (April 1836): 301–2. For a pertinent example, see (Charles Hodge), *View of the Subject of Slavery contained in the Biblical Repertory for April, 1836, in which the scriptural argument, it is believed, is very clearly and justly exhibited* (Pittsburgh, 1836). See also Charles Hodge, "The Bible Argument on Slavery," in *Cotton Is King, and Pro-slavery Arguments: Comprising the Writings of Hammond, Harper, Christy, Stringfellow, Hodge, Bledsoe, and Cartwright, on this Important Subject,* edited by E. N. Elliott (Augusta, GA: Pritchard, Abbott, & Loomis, 1860), 866, 873; Allen C. Guelzo, "Charles Hodge's Antislavery Moment," in *Charles Hodge Revisited: A Critical Appraisal of His Life and Work,* edited by John W. Stewart and James H. Moorehead (Grand Rapids, MI: William B. Eerdmans, 2002), 299–325.

19. *Minutes of the General Assembly of the Presbyterian Church in the United States of America with an Appendix,* (Philadelphia: Published by the Stated Clerk of the Assembly, 1836), 248.

20. *Minutes of the General Assembly of the Presbyterian Church,* 249.

21. *Minutes of the General Assembly of the Presbyterian Church,* 249.

22. *Minutes of the General Assembly of the Presbyterian Church,* 272–73.

23. *Presbyterian,* April 22, 1837; *Charleston Observer,* April 15, 1837. See also Smith, *In His Image, But...,* 85.

24. The four excised were the synods of Western Reserve, Utica, Geneva, and Genesee.

25. George Marsden, *The Evangelical Mind and the New School Presbyterian Experience: A Case Study of Thought and Theology in Nineteenth-Century America* (New Haven, CT: Yale University Press, 1970).

26. *Western Presbyterian Herald* (Louisville), November 15, 1838.

27. *Cincinnati Journal and Luminary,* January 15, 1837.

28. "Pro patria Deoque," *New York Observer,* June 21, 1845, 98. For earlier Old School denials of the role of slavery in the schism, see Charles Hodge, "General Assembly of 1837," *Biblical Repertory and Princeton Review* 9 (1837): 479–80.

29. Lyman Beecher, *Autobiography, correspondence, etc.,* 428–29.

30. *Minutes of the General Assembly of the Presbyterian Church in the United States of America from Its Organization, A.D. 1789 to A.D. 1820* (Philadelphia: Presbyterian Board of Publication, 1847), 692.

31. Goen, *Broken Churches, Broken Nation,* 77.

32. Theodore Clapp, *Slavery: A Sermon, Delivered in the First Congregational Church in New Orleans, April 15, 1838* (New Orleans: John GIbson, 1838), 66.

33. W. T. Hamilton, *The Duties of Masters and Slaves Respectively* (Mobile: F. H. Brooks, 1845), 18.

34. "Essex County Anti-Slavery Society," *Liberator,* Feb. 25, 1842.

35. "Report," *Liberator,* Feb. 25, 1842.

36. "The New England Anti-Slavery Convention," *Liberator,* April 8, 1842.

37. Frederick Douglass, *Narrative of the Life of Frederick Douglass, an American Slave* (Boston: Anti-Slavery Office, 1845), 117.

38. "The American Union," *Liberator,* June 3, 1842.

39. William Ellery Channing, *The Duty of the Free States* (Boston: William Crosby & Co, 1842), 53.

40. "No Union with Slaveholders," *Liberator,* May 31, 1844.

41. Cynthia Lynn Lyerly, *Methodism and the Southern Mind, 1770–1810* (New York: Oxford University Press, 1998); John H. Wigger, *Taking Heaven by Storm: Methodism and the Rise of Popular Christianity in America* (New York: Oxford University Press, 1998); Donald Mathews, *Slavery and Methodism: A Chapter in American Morality, 1780–1845* (Princeton, NJ: Princeton University Press, 1965); and Dee E. Andrews, *The Methodists and Revolutionary America, 1760–1800: The Shaping of an Evangelical Culture* (Princeton, NJ: Princeton University Press, 2010).

42. John Wesley 's Journal, Feb. 12, 1772. The latter quote comes from the very last letter of Wesley's life, penned to William Wilberforce, wherein he encouraged the abolitionist to "go on, in the name of God, and in the power of his might, till even American slavery, the vilest that ever saw the sun, shall vanish away before it." Letter to William Wilberforce, Feb. 24, 1791. Copyright 1998–2000 by the Wesley Center for Applied Theology, Northwest Nazarene University, Nampa, ID 83686. George Lyons and Michael Mattei, Digital Editors. http://wesley.nnu.edu/john-wesley/the-letters-of-john-wesley/wesleys-letters-1791/.

43. The first history of the schism was Charles Elliott, *History of the Great Secession* (Cincinnati: Swormstedt & Poe, for the Methodist Episcopal church, 1855). See also Lucius C. Matlack, *The Antislavery Struggle and Triumph in the Methodist Episcopal Church* (New York: Phillips & Hunt,1881); John Nelson Norwood, *The Schism in the Methodist Episcopal Church, 1844: A Study of Slavery and Ecclesiastical Politics* (Alfred, NY: Alfred Press, 1923); Richard Carwardine, "Methodists, Politics, and the Coming of the American Civil War," *Church History* 69, no. 3 (Sept. 2000): 578–609; Richard Cameron and Norman Spellman, "The Church Divides," in *The History of American Methodism,* vol. 2 (New York: Abingdon Press, 1964); and Mathews, *Slavery and Methodism,* esp. 246–82.

44. *Minutes of the South Carolina Conference of the Methodist Episcopal Church, For the Year 1836* (Charleston, SC, 1836), 20–21.

45. For more on Orange Scott, see his early biography by Lucius Matlack, *The Life of Rev. Orange Scott: Compiled from His Personal Narrative, Correspondence, and Other Authentic Sources of Information. In Two Parts, Volumes 1–2* (New York: C. Prindle & L. C. Matlack, 1847). See also Donald G. Mathews, "Orange Scott: The Methodist Evangelist as Revolutionary," in *The Anti-Slavery Vanguard: New Essays on the Abolitionists,* edited by Martin Duberman (Princeton, NJ: Princeton University Press, 1965).

NOTES TO PAGES 185–189

46. Letter from Orange Scott, Springfield [Massachusetts], to William Lloyd Garrison, 1836 Dec. 30, Boston Public Library.

47. *Zion's Herald—Extra,* April 8, 1835.

48. George Prentice, *Wilbur Fisk* (Boston: Houghton, Mifflin, 1890), 208.

49. Elijah Hedding and John Emory, "Address to the Ministers and Preachers of the Methodist Episcopal Church," in Charles Elliott, *History of the Great Secession* (Cincinnati, 1855), 900–901.

50. Hedding and Emory, "Address."

51. The General Conference met in May. One month earlier, white terrorists had attacked the Black community, burning a Black tenement to the ground. For more on this event, see Joe William Trotter, *River Jordan: African American Urban Life in the Ohio Valley* (Lexington: University Press of Kentucky, 1998), 35; and John Emmeus Davis, *Contested Ground: Collective Action and the Urban Neighborhood* (Ithaca, NY: Cornell University Press, 1991), 104. Just a few months later in July, another wave of terrorism destroyed James Birney's abolitionist press and the homes of several Black residents. Stanley Harold, *Border War: Fighting over Slavery before the Civil War* (Chapel Hill: University of North Carolina Press, 2010), 67.

52. *Journals of the General Conference of the Methodist Episcopal Church,* I, 447.

53. *Debate on "modern abolitionism": in the General Conference of the Methodist Episcopal Church, held in Cincinnati, May, 1836* (Cincinnati: Ohio Anti-Slavery Society, 1836).

54. Nathan Bangs, *A History of the Methodist Episcopal Church: Vol. IV, From the Year 1829 to the Year 1840* (New York: G. Lane & P. P. Sandford, 1841), 230.

55. Elliott, *History of the Great Secession,* 164.

56. John Nelson Norwood, *The Schism in the Methodist Episcopal Church, 1844: A Study of Slavery and Ecclesiastical Politics* (Albany, NY: Alfred Press, 1923), 31. For more on how American abolitionists related to Caribbean emancipation, see Gale L. Kenny, *Contentious Liberties: American Abolitionists in Post-Emancipation Jamaica, 1834–1866* (Athens: University of Georgia Press, 2011).

57. *Debate on "modern abolitionism,"* 63–64.

58. Orange Scott, *An Appeal to the Methodist Episcopal Church* (Boston: David H. Ebla, 1838), 3.

59. Scott, *An Appeal to the Methodist Episcopal Church,* 9.

60. J. R. Jacob, "La Roy Sunderland: The Alienation of an Abolitionist," *Journal of American Studies* 6, no. 1 (April 1972): 1–17.

61. Lucius Matlack, *Narrative of the Anti-Slavery Experience of a Minister in the Methodist Episcopal Church* (Philadelphia: Merrihew & Thompson, 1845).

62. "Correspondence between Gerrit Smith, esq. of Peterboro, New York and the Rev. William Winans of Mississippi," *African Repository and Colonial Journal* 14, no. 2 (Feb. 1838): 48–49.

63. "Correspondence between Gerrit Smith, esq. of Peterboro, New York and the Rev. William Winans of Mississippi," 49–52.

64. "Correspondence between Gerrit Smith, esq. of Peterboro, New York and the Rev. William Winans of Mississippi," 49–52.

65. See Matlack, *American Slavery and Methodism,* 223–25; *Zion's Herald,* Nov. 4 and 11, 1840.

66. Elliott, *History of the Great Secession,* 966.

67. Chris Padgett, "Hearing the Antislavery Rank-and-File: The Wesleyan Methodist Schism of 1843," *Journal of the Early Republic* 12, no. 1 (Spring 1992): 63–84.

68. Elliott, *History of the Great Secession,* 265.

69. Christopher H. Owen, "To Keep the Way Open for Methodism," in McKivigan and Snay, *Religion and the Problem of Slavery*, 112.

70. For more on how the Texas controversy loomed over the Methodist meeting, see Snay, *Gospel of Disunion*, 115.

71. *Journal of the General Conference of the Methodist Episcopal Church . . . 1844* (New York, 1844), 33.

72. For more on James Osgood Andrew, see George Gilman Smith, *The Life and Letters of James Osgood Andrew: Bishop of the Methodist Episcopal Church South: With Glances at His Contemporaries and at Events in Church History* (Whitefish, MT: Kessinger Pub., 1882); and Mark Auslander, *The Accidental Slaveowner: Revisiting a Myth of Race and Finding an American Family* (Athens: University of Georgia Press, 2011).

73. Robert Athow West, *Report of Debates in the General Conference of the Methodist Episcopal Church, held in the city of New York, 1844* (New York, 1844), 92.

74. West, *Report of Debates*, 143.

75. Elliott, *History of the Great Secession*, 985–86.

76. Elliott, *History of the Great Secession*, 1006.

77. West, *Report of Debates*, 179–80.

78. West, *Report of Debates*, 143.

79. Guion Griffis Johnson, *Ante-bellum North Carolina: A Social History* (Chapel Hill: University of North Carolina Press, 1937), 465.

80. For more on early Baptist antislavery, see Charles F. Irons, *The Origins of Proslavery Christianity: White and Black Evangelicals in Colonial and Antebellum Virginia* (Chapel Hill: University of North Carolina Press, 2008); Randolph Ferguson Scully, *Religion and the Making of Nat Turner's Virginia: Baptist Community and Conflict, 1740–1840* (Charlottesville: University of Virginia Press, 2008); Jewel L. Spangler, *Virginians Reborn: Anglican Monopoly, Evangelical Dissent, and the Rise of the Baptists in the Late Eighteenth Century* (Charlottesville: University of Virginia Press, 2008); and Janet Moore Lindman, *Bodies of Belief: Baptist Community in Early America* (Philadelphia: University of Pennsylvania Press, 2008).

81. *Fourth Annual Report of the American Antislavery Society* (New York: William S. Dorr, 1837), 43.

82. Smith, *In His Image, But . . .* , 115.

83. Grosvenor, Cyrus Pitt. *Address before the Anti-Slavery Society of Salem and the Vicinity: In the South Meeting-House, in Salem, February 24, 1834* (Salem, MA: W & S. B. Ives, 1834), 10.

84. "An Address to Southern Baptists," *Christian Watchman* (New York), June 19, 1840, 97.

85. John R. McKivigan, *The War against Proslavery Religion: Abolitionism and the Northern Churches, 1830–1865* (Ithaca, NY: Cornell University Press, 1984), 74–92.

86. *Baptist Missionary Magazine* 21: 200.

87. Mary Burnham Putnam, *The Baptists and Slavery, 1840–1845* (Ann Arbor, MI: George Wahr, 1913), 23.

88. "Abolition Convention," *Niles Register* 60 (March 20, 1841): 40.

89. Putnam, *Baptists and Slavery*, 25.

90. Robert Granville Gardner, *A Decade of Debate and Division: Georgia Baptists and the Formation of the Southern Baptist Convention* (Macon, GA: Mercer University Press, 1995), 7.

91. Andrew T. Foss and Edward Mathews, *Facts for Baptist Churches* (Utica, NY: American Baptist Free Mission Society, 1850), 75–76.

92. Edwin R. Warren, *The Free Missionary Principle; Or, Bible Missions: a Plea for Separate Missionary Action from Slaveholders!* (Boston: J. Howe, 1846), 10.

93. For more on Johnson, see Hortense Woodson, *Giant in the Land: A Biography of William Bullein Johnson, First President of the Southern Baptist Convention* (Nashville, TN: Boardman Press, 1950).

94. *Christian Reflector,* May 10, 1843.

95. Edwin R. Warren, *The free missionary principle, or, Bible missions: a plea for separate missionary action from slaveholders!* (Boston: J. Howe, 1847).

96. "Minutes of the Eleventh Triennial Meeting," *Baptist Missionary Magazine* 24 (July 1844): 158.

97. *Twelfth Report of the American Baptist Home Mission Society, Presented by the Executive Board at the Anniversary in Philadelphia, April 23, 1844* (New York: American Baptist Home Missionary Society, 1844), 4.

98. *Twelfth Report of the American Baptist Home Mission Society,* 5.

99. *Northwestern Baptist,* Aug. 15, 1844, and Putnam, *Baptists and Slavery,* 47–48.

100. "Baptist Anti-Slavery Convention," *Liberator,* Sept. 27, 1844.

101. "Reply of the Acting Board," December 17, 1844, in Peter George Mode, *Source Book and Bibliographical Guide for American Church History* (Menasha, WI: Collegiate Press, 1921), 591.

102. "Report Adopted by the General Board," *Baptist Missionary Magazine* 25/26 (Boston: John Putnam, 1845), 223.

103. *Report of the American Board of Commissioners for Foreign Missions: Presented at the Thirty-Sixth Annual Meeting, held in Brooklyn, New York, Sept. 9–12, 1845* (Boston: T. R. Marvin, 1845), 55–57.

104. Augustus Field Beard, *A Crusade of Brotherhood: A History of the American Missionary Association* (Boston: Pilgrim Press, 1909).

105. Edward R. Crowther, "'Religion Has Something . . . to Do with Politics': Southern Evangelicals and the North, 1845–1860," in McKivigan and Snay, *Religion and the Problem of Slavery,* 320.

106. For more on the legal contests between Methodists North and South, see Richard Carwardine, "Methodists, Politics, and the Coming of the American Civil War," *Church History* 69, no. 3 (Sept. 2000): 578–609.

107. John G. Jones, *A Complete History of Methodism as Connected with the Mississippi Conference of the Methodist Episcopal Church, South,* vol. 2 (Nashville: M. E. Church South, 1908), 500.

108. *History of the Organization of the Methodist Episcopal Church, South* (Nashville: Methodist Episcopal Church South, 1845), 253–54.

109. *Charleston Southern Christian Advocate,* Sept. 27, 1850, cited in Purifoy, "The Southern Methodist Church and the Proslavery Argument," *Journal of Southern History* 32, no. 3 (Aug. 1966), 334.

110. *Abridgment of the Debates of Congress, from 1789 to 1856, Volume 16,* Thomas Hart Benton, ed. (New York: Appleton & Company, 1861), 409.

111. Clay reportedly said this in an 1852 interview. See the *Presbyterian Herald* (Louisville), Jan. 5, 1860.

112. Robert L. Stanton, *Causes for National Humiliation: A Discourse* (Cincinnati: Moore, Wilstach, Keys & Co., 1861), 48.

Conclusion

1. Harriet Martineau, *Society in America*, 2 vols. (New York: Saunders & Otley, 1837), 2:315.

2. As historian Edward R. Crowther has recognized, "During the 1850s, southern evangelicals gradually lost the capacity to distinguish between the terms abolitionist and northerner." Crowther, "'Religion Has Something . . . to Do with Politics,'" 318.

3. Beth Barton Schweiger, "The Restructuring of Southern Religion: Slavery, Denominations, and the Clerical Profession in Virginia," in McKivigan and Snay, *Religion and the Problem of Slavery*, 297, 308.

4. William A. Smith, *Lectures on the Philosophy and Practice of Slavery as Exhibited in the Institution of Domestic Slavery in the United States* (Nashville: Stevenson & Evans, 1856), vii.

5. Smith, *Lectures on the Philosophy and Practice of Slavery*, 276–78.

6. Charles Grandison Finney, *Lectures on Systematic Theology* (London: William Tegg & Co., 1851), 369.

7. Lewis M. Purifoy, "The Southern Methodist Church and the Proslavery Argument," *Journal of Southern History* 32, no. 3 (Aug. 1966): 333–34.

8. James Henley Thornwell, "The Christian Doctrine of Slavery," in *The Collected Writings of James Thornwell*, vol. 4 (1873; Bedford, MA: Applewood Books, 1974), 383.

9. James Henley Thornwell, *The Rights and Duties of Masters* (Charleston, SC: Walker & James, 1850), 14.

10. For more on higher criticism and the decline of orthodox literalism among abolitionists, see Molly Oshatz, *Slavery and Sin: The Fight against Slavery and the Rise of Liberal Protestantism* (New York: Oxford University Press. 2012).

11. Harriet Beecher Stowe, *Uncle Tom's Cabin; or, Life Among the Lowly* (Boston, 1852), 120–23. Amos A. Lawrence to Giles Richards, June 1, 1854, quoted in Jane J. Pease and William H. Pease, eds., *The Fugitive Slave Law and Anthony Burns: A Problem in Law Enforcement* (Philadelphia: Lippincott, 1975), 43.

12. Laura L. Mitchell, "Matters of Justice between Man and Man: Northern Divines, the Bible, and the Fugitive Slave Act of 1850," in McKivigan and Snay, *Religion and the Problem of Slavery*, 139, 150.

13. John Henry Hopkins, *Slavery: Its Religious Sanction, Its Political Dangers, and the Best Mode of Doing It Away* (Buffalo: Phinney & Co., 1851), 21, 25, 32.

14. Henry C. Wright, "Michigan Anti-Slavery Society, and Disunion," *Liberator*, Oct. 24, 1856.

15. "The South Must Be Sectional," *Liberator*, July 20, 1855.

16. "Call for a Northern Convention," *Liberator*, Sept. 18, 1857.

17. "Convention at Cleveland," *Liberator*, Nov. 6, 1957.

18. O. P. Fitzgerald, *Judge Longstreet: A Life Sketch* (Nashville: Methodist Episcoal Church South, 1891), 97–106.

19. *New Orleans Christian Advocate*, January 18, 1860, cited in Lewis M. Purifoy, "The Southern Methodist Church and the Proslavery Argument," *Journal of Southern History* 32, no. 3 (Aug. 1966), 336–37.

20. Joseph Otis, "Our Nation's Ground of Hope," *Western Recorder*, June 8, 1860. Harlow, *Religion, Race*, 131.

21. Thomas Cary Johnson, ed., *The Life and Letters of Benjamin Morgan Palmer* (Richmond: Presbyterian Committee, 1906), 209, 212.

22. Thornton Stringfellow, *A Brief Examination of Scripture Testimony on the Institution of Slavery* (Richmond: Office of the Religious Herald, 1841), and *Slavery, Its Origin, Nature, and History: Its Relations to Society, to Government, and True Religion, to Human Happiness and Divine Glory, Considered in the Light of Bible Teachings, Moral Justice, and Political Wisdom* (Alexandria: Virginia Sentinel Office, 1860).

23. "Southern Secessionists and Northern Disunionists," *Liberator,* April 19, 1861.

24. David Chesebrough, ed., *"God Ordained This War": Sermons on the Sectional Crisis, 1830–1865* (Columbia: University of South Carolina Press, 1991), 59.

25. Henry Ward Beecher, *Freedom and War: Discourses on Topics Suggested by the Times* (Boston: Ticknor & Fields, 1863), 28, 45.

26. "Rev. Dr. Bellows, All Souls Church; The Crisis of Our National Disease," *New York Times,* Jan. 5, 1861.

27. See, for example, Israel E. Dwinnell, *Hope for Our Country* (Salem: Charles W. Swasey, 1862); James D. Liggett, "Our National Reverses," in Chesebrough, "God Ordained This War," 90.

28. See S. P. Leeds, *Thy kingdom come, thy will be done : a discourse delivered on the national fast, Sept. 26, 1861, in the Congregational Church at Dartmouth College* (Windsor, VT: Bishop & Tracy, 1861), 21; and S. D. Phelps, *National Symptoms: A Discourse Preached in the First Baptist Church, New Haven* (New York: Sheldon & Company, 1862), 6.

29. Nathaniel West, *Establishment in National Righteousness* (New York: J. F. Trow, 1861), 37, 10–11.

INDEX

Adams, Nehemiah, 170, 240

Andrew, James Osgood, 204

antislavery societies: American Antislavery Society, 143–44, 153, 169–71, 183; American Baptist Antislavery Convention, 193–94, 196; American Union for the Relief and Improvement of the Colored Race, 169; American Wesleyan Antislavery Society, 189; Anti-Slavery Society of Salem and Vicinity, 192; Connecticut Society for the Promotion of Freedom and for the Relief of Persons Unlawfully Holden in Bondage, 61; Maine Baptist Anti-Slavery Convention, 193; New England Antislavery Society, 144; Ohio Antislavery Society, 186–87; Pennsylvania Abolition Society, 102

African Episcopal Church, 33, 64, 71, 106–7, 147

African Masonic Lodges, 64–65, 71–72

African Methodist Episcopal Church: Bethel Church (Philadelphia), 64, 71, 106–8; bishop of (*see* Allen, Richard); Emanuel African Church (Charleston), 123; founding of, 64; Mount Zion Church (Trenton), 147

African Methodist Episcopal Church Zion, 65, 72

African Societies: African Society for the Suppression of Vice and Immorality, 71; Free African Society, 64–65; New York African Society, 65, 72; Peace and Benevolent Society of African Americans, 147

Alexander, Archibald, 125, 155

Allen, Richard: "Black Founding Father," 64; denominational organizing, 64–65, 71–72; response to colonization, 71, 93, 106–7, 134–35

American Revolution: conversionism, 9–13, 20, 22–30, 47–48, 53, 115; denominational organizing, 4, 13–14, 60–64; emancipation and manumissions, 25–26, 32–34, 38, 54–56, 88, 162; expectations of progress, 3–4, 24–36; millennialism, 7, 11, 28–29, 33, 35; purificationism, 12–13, 35, 44–45, 47–53

Appeal to the Christian Women of the South, 145

Arminianism, 96, 140–41

Asbury, Francis, 13, 47, 50–53, 61, 126

Ashmun, Jehudi, 118–21, 136

Bacon, Ephraim, 110

Bacon, Samuel, 86, 113

Baptists: Baptist Association of Wisconsin, 195; Baptized Licking-Locust Association, 75; Charleston Baptist Association, 122–23; Elkhorn Association (Kentucky), 73; First African Baptist Church in Philadelphia, 72, 108; Georgia Baptist Convention, 194, 196; Philadelphia Baptist Association, 69; Providence Baptist Church in Monrovia, 108, 121; Shaftsbury Association of Vermont, 192; South Carolina Baptist Convention, 123–24; Southern Baptist Convention, 197; Virginia Baptist antislavery petition, 164; Warren Association, 29, 62, 68. *See also* Black Baptists

Barbary Pirates, 45